Understanding Žižek, Understanding Modernism

Understanding Philosophy, Understanding Modernism

The aim of each volume in **Understanding Philosophy, Understanding Modernism** is to understand a philosophical thinker more fully through literary and cultural modernism and consequently to understand literary modernism better through a key philosophical figure. In this way, the series also rethinks the limits of modernism, calling attention to lacunae in modernist studies and sometimes in the philosophical work under examination.

Series Editors:
Paul Ardoin, S. E. Gontarski, and Laci Mattison

Volumes in the Series:

Understanding Bergson, Understanding Modernism
Edited by Paul Ardoin, S. E. Gontarski, and Laci Mattison

Understanding Deleuze, Understanding Modernism
Edited by S. E. Gontarski, Paul Ardoin and Laci Mattison

Understanding Wittgenstein, Understanding Modernism
Edited by Anat Matar

Understanding Foucault, Understanding Modernism
Edited by David Scott

Understanding James, Understanding Modernism
Edited by David H. Evans

Understanding Rancière, Understanding Modernism
Edited by Patrick M. Bray

Understanding Blanchot, Understanding Modernism
Edited by Christopher Langlois

Understanding Merleau-Ponty, Understanding Modernism
Edited by Ariane Mildenberg

Understanding Nietzsche, Understanding Modernism
Edited by Douglas Burnham and Brian Pines

Understanding Derrida, Understanding Modernism
Edited by Jean-Michel Rabaté

Understanding Adorno, Understanding Modernism
Edited by Robin Truth Goodman

Understanding Flusser, Understanding Modernism
Edited by Aaron Jaffe, Rodrigo Martini, and Michael F. Miller

Understanding Marx, Understanding Modernism
Edited by Mark Steven

Understanding Barthes, Understanding Modernism
Edited by Jeffrey R. Di Leo and Zahi Zalloua

Understanding Žižek, Understanding Modernism
Edited by Jeffrey R. Di Leo and Zahi Zalloua

Understanding Bakhtin, Understanding Modernism (forthcoming)
Edited by Philippe Birgy

Understanding Badiou, Understanding Modernism (forthcoming)
Edited by Arka Chattopadhyay and Arthur Rose

Understanding Nancy, Understanding Modernism (forthcoming)
Edited by Cosmin Toma

Understanding Cavell, Understanding Modernism (forthcoming)
Edited by Paola Marrati

Understanding Žižek, Understanding Modernism

Edited by
Jeffrey R. Di Leo and Zahi Zalloua

BLOOMSBURY ACADEMIC
NEW YORK • LONDON • OXFORD • NEW DELHI • SYDNEY

BLOOMSBURY ACADEMIC
Bloomsbury Publishing Inc
1385 Broadway, New York, NY 10018, USA
50 Bedford Square, London, WC1B 3DP, UK
29 Earlsfort Terrace, Dublin 2, Ireland

BLOOMSBURY, BLOOMSBURY ACADEMIC and the Diana logo are trademarks of
Bloomsbury Publishing Plc

First published in the United States of America 2023
This paperback edition published 2024

Copyright © Jeffrey R. Di Leo and Zahi Zalloua, 2023

Each chapter copyright © by the contributor, 2023

For legal purposes the Acknowledgments on p. vii constitute an extension
of this copyright page.

Cover design: Eleanor Rose
Cover image © Getty Images

All rights reserved. No part of this publication may be reproduced or transmitted
in any form or by any means, electronic or mechanical, including photocopying,
recording, or any information storage or retrieval system, without prior
permission in writing from the publishers.

Bloomsbury Publishing Inc does not have any control over, or responsibility for, any
third-party websites referred to or in this book. All internet addresses given in this
book were correct at the time of going to press. The author and publisher regret
any inconvenience caused if addresses have changed or sites have ceased to
exist, but can accept no responsibility for any such changes.

Library of Congress Cataloging-in-Publication Data

Names: Di Leo, Jeffrey R., editor. | Zalloua, Zahi Anbra, 1971- editor.
Title: Understanding Žižek, understanding modernism / edited by Jeffrey R. Di Leo
and Zahi Zalloua.
Description: New York: Bloomsbury Academic, 2022. | Series: Understanding
philosophy, understanding modernism | Includes bibliographical references and index. |
Summary: "Explores and illuminates Slavoj Žižek's impact on our understanding of literary
and cultural modernism"– Provided by publisher.
Identifiers: LCCN 2022018613 (print) | LCCN 2022018614 (ebook) | ISBN 9781501367441
(hardback) | ISBN 9781501393846 (paperback) | ISBN 9781501367458 (epub) |
ISBN 9781501367465 (pdf) | ISBN 9781501367472
Subjects: LCSH: Žižek, Slavoj. | Modernism (Literature) | Civilization, Modern.
Classification: LCC B4870.Z594 U53 2022 (print) | LCC B4870.Z594 (ebook) |
DDC 199/.4973–dc23/eng/20220902
LC record available at https://lccn.loc.gov/2022018613
LC ebook record available at https://lccn.loc.gov/2022018614

ISBN: HB: 978-1-5013-6744-1
PB: 978-1-5013-9384-6
ePDF: 978-1-5013-6746-5
eBook: 978-1-5013-6745-8

Series: Understanding Philosophy, Understanding Modernism

Typeset by Deanta Global Publishing Services, Chennai, India

To find out more about our authors and books visit www.bloomsbury.com and
sign up for our newsletters.

CONTENTS

Series Preface vii
Acknowledgments viii
List of Abbreviations ix

Introduction: Modernism Is "Non-All" *Jeffrey R. Di Leo and Zahi Zalloua* 1

PART I Mapping Žižek 17

1 Lacan and Žižek on the Cogito and the Modern: Galileo or Hegel? *Ed Pluth* 19

2 Žižek's Hegel, Our Hegel *Agon Hamza* 31

3 Žižek and the (Chinese Dialectic of the) Revolution *Frank Ruda* 45

4 Being Sexed: Žižek's Modern Ontology *James Penney* 61

5 *Nil Actum Credens, Si Quid Superesset Agendum:* Or, Slavoj, Can't You See I'm Burning? Žižek *avec* the Clusterfuck of 2020 *Clint Burnham* 77

6 What's Wrong with Being Happy?: Žižek's Critique of Happiness *Jeffrey R. Di Leo* 90

PART II A Leftist Plea for Modernism 105

7 Žižek *avec* Montaigne *Zahi Zalloua* 107

8 Žižek and the Bartleby Paradox: *I Would Prefer Not To? Cindy Zeiher* 122

9 Hitchcock's Modernist Hauntology
   Laurence Simmons 135

10 Žižek's Redemptive Reading of Richard Wagner's
   Ambivalent Modernity *Erik M. Vogt* 154

11 Žižek's Critique of the Authoritarian Personality
   Geoff Boucher 167

12 What Is Worth Salvaging in Modernity: A Realist
   Perspective from Non-Philosophical Marxism to Žižek's
   Universalism *Katerina Kolozova* 183

13 Are We Human? Or, Posthumanism and the Subject of
   Modernity *Matthew Flisfeder* 196

PART III Glossary 211

14 Fantasy *Todd McGowan* 213

15 Ideology *Glyn Daly* 216

16 Universality *Ilan Kapoor* 219

17 The Subject *Russell Sbriglia* 222

18 Symptom *David J. Gunkel* 226

19 Class Struggle *Matthew W. Bost* 229

20 Violence *Oxana Timofeeva* 232

21 The Death Drive *Zahi Zalloua* 235

Notes on Contributors 239
Index 244

SERIES PREFACE

Sometime in the late twentieth century, modernism, like philosophy itself, underwent something of an unmooring from (at least) linear literary history in favor of the multi-perspectival history implicit in "new historicism" or, say, varieties of "presentism." Amid current reassessments of modernism and modernity, critics have posited various "new" or alternative modernisms—postcolonial, cosmopolitan, transatlantic, transnational, geomodernism, or even "bad" modernisms. In doing so, they have not only reassessed modernism as a category, but also, more broadly, rethought epistemology and ontology, aesthetics, metaphysics, materialism, history, and being itself, opening possibilities of rethinking not only which texts we read as modernist, but also how we read those texts. Much of this new conversation constitutes something of a critique of the periodization of modernism or modernist studies in favor of modernism as mode (or mode of production) or concept. Understanding Philosophy, Understanding Modernism situates itself amid the plurality of discourses, offering collections focused on key philosophical thinkers influential both to the moment of modernism and to our current understanding of that moment's genealogy, archaeology, and becomings. Such critiques of modernism(s) and modernity afford opportunities to rethink and reassess the overlaps, folds, interrelationships, interleavings, or cross-pollinations of modernism and philosophy. Our goal in each volume of the series is to understand literary modernism better through philosophy as we also better understand a philosopher through literary modernism. The first two volumes of the series, those on Henri Bergson and Gilles Deleuze, have established a tripartite structure that serves to offer both accessibility to the philosopher's principle texts and to current new research. Each volume opens with a section focused on "conceptualizing" the philosopher through close readings of seminal texts in the thinker's oeuvre. A second section, on aesthetics, maps connections between modernist works and the philosophical figure, often surveying key modernist trends and shedding new light on authors and texts. The final section of each volume serves as an extended glossary of principal terms in the philosopher's work, each treated at length, allowing a fuller engagement with and examination of the many, sometimes contradictory ways terms are deployed. The series is thus designed both to introduce philosophers and to rethink their relationship to modernist studies, revising our understandings of both modernism and philosophy, and offering resources that will be of use across disciplines, from philosophy, theory, and literature, to religion, the visual and performing arts, and often to the sciences as well.

ACKNOWLEDGMENTS

We would like to thank the contributors to this volume for sharing their essays and insights with us. Thanks also go to Nicole Simek and Vlad Voinich for the help they have given us in editing and preparing this manuscript for production. At Bloomsbury, we owe a debt of gratitude to Paul Ardoin, S. E. Gontarski, and Laci Mattison, the editors of this series, *Understanding Philosophy, Understanding Modernism*. Their helpful suggestions and steadfast encouragement at every stage of this project were most appreciated. Finally, thanks as well to Haaris Naqvi and Rachel Moore of Bloomsbury for steering this manuscript through the publication process.

ABBREVIATIONS

ARDM   *Absolute Recoil: Towards a New Foundation of Dialectical Materialism* (London: Verso, 2014).

A   *Antigone* (New York: Bloomsbury, 2016).

AR   *The Art of the Ridiculous Sublime: On David Lynch's Lost Highway* (London: Verso, 2000).

CU   *Cogito and the Unconscious* (Durham: Duke University Press, 1998).

CHU   *Contingency, Hegemony, Universality: Contemporary Dialogues on the Left* (with Ernesto Laclau and Judith Butler) (London: Verso, 2000).

CH   *The Courage of Hopelessness* (London: Penguin, 2018).

CZ   *Conversations with Žižek* (with Glyn Daly) (London: Polity, 2004).

D   *Disparities* (London: Bloomsbury, 2016).

WDR   *Welcome to the Desert of the Real: Five Essays on 9/11 and Related Dates* (London: Verso, 2002).

E   *Enjoy Your Symptom! Jacques Lacan in Hollywood and Out* (New York: Routledge, 1992).

EY   *Everything You Always Wanted to Know About Lacan (But Were Afraid To Ask Hitchcock)*, Slavoj Žižek (ed.) (London: Verso, 2010).

FA   *The Fragile Absolute, or, Why Is the Christian Legacy Worth Fighting For?* (London: Verso, 2000).

FR   *The Fright of Real Tears: Krzysztof Kieślowski between Theory and Post-Theory* (London: British Film Institute, 2001).

FT   *First as Tragedy, Then as Farce* (London: Verso, 2009).

HRL   *How to Read Lacan* (London: Granta Books, 2006).

HWB	*Hegel in a Wired Brain* (London: Bloomsbury Academic, 2020).
I	*Iraq: The Borrowed Kettle* (London: Verso, 2004).
IC	*The Idea of Communism; Douzinas, Costas, and Slavoj Žižek* (London: Verso, 2010).
IR	*The Indivisible Remainder: An Essay on Schelling and Related Matters* (London: Verso, 1996).
ITR	*Interrogating the Real*, Rex Butler and Scott Stephens (eds.) (London: Continuum, 2005).
LTBD	*Like a Thief in Broad Daylight: Power in the Era of Post-Humanity* (London: Penguin, 2018).
LA	*Looking Awry: An Introduction to Jacques Lacan through Popular Culture* (Cambridge: MIT Press, 1994).
LTD	*A Left that Dares to Speak Its Name* (Medford: Polity, 2020).
LC	*In Defense of Lost Causes* (London: Verso, 2008).
LN	*Less Than Nothing: Hegel and the Shadow of Dialectical Materialism* (New York: Verso, 2012).
MC	*The Monstrosity of Christ: Paradox or Dialectic?*, with John Milbank (Cambridge: MIT Press, 2009).
ME	*The Metastases of Enjoyment: Six Essays on Woman and Causality* (London: Verso, 1994).
MSH	*The Most Sublime Hysteric: Hegel with Lacan* (Cambridge: Polity, 2014).
N	*The Neighbor: Three Inquiries in Political Theology*, with Eric Santner and Kenneth Reinhard (Chicago: University of Chicago Press, 2010).
OB	*On Belief* (London: Routledge, 2001).
OSD	*Opera's Second Death*, with Mladen Dolar (London: Routledge, 2002).
OWB	*Organs without Bodies: On Deleuze and Consequences* (New York: Routledge, 2004).
PC	*Slavoj Žižek presents Mao Tse-Tung: On Practice and Contradiction* (London: Verso, 2007).
PD	*The Puppet and the Dwarf: The Perverse Core of Christianity* (Cambridge: MIT Press, 2003).

PF	*The Plague of Fantasies* (London: Verso, 1997).
PV	*The Parallax View* (Cambridge: MIT Press, 2006).
SFA	*Sex and the Failed Absolute* (London: Bloomsbury, 2019).
SOI	*The Sublime Object of Ideology* (London: Verso, 1989).
DSST	*Did Somebody Say Totalitarianism? Five Interventions in the (Mis)use of a Notion* (London: Verso, 2001).
TK	*For They Know Not What They Do: Enjoyment as a Political Factor* (London: Verso, 2002).
TN	*Tarrying with the Negative: Kant, Hegel, and the Critique of Ideology* (Durham, NC: Duke University Press, 1993).
TS	*The Ticklish Subject: The Absent Centre of Political Ontology* (London: Verso, 1999).
V	*Violence* (New York: Picador, 2008).
ZR	*The Žižek Reader*, Elizabeth and Edmond Wright (eds) (Oxford: Blackwell, 1999).
ZPM	*Slavoj Žižek présente Mao, De la pratique et de la contradiction. Avec une lettre d'Alain Badiou et la réponse de Slavoj Žižek* (Paris: La fabrique, 2008).
TWIH	"'The Wound Is Healed Only by the Spear That Smote You: The Operatic Subject and Its Vicissitudes." *Opera Through Other Eyes*, ed. David J. Levin (Stanford: Stanford University Press, 1994), 177–214.
WWWS	"Foreword: Why Is Wagner Worth Saving?" Theodor W. Adorno, *In Search of Wagner*. With a new foreword by Slavoj Žižek; trans. Rodney Livingstone (London: Verso, 2009), viii–xxvii.
WAG	"Afterword: Wagner, Anti-Semitism and 'German Ideology,'" in Alain Badiou, *Five Lessons on Wagner*. Trans. Susan Spitzer. With and Afterword by Slavoj Žižek (London: Verso, 2010), 161–225.
WC	*Wagner and the Consequences*. Lacanian Ink, special issue 41/42, September 2013.
WS	*The Wagnerian Sublime: Four Lacanian Readings of Classic Operas* (Berlin: August Verlag, 2016).

Introduction

Modernism Is "Non-All"

Jeffrey R. Di Leo and Zahi Zalloua

Slovenian philosopher and cultural theorist Slavoj Žižek (1949–) is a leading thinker today, whose polemical works span topics from Hegel to Lacan, from Shakespeare to Beckett, and from Hitchcock to Lynch. Critical through and through of both postmodern ideological complacencies—for example, the death of the subject and the return to ethics—and premodern ones—for example, the re-enchantment of the world, the embrace of postcritique—Žižek doubles down on his commitment to modernism/modernity, to what it means to be modern, and on the necessity of asking modern questions (about the subject, nature, and political economy) in the age of the Anthropocene, this unprecedented global state in which human activity has become the determining factor impacting the climate and the environment. To that end, Žižek infuses standard Marxist thought with German Idealism and Lacanian psychoanalysis. Against the twin deceptive attitudes of pessimism and optimism—postmodern pessimism about the prospects of transformative critique and optimism about the end of history à la Fukuyama, that is, the fantasy of a postpolitical or post-ideological stance—Žižek vigorously argues that ideology is not a totalizing force and that modernism's negativity still has an urgent role to play in today's society, countering the postmodern pull toward cynicism.

Whereas postmodernists like Michel Foucault moved critique away from ideology and toward power, Žižek sticks to the virtues of *Ideologiekritik*, endeavoring to save the concept from its relegation to a relic of a prior, outdated critical toolbox. Working in a post-Althusserian vein, Žižek does not treat ideology merely as a matter of cognitive distortion. Rather, Žižek stresses the ways in which ideology takes hold on us at the level of the unconscious, soliciting and securing our libidinal investment. Going beyond the traditional identification of ideology with false consciousness—"They do not know it, but they are doing it," as Marx famously puts it in *Das Capital*—Žižek modernizes this saying, rewriting and reconfiguring its psychoanalytic bases and implications by foregrounding the problem of fetishistic disavowal: "They know that, in their activity, they are following an illusion, but still they are doing it" (*SOI*, 33). Ideology critique, *mutatis mutandis*, proceeds through the exposure of such a disavowal ("I know very well, but still . . .") on the part of the allegedly post-ideological, postmodernist subject of late capitalism.

We might say that Žižek re-modernizes philosophy by returning to the legacy of the Cartesian subject, favoring the emancipatory potential of self-reflexivity, the capacity to unplug from the organic given, as opposed to the received view of the *cogito* as a thinking substance—the template of human knowers as "masters and possessors of nature"[1]—and the site of full positivity, of the privileges of certainty and self-transparency. More importantly still, Žižek's modernist commitment opens to a Lacanian register. The modernist subject is the psychoanalytic subject; it is out-of-joint, empty, and fraught, a non-substantial entity, and a locus of "the infinite power of absolute negativity" (*TWN*, 23). This modernist negativity is perhaps most visible in Žižek's use of the Lacanian notion of the act. Unlike what Lacan calls a *passage à l'acte*—which typically registers only the agent's frustration and thus remains an impotent political intervention[2]—the act succeeds in changing the coordinates of the subject's social being. It violently transforms the subject ontologically—you are no longer the same as before. The act subverts the hegemonic order, resulting in a momentary eclipsing or *aphanisis* of the humanist subject. As a locus of negativity, the act touches the Real, troubling the system's coherence and sanctioned reality. The act reveals what Lacan calls the *pas-tout*, "non-all" or "not-all" of symbolic reality.

The title of our Introduction, "Modernism Is Non-All," takes up the implications of this "non-all" for an understanding of modernism/modernity. In Seminar XX, Lacan famously lays out four formulas of sexuation.[3] On the masculine side, there are two: (1) there is at least one X that says no to the phallic function, and (2) all Xs are subject to the phallic function. And on the feminine side, there are two more: (1) there is no X that says no to the phallic function, and (2) not all Xs are subject to the phallic function. Unlike the masculine side, there is no claim of universality rooted in exception here; woman (unlike Man) does not constitute a totality. If there is no exception that stands outside the social system, then the system as such is never whole or complete. And because there is nothing of woman *outside* the Law (no constitutive exception), woman is also "non-all," incomplete and imperfect, inside of the Symbolic.

Žižek critically reinterprets the Lacanian logic of the feminine "non-all" as referring to the ways a subject's enjoyment (*jouissance*) is structured and organized. The words "masculine" and "feminine" do not refer to anatomical differences but to a subject's relation to the phallus. In other words, the masculine and feminine sides represent competing logics and different structures of enjoyment. It might be helpful to expand on this idea a bit. The masculine logic is first and foremost a logic of the exception: the exception that proves the rule, that closes the set. While all men are symbolically castrated due to their entry into the symbolic order, a masculine logic hangs on to the notion that there is always one "Man" who does not sacrifice his enjoyment, one Man who must remain immune to the law of castration. For Lacan, the mythical primal father of Freud's *Totem and Taboo* incarnates such a figure. While the primal father—who enjoyed all women at will, "achieving complete satisfaction" (*TK*, 123)—had to be killed for the symbolic order to be erected, his exceptional subject-position lives on in the cultural imaginary. The masculine logic does not give up on perfection (from the Latin *perfectio*, meaning completion). Such a logic always holds on to the phantasmatic promise or hope of returning to the prior, full plenitude of a pre-symbolic enjoyment.

In the feminine logic, there is no claim of universality rooted in exception. So if there is no exception that stands outside the system, then the system as such is never whole or complete. And because there is nothing of woman outside the Law, "woman" is said to be "non-all" inside of the symbolic order. Again, there is always a risk misreading Lacan/Žižek here. The feminine seems to evoke a biological register, but it actually denotes a logic and structure of enjoyment, and one that potentially applies to all subjects. Whereas the masculine logic of exception posits a sovereign subject, a subject who has unlimited enjoyment, who stands outside the law of castration that governs social symbolic existence and whose self-presence is transparent, the feminine logic, by contrast, sees no exception to the law of castration. It declines the illusion of an uncastrated Man (and with it the possibility of absolute enjoyment) but at the same time takes castration to be "non-all," never complete or whole. This is why Žižek says, "*subjectivity as such . . . is feminine*" (*TK*, xxii). The question, of course, is whether or not individuals avow this ontological reality, the unsettling reality of "the void of the 'barred subject'" (*TK*, xxii), whether or not they decline their interpellation as a mystified, undivided, sovereign subject.

Žižek's modernism follows the path of the "non-all." Or rather, his Lacanian approach allows him to implicitly cast the modern not as an exception to tradition, to what lies outside its reach and governance, but as an unsettling source of de-completion. In other words, the "non-all" (of modernism/modernity) articulates the logic of the Real, pointing to what is irreducible to a society's symbolic representation of reality. The Real does not lie outside the Symbolic, external to its mechanisms; rather, "the Real is the Symbolic itself in the modality of non-All, lacking an external Limit/Exception" (*PD*, 69). The Real, Žižek insists, lacks a fixed ontology, "the very field of ontology, of the positive order of Being, emerges through the subtraction of the Real. The order of Being and the Real are mutually exclusive: The Real is the immanent blockage or impediment of the order of Being, what makes the order of Being inconsistent" (*LN*, 958).

Žižek's modernism as a logic/hermeneutics aligns with this ontological incompleteness. To be modern is to embrace the "non-all" and infect with doubt what passes for natural and stable in our social reality. To be modern is to be skeptical of any culture's phantasmatic and ideological pretension of wholeness. The logic of the "non-all" enables Žižek to theorize modern subjectivity and otherness, along with the signifying order, differently, underscoring the dynamism and mutability of ontology. In a political register, this logic can be said to inform the "proletarian position," the position occupied by society's marginalized subjects, its "parts of no-part," a notion Žižek freely borrows from Jacques Rancière.[4] The "part of no-part" stands for the Others who are systematically excluded and/or racialized by society's laws and norms, falling outside the protection of the liberal and humanist umbrella. They are the "'supernumerary' elements" of their respective societies: "those who belong to a situation without having a specific 'place' in it; they are included but have no part to play in the social edifice" (*DI*, 60). As a given order's constitutive outsiders, they stand for "true universality,"[5] since their interests are not predetermined by their subject positions. Indeed, when the "parts of no-part" seek to remedy wrongs, they are actually speaking to universal concerns (rather than to the particular interests of a group; the slogan "Women rights are human rights" captures this sentiment). Not attached to the status quo in the same libidinal and ideological way, the "parts of no-part" hold the promise of transformative change—of enacting politics as such. They articulate and affirm what Étienne Balibar calls *égaliberté*, equality-freedom, as an unconditional demand.[6]

To be sure, the masculine logic is also implicated in universal claims. An example can help shed some light on the fault lines between the logic of the exception and that of the "non-all." Let's consider the universality of humanity along with its ambivalent relation to racism or anti-Blackness, more specifically. A masculine logic would read Black folks as the remainders of a white supremacist-sanctioned humanity. That is to say, Black people stand outside the closed set of (white) humanity, dreaming one day of their inclusion in white civil society, of belonging to the "symbolic family" of humanity. A feminine logic, in contrast, would complicate this inside/outside opposition. The disruptive presence of Black subjects discloses the "non-all" of the Symbolic, of the American order of things. Take, for example, the antiracist movement Black Lives Matter (BLM). In their global protests, BLM activists are implicitly affirming that humanity is "non-all"—opening a space for thinking who or what might also count in or belong to this community, in what Achille Mbembe calls this "common world."[7] BLM is not after more rights or the full inclusion of Blacks into a ready-made humanity. The movement flatly rejects the ideological inclusivity of liberal democracy. What BLM is after is nothing short of a new humanity, what Frantz Fanon imagined as a new "species"[8] of humanity, a humanity that is predicated on negativity and/as invention, on the modern political project to "redefine the very universality of what it means to be human."[9]

In his works, Žižek often turns the figure the "unruly Jew" (*LC*, 6) as exemplifying not only society's "part of no-part" but also philosophy's "constitutive homelessness" (*PV*, 9), its perpetual state of out-of-jointness, its unwillingness to conform to the popular beliefs and suppositions of the day. In "What Is Enlightenment?" Immanuel Kant argued that while individuals in an official capacity have to obey orders (in the domain of the "private use of reason"), individuals (as would-be philosophers) must not compromise on their "public use of reason," that is, they must not censure themselves and give up their right to address their views, to speak as "*a scholar . . . before the entire public of the reading world.*"[10] As Žižek explains, the public use of reason, "in a kind of short-circuit, by-passing the mediation of the particular, directly participates in the universal," enabling the individual to be modern and cosmopolitan, to break with the "communal-institutional order of one's particular identification" (*V*, 143).

This is precisely the position adopted by the cosmopolitan Jew, who maintains and nurtures a critical distance from the organic given, from community as such:

> The privileged role of Jews in the establishment of the sphere of the "public use of reason" hinges on their subtraction from every state power—this position of the "part of no-part" of every organic nation-state community, not the abstract-universal nature of their monotheism, makes them the immediate embodiment of universality. No wonder, then, that, with the establishment of the Jewish nation-state, a new figure of the Jew emerged: a Jew resisting identification with the State of Israel, refusing to accept the State of Israel as his true home, a Jew who "subtracts" himself from this state, and who includes the State of Israel among the states towards which he insists on maintaining a distance, living in their interstices. (*LC*, 6)

Occupying the position of the "part of no-part," the cosmopolitan Jew stands for "the empty principle of universality."[11]

To be modern is to insist on this gap between the subject and the given. Postmodern philosophers, in contrast, have sought to escape the treacherous orbit of the subject. They blame the "subject," its hubris and narcissistic predilections. Many have rallied behind Emmanuel Levinas's philosophy of the Other, in which the "face" is said to effect a rupture with philosophy as usual. *Pace* Heidegger, Levinas boldly affirms "ethics as first philosophy,"[12] elevating the encounter with the concrete Other above all else. With Levinas, the face is that which transcends the economy of the Same, the reduction of the unknown to the known, the unfamiliar to the familiar. The face exceeds any phenomenological containment; it possesses a pre-discursive purity, escaping the principle of cognitive mastery. We might say that the face obeys a masculine logic; it is the exception that closes the set of what is knowable, separating ethics from the realms of epistemology and ontology. Jacques Derrida voiced an early critique of Levinas by arguing that for the face to be recognized as a face it must retain *some* relation to language and meaning, to that which Levinas claims to have left behind.[13] Žižek pursues this line of critique, though in a much more polemical tone, arguing that Levinas's radical alterity is still subjected to mediation, to the workings of the symbolic order. As an alternative to Levinas, Žižek turns to Primo Levi and his account of the *Muselmann*, which helps to recast the Other beyond a postmodern Levinasian-inflected ethics.

If Žižek criticizes Levinas's "ethical petrification" (*LC*, 165) of otherness, he praises Levi's disclosure of the Other—the *Muselmann*—a being radically stripped of its symbolic veneer, resistant to the subject's imaginary projection (the Other as alter ego), and refused the human privilege of intersubjectivity. In contrast to Levinas's gentrification of the face—what amounts to an imaginary-symbolic Other—Levi portrays the *Muselmann* as faceless: "When confronted with a Muselmann, one cannot discern in his face the trace of the abyss of the Other in his/her vulnerability, addressing us with the infinite call of our responsibility. What one gets instead is a kind of blind wall, lack of depth" (*N*, 161). This "'faceless' face," as Žižek further explains, is a "neighbor with whom no empathetic relationship is possible" (*N*, 162).

Who is this neighbor? It is Žižek's ethico-political response to the Levinasian Other; it is the real Other. Žižek considers the biblical figure of the neighbor the "most precious and revolutionary aspect of the Jewish legacy," underscoring the ways in which the neighbor "remains an inert, impenetrable, enigmatic presence that hystericizes" (*N*, 140–1). Žižek takes up the provocation posed by the injunction "Love thy neighbor!"

This injunction is fundamentally at odds with the ethical tradition. Here Žižek follows Lacan and quotes him saying that "nothing is farther from the message of Socrates than *you shall love your neighbor as yourself, a formula that is remarkably absent* from all that he says" (*N*, 4). Jewish law acknowledges the Real of the neighbor: the neighbor as the "bearer of a monstrous Otherness, this properly *inhuman* neighbor" (*N*, 162). The biblical injunction contradicts an idealized vision of Man—the ethical Other (the "neighbor" in "love thy neighbor") is not a being endowed with rights and moral sensibility *like me*. The figure of neighbor is the unsettling presence that the signifiers "man" and "human person" cover over: "'Man,' 'human person,' is a mask that conceals the pure subjectivity of the Neighbor" (*LC*, 16). The injunction is thus better understood as inaugurating an "anti-ethics" (*DL*, 16), an ethics that radically deviates from philosophy's long humanist orientation. In the faceless/real neighbor, it is not my sovereignty and humanity that I find confirmed but my own fundamental otherness: myself as neighbor, making me cognizant of "the gap between what I am as a determinate being and the unfathomable X" (*HRL*, 44).

Another unexpected example of the neighbor can be found in Žižek's engagement with Derrida's cat (encounter). Interpellated by his little female cat as he was naked and coming out of the shower,[14] Derrida muses on his feline's alternity and the inadequacies of language to account for the cat's singularity:

> If I say "it is a real cat" that sees me naked, this is in order to mark its unsubstitutable singularity. When it responds in its name . . . it doesn't do so as the exemplar of a species called "cat," even less so of an "animal" genus or kingdom. It is true that I identify it as a male or female cat. But even before that identification, it comes to me as this irreplaceable living being that one day enters my space, into this place where it can encounter me, see me, even see me naked. Nothing can ever rob me of the certainty that what we have here is an existence that refuses to be conceptualized [*rebelle à tout concept*].[15]

But unlike Derrida who is fascinated by the cat's radical otherness, Žižek speculates about the subject's own animality:

> The cat's gaze stands for the gaze of the Other—an inhuman gaze, but for this reason all the more the Other's gaze in all its abyssal impenetrability. Seeing oneself being seen by an animal is an abyssal encounter with the Other's gaze, since—precisely because we should not simply project onto the animal our inner experience—something is returning the gaze which is radically Other. The entire history of philosophy is based upon a disavowal of such an encounter. (*LN*, 411)

Philosophy is deeply invested in safeguarding its cherished subject, the proper subject of humanism. Philosophers, in general, are traumatophobic, ceaselessly working to shield the subject, to immunize it from trauma, from disturbing exposures, disavowing any encounter with the faceless face neighbor, the animal, the animalized human. But whereas a new humanism may want to include the nonhuman under its tent, Žižek moves in the other direction; rather than save the other-subject by recognizing/extending a face to the destitute, Žižek ponders about what the cat sees, degrading the human(ist) subject from its self-appointed position of the *seer* to that of the *seen*.

Žižek continues his meditation and proposes his own cat example: "I remember seeing a photo of a cat after it had been subjected to some lab experiment in a centrifuge, its bones half broken, its skin half hairless, its eyes looking helplessly into the camera—this is the gaze of the Other disavowed not only by philosophers, but by humans 'as such'" (*LN*, 411). Žižek's cat cannot but evoke Levi's *Muselmann*. The lab cat recalls Levi's description of the living dead of Auschwitz. In both cases, the symbolic veneer dissolves. Not unlike the *Muselmann*, the lab cat no longer conforms to its image within the symbolic order. It is unrecognizable as a pet, far removed from the all-too-familiar fuzzy and cute cat of domesticity.

The cat as real neighbor is neither *like* other cats nor a radical alterity mysteriously exempt from symbolic mediation (as would be a posthumanist Levinasian account of the cat, informed by masculine logic of the exception). This lab cat hystericizes Žižek:

> What if that which characterizes humans is this very openness to the abyss of the radical Other, this perplexity of "What does the Other really want from me?" In other words, what if we turn the perspective around here? What if the perplexity a human sees in the animal's gaze is the perplexity aroused by the monstrosity of the human being itself? What if it is my own abyss I see reflected in the abyss of the Other's gaze . . .? (*LN*, 414)

What do the *Muselmann* and the lab cat want from me? Žižek's answer to this version of "*Che vuoi?*" turns the question on its head. The terrifying abyss, the irreducible alterity, that the subject witnesses in their gaze, that provokes the subject's hystericization, is paradoxically *also* the subject's.

Žižek's examples of the neighbor (the *Muselmann*, the cat, the subject as such) also tell us something about his brand of exemplarity. Representations of the neighbor—of the Other/otherness—are always to some extent inadequate, deficient, or lacking. They are never identical to the matter at hand. Examples can never ground a pure heterology. Žižek, however, proposes to reframe exemplarity as a materialist practice:

> The difference between the Idealist and the materialist use of examples is that, in the Platonic-Idealist approach, examples are always imperfect, they never perfectly render what they are supposed to exemplify, so that we should take care not to take them too literally, while, for a materialist, there is always more in the example than in what it exemplifies: that is, an example always threatens to undermine what it is supposed to exemplify since it gives body to what the exemplified notion itself represses, is unable to cope with.[16]

This materialist use of examples expresses the logic of the "non-all" and defines Žižek's unapologetic modernism, a modernist hermeneutics that tirelessly circles around the traumatic kernel of the Real at the heart of the being that each example lays bare.

This volume takes up the challenges laid out by Žižek's iconoclastic thinking and its reverberations in an array of fields: philosophy, psychoanalysis, political theory, literary studies, and film studies, among others. Žižek's multidisciplinary appeal attests to the provocation, if not scandal, of his politically incorrect thought. *Understanding Žižek, Understanding Modernism* makes the force and inventiveness of Žižek's writings accessible to a wide range of students and scholars invested in the open question of modernism and its legacies. The volume is divided into three parts. The first part, "Mapping Žižek," situates and assesses Žižek's contributions to philosophy and critique since his groundbreaking 1989 *The Sublime Object of Ideology*. The second part, "A Leftist Plea for Modernism/Modernity," which takes its inspiration from Žižek's 1998 article "A Leftist Plea for Eurocentrism," focuses on Žižek's explicit engagement with modern literary texts as well as the ways in which he doubles down on the virtues of the modern, on what it means to be modern and ask modern questions. The third part, "Glossary," is devoted to Žižek's critical vocabulary.

Part I: Mapping Žižek

Part I begins with two pieces that engage Žižek's use of Hegel. In "Lacan and Žižek on the Cogito and the Modern: Galileo, or Hegel?" Ed Pluth situates the key Žižekian theme of the Cartesian *cogito*, as reworked by Lacan, in relation to another aspect of the modern that Lacan himself focused on, just as much as he did Descartes and the negative: the Galilean theme of the mathematization of nature. Pluth explores this relationship to elucidate the differing paths Žižek and Lacan take with respect to philosophy, which Žižek embraces while Lacan explicitly distances himself from it. To what extent, Pluth asks, is this because Lacan thought that in order to be modern, psychoanalysis needed a recourse to mathematization, precisely because that is its best chance to avoid the auras of sense and meaning, always religious according to Lacan? And to what extent does Žižek's use of Hegel fix the problem, challenging Lacan's view that there can be no philosophy that is truly allied to modernity? In Chapter 2, "Žižek's Hegel, Our Hegel," Agon Hamza turns to Žižek's reading of Hegel as "the most radical thinker of *parallax*." Radically reconfiguring the Kantian distinction between phenomena/noumena, Hegel renders Being itself incomplete. That is to say, the non-all of Being is constitutive of Being itself. Impossibility is not an epistemological condition but an ontological fact: the gaps in knowledge are gaps in being as being. Hamza unpacks the full force of Žižek's "return to Hegel," and more concretely, the notion of *absolute recoil*, as it relates to dialectical materialism and its implications for Žižek's Hegelian reading of Christianity. In doing so, this chapter argues that the fundamental axiom of the "return to Hegel" is an intellectual and political imperative of our era.

In Chapter 3, "Žižek and the (Chinese Dialectic of the) Revolution" Frank Ruda thinks through Žižek's critical account of the Chinese Cultural Revolution. Using an exchange between Žižek and the French philosopher Alain Badiou as a prism to examine in what precise way this last grand revolution failed and what can be learned from it, Ruda moves the discussion into a more general reflection on how to conceive of a politics of negation and how it is connected to the modern problem of egalitarian organization in Žižek's perspective. Chapters 4 and 5 each take up the role of Freud's work in Žižek's project. As a quintessentially psychoanalytic thinker, James Penney observes in "Being Sexed: Žižek's Modern Ontology," Žižek has been concerned since his earliest work with the epistemological implications of Freud's theory of sexuality, including its formalization by Lacan, for how we conceive of the limits of knowledge. Lately, however, alongside intellectual allies like Joan Copjec and Alenka Zupančič, his focus has shifted from sex conceived as a fault or inconsistency in the forms of knowledge to sex as a disruption or torsion in the very fabric, so to speak, of being. Staging a critical encounter with the most modern postmillennial discourses, from so-called object-oriented ontology and speculative realism to quantum physics and queer theory, Žižek has reintroduced the subject of the unconscious into the interrogation of being, insisting with great consequence that this being, or more precisely its failure or inconsistency, is not one, non-all; that it is necessarily, in other words, *sexed*. Penny traces the relinking of being and sex in Žižek's recent work, situating it within a broader project premised on the contention that the consequences of psychoanalysis for ontology have only just begun to be developed. Penny takes stock of the significance of these consequences for philosophy and contemporary sexuality theory, then explores how they echo across Žižek's provocative and controversial engagement with MeToo discourse and queer theory. In "*Nil Actum Credens, Si Quid Superesset Agendum*: Or, Slavoj, Can't You See I'm Burning? Žižek *avec* the Clusterfuck of 2020,*"* Clint Burnham sets out to develop a way of understanding what can suggestively be termed the "clusterfuck" of 2020. To do so he draws on Žižek's combination of two paradigmatic dreams in the Freudian canon—"father, can't you see I'm burning?" and "he was dead but did not know it"—and adds to these a third well-known utterance, "a child is being beaten." In this tripartite analysis, Burnham proposes that we can not only comprehend the dawning awareness of racialized state violence (*après* George Floyd), the sudden arrival of a pandemic, and the ongoing climate crisis by analyzing *jouissance*-laden voyeurism and the status of knowledge in the unconscious/dream state, but also that the unwieldly harnessing of these forms of critique can aid in sussing out whether each crisis replaces another (as Covid-19 seemed, briefly, to replace the environmental crisis), whether they intensify one another, or whether they relate to one another in some other way.

Part I closes with Jeffrey R. Di Leo's engagement with Žižek's analyses of neoliberal capitalism in "What's Wrong with Being Happy? Žižek's Critique of Happiness." Di Leo examines Žižek's argument for saying "No Thanks!" to happiness within the philosophical and psychological traditions, as well as its importance as an act of public philosophy, particularly via arenas such as YouTube. As an important public advocate of a modern—and highly unpopular—"tragic" view of happiness, Žižek stands squarely against the celebration of happiness in American society. What, asks Di Leo, is the price of pursuing happiness under late capitalism? Is it one worth paying? Or should we follow Žižek and reject happiness—along with its humanist framework which constantly covers over or obfuscates the Real, the sabotaging role of the death drive in human affairs? For Žižek, the answer is clear, but is his argument convincing enough to persuade more than the tragic few? To answer these questions Di Leo begins by reviewing the typically modern position on happiness found in the writings of Sigmund Freud, and their further development in Lacan, before turning to Žižek's psychoanalytic critique. As a public philosopher, Žižek's critique of happiness extends to a wide audience an updated version of one key aspect of the modern condition of civilization touted by Freud a century ago. Di Leo concludes that Žižek's analysis brilliantly reveals how the devolving conditions of neoliberal capital in the new millennium underwrite unprecedented levels of social control and manipulation under the guise of the pursuit of happiness. In short, much of what's wrong with happiness is the same as what's wrong with neoliberal capitalism.

Part II: A Leftist Plea for Modernism/Modernity

Part II begins with Zahi Zalloua's "Žižek *avec* Montaigne." In this chapter, Zalloua takes up Lacan's and Žižek's turns to early modern philosophers as a way to recast both the philosophical subject and the project of philosophy. If Žižek, repeating the late Lacan, rehabilitates the Cartesian subject, rejecting its too hasty postmodern dismissal, Lacan finds in Montaigne a remarkable instance of the *aphanisis* of the subject, foreshadowing the split subject of psychoanalysis. In an innovative reading of the *cogito*, Žižek foregrounds the emptiness of the Cartesian subject. What emerges is not a substantial subject but as Žižek puts it *"a subject bereft of subjectivity."* Zalloua argues that this Žižekian view of the subject better describes or, at least, is already anticipated by Lacan's Montaigne. Ontological incompleteness and hermeneutic slipperiness indeed characterize the Montaignian subject. The essay form illustrates and enacts the feminine logic of the non-all. While Lacan praises Montaigne for his disclosure of the provisional character of the subject, Žižek surprisingly remains silent on this Montaignian intertext. In reading Žižek *with* Montaigne, Zalloua explores what this encounter might look like, staging Montaigne's brand of skepticism as an inventive locus of negativity that not only unsettles the ego by inducing moments of *aphanisis* but also supplements philosophy's cognitive norms and procedures with psychoanalysis and its praise of hysterical doubt.

In Chapter 8, "Žižek and the Bartleby Paradox: *I Would Prefer Not To?*" Cindy Zeiher takes up the perplexing, frustrating, yet curiously admirable mantra repeatedly uttered by Melville's Bartleby: "I'd prefer not to." Žižek sees Bartleby as the melancholic subject of politics whose mantra implies passive resistance to the never-ending flow of capital. Employed initially as a skilled scrivener, Bartleby gradually withdraws into a world of his own, finally refusing either to perform his duties or to leave the office—as his mantra states, he simply prefers to do nothing, to opt out. Such loyalty to nothingness reveals Bartleby's ultimately negative mode of being, his non-all, one which refuses subjectivity of almost any sort for himself, although he certainly stands in for the mirror to reflect the quandary of subjectivity of his employer/narrator. In this position, he adopts language as the sole condition for his existence. Bartleby presents, Zeiher argues, not only as an existential subject in crisis but also as a thoroughly modern figure whose ultimate refusal of life short-circuits speech while nevertheless remaining focused on the problem of language. Bartleby's retention of language deliberately hystericizes the ambivalent subjectivity of his employer who agonizes between offering resistance and doing nothing. Here we may, like Žižek, read Bartley as a figure of resistance to capitalist politics who at the same time invites the ambivalent and frustrated modern subject to opt in, but no further than to the command of the speech act.

In Chapter 9, "Hitchcock's Modernist Hauntology," Laurence Simmons takes up Hitchcock's film *Rebecca* in an attempt to address a criticism of Žižek related to his account of the "Selznick period" of Hitchcock's films. Formally, the modernist qualities of these films are visible in the presence of long, anamorphically distorted tracking shots that are thematically framed around the point of view of a traumatized female heroine. For Žižek, Hitchcock's films put on display "feminine masochism," a woman taking pleasure in her own ruin and finding a tortured satisfaction in her subjection and humiliation. For Tania Modleski, however, Žižek's readings of Hitchcock focus too much on men and women, and neglect "women in relation to one another," a concern of Hitchcock's *Rebecca*. Simmons proposes to redeem this lack, the absence of a sustained Žižekian engagement with *Rebecca*, by analyzing *Rebecca*'s disjointing, mixing, and disarticulation of genres (Gothic, Modern, Popular Romance)—all of which in turn unsettle the stability of representation on which those very genres are premised. Simmons argues that what makes Hitchcock's film appear "old-fashioned" and even ridiculous is ironically what renders it "modern" and dynamic—and we might add non-all.

Moving from cinema to music, "Žižek's Redemptive Reading of Richard Wagner's Ambivalent Modernity" examines Žižek's repeated working through of Wagner's œuvre, which, Erik Vogt notes, often proceeds by affirming and critically reevaluating central claims found in Theodor W. Adorno's complex and groundbreaking interpretation of Wagnerian art. If Adorno reads this work in terms of an ambivalent modernity that must be grasped both in its regressive and progressive aspects, Žižek pursues and expands on Adorno's ideologico-critical analysis of sexual politics in Wagnerian music dramas by putting forth the hypothesis—in his early texts—that the ways in which Wagner stages the sexual relationship form the matrix of anti-Semitic proto-fascism. What is more, Vogt argues, Žižek's more recent texts on Wagner seem to perform a kind of parallactic perspective shift analogous to the interventions into the "case of Wagner" that characterize Adorno's own late essays on Wagner from the 1960s. This shift provides the possibility for Žižek to present the Wagnerian music dramas not only as coded ciphers for the antagonisms of modern capitalist society that Wagner—"as theoretician of fascism"—articulates and disavows at the same time but also as instantiations of an excess that becomes legible as a version of Pauline modernist art.

In Chapter 11, "Žižek's Critique of the Authoritarian Personality," Geoff Boucher offers a Žižekian interpretation of the authoritarian personality at the center of urgent contemporary social and political questions. By recasting the authoritarian personality as a perverse form of subjective structuration rather than a "sado-masochistic character," Žižek, Boucher argues, highlights a psychodynamic model of authoritarian subjectivity, a model primarily fueled by anxiety. Here, perverse subjectivity is not considered as a reified "thing," or a fixed "character," but conceived as a subject-position taken up in reaction to heightened anxiety. What interests Boucher are the regressive responses found in the mechanisms of repression, disavowal, and foreclosure to an anxiety produced by "enjoyment," the name for this unruly desire "beyond the pleasure principle." Boucher argues that when a subject is overwhelmed, the increase in anxiety generates regressive defenses, which, in turn, shifts the positionality of individuals and makes them more vulnerable to new ideological narratives and conceptions about social reality. Perverse subjectivity, continues Boucher, has everything to do with the shifting relationship between authority, transgression, and anxiety, within which the effort of the pervert/authoritarian is to enact a supreme transgression in order to bring an effective authority into being.

Next, in "What Is Worth Salvaging in Modernity: A Realist Perspective from Non-Philosophical Marxism to Žižek's Universalism," Katerina Kolozova situates Žižek's writings in relation to two strands of modernism's legacy: the objectivist and subjectivist, the materialist and the idealist. Kolozova proposes a comparative reading of two vantage points on the notion of subjectivity— that of non-Marxism and that of Žižek's universalism, as conceived in his works of the early 2000s—that both proclaim the possibility of thinking of or in relation to the real, albeit by conceding its radical foreclosure.

Building on Karl Marx's writings and aided by the methodological organon of François Laruelle's non-philosophy, Kolozova maintains that subjectivity-centered modern rationality is the point of bifurcation at which two clearly delineated traditions of modernity emerge. It is a point of split between Marx's radical materialism as politico-epistemic project and its economic foundation, on the one hand, and that of the republican vision of the Enlightenment, on the other. Thanks to the Diamat (dialectical materialism) doctrine that pervaded and dominated both Eastern and Western traditions of Marxism, Kolozava continues, Marx's project of radical materialism has hitherto failed to see fruition. The early modern republicanism, turned into the liberal-democratic legacy as we know it nowadays (with the individualist metaphysical foundation of its political-economic horizon), has prevailed as that which undergirds modernity to this day.

Finally, in "Are We Human? Or, Posthumanism and the Subject of Modernity," Matthew Flisfeder offers a counterintuitive reading of Žižek's modernism, tying it to an inventive variation on humanism predicated on the inhuman and informed by the logic of the non-all. Flisfeder locates this "inhuman humanism" in Žižek's more recent critical engagement with posthumanism, transhumanism, and new materialism, as well as in his defense of Cartesianism and his Hegelian rereading of Lacan, with a special interest in the latter's feminine logic of sexuation. Flisfeder carefully distinguishes Žižek's inhuman humanism from its Marxist-humanist versions in the French tradition, represented, for example, by Sartre and Lefebvre, as well as from the antihumanist camps of Althusser and their followers. Žižek's *inhuman* humanism springs from his understanding of Human subjectivity as constitutively alienated, while his inhuman *humanism* is also grounded in the free choice of the subject, placing his work squarely in the Enlightenment tradition and the modern understanding of universal emancipation.

Part III: Glossary

Entries include "Fantasy," "Ideology," "Universality," "The Subject," "Symptom," "Class Struggle," "Violence," and "The Death Drive."

Notes

1 René Descartes, *Discourse on Method and Meditations on First Philosophy*, trans. Donald A. Cress (Indianapolis: Hackett, 1998), 35.

2 As an example of the *passage à l'acte*, Žižek gives the 2005 Paris riots, sparked by the deaths of Ziad Benna and Bouna Traoré, who were electrocuted as they fled the police in the Parisian suburb of Clichy-sous-Bois. As Žižek observes: "What needs to be resisted when faced with shocking reports and images of

the burning Paris suburbs is what I call the hermeneutic temptation: the search for some deeper meaning or message hidden in these outbursts. What is most difficult to accept is precisely the riots' meaninglessness: more than a form of protest, they are what Lacan called a *passage a l'acte*—an impulsive movement into action which can't be translated into speech or thought and carries with it an intolerable weight of frustration" (*V*, 76).

3   Jacques Lacan, *On Feminine Sexuality, The Limits of Love and Knowledge, 1972-1973: Encore, The Seminar of Jacques Lacan, Book XX*, trans. Bruce Fink (New York: Norton, 1998).

4   Jacques Rancière, *Disagreement: Politics and Philosophy*, trans. J. Rose (Minneapolis: University of Minnesota Press, 1999), 11.

5   "One pathetically asserts (and identifies with) *the point of inherent exception/ exclusion, the 'abject,' of the concrete positive order, as the only point of true universality, as the point which belies the existing concrete universality*" (UE, 178–9).

6   Slavoj Žižek, "A Leftist Plea for 'Eurocentrism,'" *Critical Inquiry* 24, no. 4 (1998): 988. See Étienne Balibar, *Equaliberty: Political Essays*, trans. James Ingram (Durham: Duke University Press, 2014).

7   Achille Mbembe, *Critique of Black Reason*, trans. Laurent Dubois (Durham: Duke University Press, 2017), 1.

8   Frantz Fanon, *The Wretched of the Earth*, trans. Richard Philcox (New York: Grove Press, 2004), 1.

9   Slavoj Žižek, "Human Rights and Its Discontents," *Lecture at Bard College*, November 15, 1999, available online: http://www.lacan.com/zizek-human.htm (accessed June 15, 2021).

10 Immanuel Kant, "An Answer to the Question: What Is Enlightenment?" in *What Is Enlightenment? Eighteenth-Century Answers and Twentieth-Century Questions*, ed. James Schmidt (Berkeley: University of California Press, 1996), 60.

11 Žižek, "A Leftist Plea for 'Eurocentrism,'" 988.

12 Emmanuel Levinas, "Is Ontology Fundamental?" in *Entre Nous: On Thinking-of-the Other*, trans. Michael B. Smith and Barbara Harshav (New York: Columbia University Press, 1998), 1–11.

13 Jacques Derrida, "Violence and Metaphysics," in *Writing and Difference*, trans. Alan Bass (Chicago: University of Chicago Press, 1978), 151.

14 Jacques Derrida, *The Animal that Therefore I Am*, trans. David Willis (New York: Fordham University Press, 2008), 6.

15 Derrida, *The Animal*, 9.

16 Slavoj Žižek, "Afterword: With Defenders Like These, Who Needs Attackers?" in *The Truth of Žižek*, ed. Paul Bowman and Richard Stamp (New York: Continuum, 2007), 234.

PART I

Mapping Žižek

1

Lacan and Žižek on the Cogito and the Modern

Galileo or Hegel?

Ed Pluth

It would likely be impossible to cover the relationship between Žižek and Hegel in a comprehensive fashion without basically duplicating Žižek's entire corpus. With the obvious exception of Lacan, certainly no other figure receives as much of his attention. Furthermore, trying to handle just some of what he does focus on in Hegel would be a challenge, as there are simply too many topics one could choose from, and the choice would seem arbitrary: absolute knowing, teleology, contingency and necessity, freedom, the cunning of reason—all of these are good Hegelian chestnuts that Žižek rereads, and reworks, in noteworthy ways. Fortunately, there is an organizing principle behind Žižek's widespread references to Hegel that one can focus on: the theme of the negative.

Focusing on this theme also allows us to spot some interesting differences between Lacan and Žižek when it comes to thinking the modern, and I believe this accounts for some of their differing trajectories: Žižek is overtly philosophical, and Lacan keeps philosophy at some distance. When Lacan himself thought about the modern he thought of two figures primarily: Descartes and Galileo. Descartes for the cogito and Galileo for the mathematization of nature, both of which Lacan thought were critical conditions for the possibility of psychoanalysis. When Žižek thinks about the modern he thinks of the cogito as well, but also, of course, Hegel (and other German Idealists as well like Kant, and Schelling, to a lesser extent), which is something Lacan does not do. Furthermore, he gives the cogito a slightly different spin compared to Lacan by reading it as a moment of negativity: not that Lacan does not do this, but Lacan's take on the cogito is more Galileo-inflected than Žižek's. Why is this?

I would like to use one of Žižek's early mission statements, found in *The Most Sublime Hysteric*, originally published in French in 1982, and appearing in different guises after that, to begin to get at an answer. It is a statement largely about misreadings, and I will paraphrase it here. It starts with the observation that among philosophers and theorists in the post-1968 French context especially (Žižek started this project in the early 1980s, at the latest), there is near-universal mistrust of Hegel and his central goal of absolute knowledge—it is totalizing, repressive, intolerant of difference and alterity, and impossible to achieve anyway. Yet, Žižek claims, this Hegel—call it the "panlogicist" Hegel, a Hegel according to whom nothing escapes the keen eye of Reason—is not the real Hegel but a caricature (*MSH*, 2). Absolute knowledge (for Hegel the goal of philosophy: or, better, the overcoming of philosophy as a "desire for wisdom" by the actual attainment of wisdom itself) can be read or thought quite differently, and in fact in a way that resonates with and can shed light on contemporary themes, impasses, and concerns (even post- and anticolonial ones). Fredric Jameson has recently summed up the issue well, in a text otherwise mostly defending Hegel, by concluding that the one thing that cannot be countenanced or brushed away in Hegel is what he calls the narcissism of the absolute: the absolute sees only itself, everywhere; there is no outside, no true other.[1] According to readings like this (not Jameson's but the ones Žižek mentions), Hegel might not even qualify as a modern thinker and could be portrayed instead as a reactionary premodern, hanging on to an antiquated metaphysics of totality. The Christian structure of Hegel's philosophy is indeed hard to overlook, and Žižek has even written about it (see especially *The Puppet and the Dwarf: The Perverse Core of Christianity* as well as the volume he appears in with the theologian John Milbank, *The Monstrosity of Christ*).

As for Lacan, the take on him at the time (and notice that this is shortly after his death in 1981) was that, while certainly no partisan for absolute knowledge (his embrace of the unconscious would likely rule this out) the phallus, however, as the privileged signifier of desire, guiding Lacan's understanding of the unconscious and sexual difference, plays a role similar to that of Reason in Hegel. To be a bit glib about it, where Hegel sees Reason everywhere, Lacan sees phalluses: acres and acres of phalluses. Lacan is, in short, a closeted and reconfigured Hegelian, adhering to the same colonizing (because applying the same model to everything), totalizing, and reductive model or image of thinking that Hegel does, just with different terms.

Žižek sets all this up in his typically engaging way and what comes next is a classic Žižekian twist. He in fact says to the point about Lacan and

Hegel: "yes, but." Yes, Lacan is a Hegelian but not in the sense that this (mostly deconstructive/Heideggerian inflected) reading of Lacan gives. Both the form and the content of Hegel's and Lacan's works are understood incorrectly by this reading. Žižek proposes a reading of Lacan with Hegel in which each sheds light on the other—a new/better Hegel made more visible when read through Lacan, where the emphasis is on topics like the negative and lack in the Other: topics that make impossible the very things critics of both Hegel and Lacan accuse them of. And a better Lacan, in which the topics of nontotality and alterity come to the fore as well:

> To my eyes, Lacan was fundamentally Hegelian, but did not know it. His Hegelianism is not to be found where we might expect it to be, in his overt references to Hegel, but rather in the final stage of his teachings, in the logic of the *pas-tout*, in the importance he placed on the Real, on the Lack in the Other. And, reciprocally, a reading of Hegel through the lens of Lacan gives us a picture of Hegel that is radically different from the common accepted view of him as a "panlogicist." It will bring out a Hegel of the logic of the "signifier," of a self-referential process articulated as the repeated positivation of a central Void. (*MSH*, 3)

Interestingly, what is not mentioned here is what I think is a central character in this drama between Hegel, Lacan, and Žižek when it comes to thinking the modern: the cogito. Insofar as the negative is a hallmark of the modern, Žižek's return to a Hegel for whom the negative is a key concept can be read as an effort to get something about the modern right, something that is arguably not emphasized in Lacan's own reading of the cogito (as I will try to show here). Žižek returns to Hegel not only to save Lacan from bad readings, or to save Lacan from his own bad reading of Hegel, but to hang on to something crucial about the modern itself. And, given that Lacan associates psychoanalysis so closely with modernity, something about psychoanalysis itself is at stake here as well—or, as I shall suggest in my conclusion, something is certainly at stake as far as the relationship between psychoanalysis and philosophy goes. Lacan did choose a partner for aligning psychoanalysis with modernity: not Hegel, a philosopher, but Galileo. The difference between Lacan and Žižek on this point is important and revealing, and it will be another one of my focal points here.

For Žižek the cogito arguably serves as the gateway to modernity. In a parody of the opening of *The Communist Manifesto* that opens his own *The Ticklish Subject*, Žižek writes that a specter is haunting Western academia, "the specter of the Cartesian subject":

> This book endeavors to reassert the Cartesian subject, whose rejection forms the silent pact of all the struggling parties of today's academia. [. . .]. The point, of course, is not to return to the *cogito* in the guise in

which this notion has dominated modern thought (the self-transparent thinking subject), but to bring to light its forgotten obverse, the excessive, unacknowledged kernel of the *cogito*, which is far from the pacifying image of the transparent Self. (*TS*, 2)

This "excessive, unacknowledged kernel" of the cogito is, of course, for Žižek its radical negativity. The more recent *Absolute Recoil* lists the cogito as one of the three great events in the history of philosophy, situated between antiquity's Platonic idealism and our contemporary, Hegel (179). And Lacan himself claimed that the new theoretical continent revealed by Freud's discovery of the unconscious would not have been found without the Cartesian cogito as a compass. Referring to his work in a previous year's seminar, Lacan writes that "I took my lead last year from a certain moment of the subject that I consider to be an essential correlate of science, a historically defined moment . . .: the moment Descartes inaugurates that goes by the name of *cogito*."[2] Yet Lacan and Žižek treat the cogito in different ways, with Žižek focusing on its negativity (a Hegelian inflection), and Lacan on something a bit harder to characterize, something that can certainly be thought of in terms of negativity, but that I am arguing receives a different emphasis, one in which his Galilean inspiration is evident.

Lacan's reading of Descartes goes against most conventional readings, according to which the point is to bring thinking and being together, making the cogito into a thinking substance, a thing-that-thinks.[3] Žižek certainly does follow Lacan on this point. Lacan's strategic rereading of the cogito asserts that, logically and chronologically, the cogito is essentially empty before it gets around to assuring itself of its own substantial being. He even rewrites the famous phrase *cogito ergo sum* such that this void-like emptiness is highlighted. Lacan alters the phrase by punctuating it differently, much as a Lacanian psychoanalyst will call to your attention a slip of the tongue by means of a sort of verbal punctuation, like an "mmm" or the repetition of a word. What Lacan does is (1) add a colon between the *I think* and the *I am*, and (2) put quotation marks around the last part of the phrase, such that it reads cogito*: "ergo sum"* or *I think: "therefore I am."* He discusses this change in some detail in his still unpublished seminars from the mid-1960s, but a canonical treatment of it does also occur in "Science and Truth," the most recent essay to have been included in the 1966 *Ecrits* (it was in fact read out loud at the opening session of his thirteenth seminar in late 1965):

> Which is why it is worth restating that in the test of writing *I am thinking: "therefore I am,"* with quotes around the second clause, it is legible that thought only grounds being by knotting itself in speech where every operation goes right to the essence of language.[4]

What is translated as "test" here could also be rendered as an ordeal or a trial (*épreuve*): perhaps Lacan is alluding to the strain he is putting the Cartesian formula under by writing it and punctuating it in such an unconventional manner. But notice that doing so does clearly move the formula away from the assertion of a *fusion* of thinking and being: being slips away into something *cited* by a thought. We could even say that being becomes something like the elusive metonymic object of thinking's desire, always called upon but never attained!

While it does make sense to think of this as an insertion of negativity into what is usually taken to be an assertion of full being, things get more complicated when it becomes a question of *which* thinking is involved here: if the cogito is of any relevance for psychoanalysis, it must be because it is somehow a precondition for the unconscious. But how does the move from the cogito as a self-conscious assertive act to the cogito as a precursor to the unconscious happen? Lacan's claim in "The Instance of the Letter" (1957) that "I am thinking where I am not, therefore I am where I am not thinking" does echo the cogito's phrasing and displays a disjunction between thinking and being as well.[5] The "thinking where I am not" is the unconscious (insofar as I associate my being with the ego and conscious life) and the "I am" where I am "not thinking" indicates that my true being is, nevertheless, there where I do not *think* I am thinking: precisely the unconscious again. One must be careful reading the relation this way, however, and not turn Lacan into a Kantian, for whom there is arguably no relation between thinking and being (or appearances and things in themselves) at all. More on this in a bit, since I think Žižek's use of Hegel to read Lacan, emphasizing the theme of negativity, is driven by a concern to avoid any semblance of Kantian, let alone Cartesian, dualism.

Later variations on the cogito occur in Lacan's work in which he tries to articulate the relevance of the cogito for psychoanalysis further, such as when Lacan establishes an "alienating vel" or either/or as the very beginning of subjectivity and its partner, the unconscious. Lacan had previously discussed the idea of an alienating vel in his eleventh seminar, in terms of a forced choice between being and *meaning* (interestingly, not *thinking*).[6] But then, starting with a negation of the Cartesian fusion of being and thinking, which in logical terms can be read as the negation of a conjunction (it is not the case that "I think AND I am"), Lacan then uses DeMorgan's law to arrive at a logically equivalent statement in the form of an alternative: "Either I am not thinking, OR I am not." While the seminar sources are sketchy and the record is not entirely clear, it seems that what Lacan is arguing in these sessions is that the only real choice is "I am not thinking," which is how he accounts for the origin of a refused thinking that returns in the Real: the unconscious, precisely.[7] As Fink points out in his commentary on this aspect of Lacan's views, the forced choice of "I am not thinking" does allow one to hang on to a semblance of being—the option "I am not" is avoided, and access to being is granted, albeit at the cost of rejecting a certain thinking and certain thoughts.[8]

While the separation of being and thinking in the cogito is emphasized by both Lacan and Žižek, where there seems to be a slight, but noteworthy I will say, divergence, can be found in Lacan's idea that, when coupled with the Galilean move toward mathematization and quantification, stripping natural physical objects of their qualities and reducing them to what is measurable, the cogito can be seen not simply, or not just, in terms of a separation of thinking and being but as a reduced thinking, a thinking-point blank, a thinking without qualities (a thinking that does not yet doubt, perceive, or judge, it merely thinks "that I am . . . "): a thinking that is all the same not without a subject. This is what Jean-Claude Milner also takes to be the upshot of Lacan's rewriting of the cogito, emphasizing its Galilean heritage:

> mathematized physics eliminates all the qualities of beings . . . ; a theory of the subject that wishes to answer to such a physics must also strip the subject of all its qualities. This subject, constituted according to what characterizes science, is the subject of science. . . . The qualitative markers of empirical individuality, whether psychic or somatic, do not apply to this subject; the qualitative properties of the soul do not apply to it either: this subject is neither mortal nor immortal, pure nor impure, just or unjust, sinner or saint, damned or saved; not even the formal properties that for such a long time were thought to be constitutive of subjectivity itself apply to it: it has neither Self, nor reflexivity, nor consciousness.
>
> Such is precisely the being that the *cogito* makes emerge.[9]

This cogito can be considered negative from this perspective, certainly, but more because of the fact that it is a thinking without qualities, not because it is a void or an abyss. And it is certainly significant that, with Galileo as a partner rather than Hegel, Lacan is able to drive this specific point about the cogito home by the imposition of a writing, by the mere addition of punctuation marks. While not perhaps strictly a mathematization, or an algebra, or even a topology (Lacan would develop all these more explicitly, and I will say more about them in a bit) it is certainly noteworthy that he opens up a new meaning for the cogito by means of written punctuation marks. Read this way, his treatment of the cogito fits in with his career-spanning anti-imaginary campaign, his suspicion of philosophical forms of expression, along with his fondness for nonintuitive mathematizations and topologies (imaginary numbers, Klein bottles, cross-caps).

If we look at Hegel's own remarks on the Cartesian cogito, we see that what Lacan embraces about the cogito is more or less exactly what Hegel criticizes about it: its quality-less status as a mere thinking-point, a thinking "that I am." At first, Hegel's seems like it is going to be a fairly conventional reading of Descartes. For example, Hegel takes *cogito ergo sum* to assert that "Thought and Being [are] inseparably bound together."[10] Where things get interesting is in his discussion of how the phrase should not be read as a syllogism: a claim that comes straight from Descartes himself. For there is no third, mediating term between thinking and being. *Cogito ergo sum* is not to be read as a bit of deductive argumentation. If this is the case, then the assertion instead needs to be taken as an "immediacy."[11] And for Hegel, the great enemy of immediacy, this is exactly its flaw:

> In thought we thus have Being; Being is, however, a poor determination, it is the abstraction from the concrete of thought. This identity of Being and Thought, which constitutes the most interesting idea of modern times, has not been further worked out by Descartes.[12]

Hegel is saying here that while the cogito is a fusion of being and thinking ("the most interesting idea of modern times" yet also the culmination of the Parmenidean dream, and thus not really a *break*), the problem is that the being asserted is a minimal, abstract, being-without-qualities: we could say, under the influence of Lacan's reading, that it is a reduced, Galilean cogito-point. Lacan, in contrast to Hegel, takes the further step of pointing out that the Cartesian move effectively disjoins thinking from being—it is anti-Parmenidean and truly modern—and as such it opens the door to the unconscious as an Other thinking. The point, of course, for Hegel, will be to develop a philosophy that fleshes out the contents of the cogito (a Logic): this would constitute a continuation of the modern, Cartesian project, doing true justice to "the most interesting idea of modern times." And, moreover, it would somehow get the relation between thinking and being right.

Despite Hegel's own take on the cogito, Žižek credits Hegel with associating subjectivity with negativity. In the chapter "I, or He, or It (the Thing) Which Thinks" from *Tarrying with the Negative*, Žižek places Descartes himself on the hither side of the modern. "The Cartesian universe stays within the confines of what Foucault, in his *The Order of Things*, called 'classical episteme,' that epistemological field regulated by the problematic of representations—their causal enchainment, their clarity and evidence, the connection between representation and represented content, etc" (*TN*, 12–13). This seems right, but with Lacan's reading in mind, Descartes is also credited in these pages with unintentionally wounding the premodern texture of reality with the cogito: only to patch it up right away. "Descartes [. . .] patches up the wound he cut into the texture of reality" by asserting that to think is to be, to be assured of existing: "only Kant fully articulates the inherent paradoxes of self-consciousness" (12). Here credit is given to Kant, yet Hegel is dubbed later in the same chapter "the most consequential of Kantians" (21). For

> the Hegelian subject—i.e., what Hegel designates as absolute, self-relating negativity—is nothing but the very gap which separates phenomena from

the Thing, the abyss beyond phenomena conceived in its negative mode, i.e., the purely negative gesture of limiting phenomena without providing any positive content which would fill out the space beyond the limit. (21)

Similar points are developed later in *Less Than Nothing*, this time not in the context of German Idealism but of Lacan's use of the cogito. Žižek points out what is consistent among the differing manipulations and permutations Lacan's treatment of the cogito underwent: that the cogito shows us in fact a separation of thinking and being.

What all these versions share is their accent on the gap that separates *cogito* from *sum*, thought from being—Lacan's aim was to undermine the illusion of their overlap by pointing to a fissure in the apparent homogeneity of thinking-being.

Yet Žižek is quick to point out in the very next sentence that this is not an absolute split, that there is nevertheless some sort of overlap (Lacan is not Kant):

It was only towards the end of his teaching that he asserted their overlap—a negative one, for sure. In other words, Lacan finally grasps the most radical zero-point of the Cartesian *cogito* as the negative intersection between being and thinking: the vanishing point at which I don't think *and* I *am not*: I am not a substance, a thing, an entity, I am reduced to a void in the order of being, to a gap, a *béance*. I *do not think*. (*LN*, 876–77)

Žižek is surely right to claim that even for Lacan being and thinking are still topologically linked somehow, but much hangs on how to get at this! Drawing on Hegel, he uses the concept of the negative to get at the relation, writing here of a "negative" overlap and a "negative intersection": ideas that one could certainly puzzle over. But it is a point often repeated in Žižek's work that gaps, fissures, faults, lacks are not, in an idealist fashion, the results of a projecting subject (or, from a religious perspective, the fault of Sin): rather, they are intrinsic to being itself, and the structure of the subject echoes them. If there is an overlap to be described, in philosophical terms using the word "negative" is not a terrible way to describe it! If it is an overlap at all, it is more like a repetition or an echoing than a fusion. But one sees the difficulty here I hope: it is difficult to use the resources of ordinary language to get such ideas across. I will return to this point in my conclusion.

This is why it is interesting to take Lacan's Galilean flirtations seriously and consider again why Lacan did not turn to Hegel. There is an easy answer as to why Lacan himself did not use Hegel as a resource for psychoanalysis:

it was for nonessential, contingent reasons. Lacan had no reason to disagree with the dominant pan-logicist reading of Hegel from the twentieth-century Hegelians he knew and respected, Hyppolite and Kojève. Žižek suggests as much in the mission statement I paraphrased from at the start of this essay: "Lacan 'did not know where he was a Hegelian,' because his reading of Hegel followed in the tradition of Kojève and Hyppolite" (*MSH*, 4). But there are deeper reasons, ones that are not only attributable to a misreading of Hegel, or even a nonreading of Hegel, but rather to Lacan's overall perspective on philosophy generally.

Without Hegel as a partner and, significantly, without philosophy as a partner, Lacan develops an alternative modernist route for psychoanalysis, using new "writings" and topologies. This is a consequence of Lacan's pessimism about philosophy and what he took to be its intrinsic weddedness to the resources of the Imaginary. When Lacan, in a variety of places, called for a new "transcendental aesthetic," he looked to use nonintuitive geometries and topologies that would avoid the lures of classical geometrical forms, with their obvious distinctions between inner and outer spaces: completely inadequate for thinking the status of such things as drives and the unconscious, and treacherously misleading as well. A new "transcendental aesthetic" was necessary for psychoanalysis then because the Kantian rules for perception and experience don't apply to the spaces psychoanalysis works in, on, and with. Lacan himself seems to have considered quantification and writing (cf. Galileo's idea that the book of nature is written in the language of mathematics) to be as, if not more, important, than the negative for securing the position of psychoanalysis.

I think the difference here—the choice, between Galileo or Hegel—is significant, since the partnership with Hegel rather than Galileo is probably necessary for any approach that is going to try to bring a Lacanian orientation into philosophy. I certainly cannot think of any better philosopher for the purpose! Lacan, we know, however, preferred to associate himself with anti-philosophy.[13] Lacan's alliance with Galileo (indeed a short-lived one, if Milner's reading is correct, spanning only the period of what he calls Lacan's "first classicism," roughly 1955 to 1966, notably overlapping with his efforts to rewrite the cogito) was consistent with developing psychoanalysis as some sort of science.[14] Not a typical natural science, of course, but something new and mathematized, applying to a different category of objects, yet a science insofar as its mathematization would assure its ability to be transmitted integrally.

I think this discussion can help us to appreciate the importance of a recent revision to Žižek's mission statement from 2012's *Less Than Nothing*, which will return us to the theme of why Žižek uses Hegel. It includes a reference to the work of the Slovenian "Party Troika" (including Mladen Dolar and Alenka Zupančič) and also refers to "limitations" that the project has "recently" encountered:

> Whatever we were doing, the underlying axiom was that reading Hegel through Lacan (and vice versa) was our unsurpassable horizon. Recently, however, limitations of this horizon have appeared: with Hegel, his inability to think pure repetition and to render thematic the singularity of what Lacan called the *objet a*; with Lacan, the fact that his work ended in an inconsistent opening: *Seminar XX (Encore)* stands for his ultimate achievement and deadlock—in the years after, he desperately concocted different ways out (the *sinthome,* knots . . .) all of which failed. (*LN*, 18)

It is rare to see points like this about either Hegel or Lacan coming from Žižek! After several decades, he observes that there are limits to the project he outlined in 1982. There may be a Hegel irreducible to Lacan, and vice versa. This would not be surprising. He references Hegel's incapacity to think the status of such psychoanalytic concepts as repetition and object a. As for Lacan, it is a bit harder to say. The deadlocks Žižek refers to, I believe, involve some notorious impasses in formalization (always a hallmark of the Real). Žižek suggests that these persistent encounters resulted in a sort of repetition compulsion on Lacan's part: I would say, he tried to handle this problem by developing multiple, different writing techniques. And I am not referring to Lacan's difficult style but rather to the multitude of letters, symbols, formulas, graphs, and so on deployed across the Lacanian corpus. Žižek refers to the *sinthome* and Borromean knots: but we could add the better known Lacanian algebra itself (barred-S, a, A, S◊D, S(barred-A), and so on, and even his discourse theory (involving permutations of S1, S2, barred-S, and a), which all, of course, involve the manipulation of letters. Even the Borromean knots can be read as a use of letters (they are typically labeled R, S, I), and I want to point out again how Lacan's manipulation of *cogito ergo sum* itself occurs by means of the creative insertion of punctuation marks.

Jean-Claude Milner's suggestion is that after Lacan's Galilean project collapses (it does not seem possible to integrally transmit psychoanalytic knowledge, through mathemes or schools), at the end of his career Lacan was increasingly drawn to silence and showing: the silent manipulation of Borromean knots before some rather puzzled seminar audience members.[15] While this can be contested, and should be (it even is by Milner himself), it does indeed seem as if Lacan was caught between the horns of a dilemma: the use of ordinary language generates meaning, meaning is "religious" and imaginary, the errors of philosophy need to be avoided, a new transcendental aesthetic is needed, so what we need is a writing that targets the Real in a more efficacious manner. If that doesn't work, where else can one go but to silence and showing? Žižek's use of Hegel, I suggest, is an effort to find a way out of this dilemma, one that embraces the unique manner in which philosophy can use language.

The following passage gives us some sense of what Žižek is up to: regarding the truths psychoanalysis reveals, he notes that "of course, the only way for us to articulate this truth is within language—by way of torturing language. As Hegel already knew, when we think, we think in language against language" (*LN*, 877–78). Hegel of course is famous for using ordinary German words in a way that stretched them out, making them unfamiliar. Hegel's jargon does not consist of alien made-up technical terms but rather just ordinary German words used in an idiosyncratic way. Previously, Žižek had been talking about Walter Benjamin's *Critique of Violence* and whether language is a nonviolent medium. Žižek's agreement with Benjamin is one of his typically ironic ones:

> there *is* a "language" which is outside violence, but Benjamin looks for it in the wrong place. It is not the language of peaceful communication among subjects, but the language of pure mathematics, this joyful study of multiplicities. Should we still call it language? Lacan's answer was no: he played with terms like "matheme" or "writing." (878)

Žižek seems to be thinking of Alain Badiou's use of set theory here, but indeed, the point of Lacan's flirtations with different mathemes and writings was to circumvent meaning, the Imaginary, and the intuitive as much as possible. Žižek's detour through Hegel arrives at the idea of a language use against language—let's call that philosophy, when it is at its best. This is a possibility for philosophy that Lacan did not seem to put any confidence in, yet it is a practice, a language use, that we can certainly say that he engaged in. But what is an open question for me still is whether a focus on the negative is adequate to the task Lacan envisioned for the development of the kind of new transcendental aesthetic psychoanalysis needed: Can it take us to the kind of topological spaces Lacan thought were necessary for getting the psychoanalytic domain right? Is the negative enough or for the furtherance of the modern project that is psychoanalysis is not some Galilean flirtation needed as well?

Notes

1 Fredric Jameson, *The Hegel Variations: On the Phenomenology of Spirit* (London: Verso, 2010), 130.

2 Jacques Lacan, *Écrits: The First Complete Edition in English*, trans. Bruce Fink (New York: Norton, 2007), 727.

3 According to Jean-Claude Milner, Lacan's reading of the cogito is indebted to the "instantaneist" reading of it by the Descartes scholar Martial Gueroult. (*A Search for Clarity: Science and Philosophy in Lacan's Oeuvre*, trans. Ed Pluth (Evanston: Northwestern University Press, 2020), 129, n. 10). I will comment

on this reading a bit later on: it seems to me Hegel may also have had this view!

4   Lacan, *Écrits*, 734.
5   Lacan, *Écrits*, 430.
6   Lacan, *The Seminar of Jacques Lacan. The Four Fundamental Concepts of Psychoanalysis*, ed. Jacques-Alain Miller, trans. Alan Sheridan (New York: Norton, 1998), 211.
7   Lacan, *Logique du fantasme*. Unpublished seminar (volume XIV). Session of April 12, 1967.
8   Bruce Fink, *The Lacanian Subject* (Princeton: Princeton University Press, 1996), 45.
9   Milner, *A Search for Clarity*, 22.
10 G. W. F. Hegel, *Lectures on the History of Philosophy, Volume 3: Medieval and Modern Philosophy*, trans. E. S. Haldane and Frances H. Simon (Lincoln: University of Nebraska Press, 1996), 228.
11 Hegel, *Lectures*, 229.
12 Hegel, *Lectures*, 230.
13 See Alain Badiou's definitive study of this issue. *Lacan: Anti-Philosophy 3 (The Seminars of Alain Badiou)*, trans. Kenneth Reinhard and Susan Spitzer (New York: Columbia University Press, 2018).
14 Milner in fact refers to Lacan's first "classicism" period as an "extended Galileism," one that he argues is replaced in a second "classicism" by a use of mathemes and letters (Milner, *A Search for Clarity*, 72). If I am blending the two together here, it is perhaps because I am not as convinced of the discontinuity between the two periods as Milner is. Certainly what is happening, and increasing during this time, are Lacan's frustrations with the transmissibility of psychoanalysis, culminating with his use of Borromean knots and ultimately the dissolution of his school.
15 In an afterward to *A Search for Clarity*, Milner now argues that he overlooked the importance of Joyce and lalangue for Lacan during this period, such that a concept like creative or active homophony might be what Lacan was truly after (Milner, *A Search for Clarity*, 118–23).

2

Žižek's Hegel, Our Hegel

Agon Hamza

> *It is necessary to study a system of philosophy as a whole. The principle of a philosophy contains everything in undeveloped form, but only as undeveloped, latent, as the empty formal concept, not the thing itself. Just like a miser, keeps all his enjoyments in his purse as possibility, and spares himself the actuality, the toil of enjoyment itself.*
>
> HEGEL

Referring to Slavoj Žižek as *our* Hegel can be considered as quite a bold claim. One can think of many reproaches to this thesis, beginning with the most frequent one, which points to Žižek's performative contradiction, which indicates his ability to jump from the highest register (discussions of Hegel, Lacan, Schelling, etc.) to the lowest (popular culture, obscenities, and vulgarities of everyday life . . .) while paying crucial attention, in between, to the politics of emancipation. How can one take such an approach seriously, especially coming from a philosopher who tries to defend and rethink Hegel? Isn't Hegel the very name of the systematicity and coherence of philosophy and philosophical thinking?

To this, one can reply with Žižek. For him, contradiction is itself the constitutive dimension of his thinking, that is to say, of dialectical thinking. His example is Hegel's *Phenomenology of Spirit*, which is an inconsistent book; it is full of contradictions, and what is more interesting is that *Phenomenology* is perhaps one of the most nonsystematic "big books" in the history of philosophy. Its content is highly rich in terms of what Hegel discusses there, ranging from self-certainty and the master-slave dialectic all the way to a discussion of Antigone, the French Revolution, art, and religion. The wide variety of topics discussed here cannot have any consistent systematicity whatsoever, but this contradiction is the very foundation of Hegelian thinking, an observation that holds for Žižek as well. The lack of great systematization for which Hegel was continuously accused of: the grand totalizer, whose system absorbs and swallows everything within itself. Hegel's thought exists on contradictions, which means that it also embodies it. This is where we should locate and understand Žižek's inconsistency: both as his *forte* as well as his compatibility with Hegel and fidelity to his work.

This is his principle of dialectical materialism. Dialectical materialism is not a system of thought nor a preconfigured system. In traditional understanding, dialectic is conceived of either as a method or as a system. However, this is not the case with Žižek. For him, putting dialectical materialism to work means interpenetrating it with an object. In other words, there is no distinction between the method and an object: they are mediated. This means that the method appears within what it studied as an object, and the object is nothing other than a "distortion," a particular logic which spells out the method. In what follows, I will discuss the concept of dialectical materialism through the notion of *absolute recoil* and, from this standpoint, its implications in Žižek's Hegelian reading of Christianity. In this sense, this chapter follows his fundamental axiom of "returning to Hegel," as an intellectual and political imperative of our era.

Absolute Recoil

In recent years, Slavoj Žižek has set out to rework the tenets of dialectical materialism, after the disastrous failure of the socialist and communist experiments of the previous century.

Žižek's name for the dialectic is *absolute recoil*. Hegel uses this term twice in his *Science of Logic*, through which he philosophizes about "the speculative coincidence of opposites in the movement by which a thing emerges out of its own loss" (AR, 1). In a longer paragraph from *Logic*, Hegel writes that the ground is

> itself *one of the reflected determinations* of essence; but it is the last of them, or rather the meaning of this determination is merely that it is a sublated determination. The reflected determination, in falling to the ground, acquires its true meaning, namely, to be within itself the absolute recoil upon itself, that is to say, the positedness that belongs to essence is only a sublated positedness, and conversely, only self-sublating positedness is the positedness of essence. Essence, in determining itself as

ground, is determined as the non-determined; its determining is only the sublating of its being determined. Essence, in being determined thus as self-sublating, has not proceeded from another, but is, in its negativity, self-identical essence.[1]

Hegel argues that in a logic of reflection, there is nothing before the loss; that is to say that "becoming is essence, its reflective movement, is the movement of nothing to nothing, and so back to itself."[2] For Hegel, the becoming as transition sublates itself in becoming, which means that when something (say, origin, or cultural or national roots, etc.) is negated, and through the very act of negation, that thing is posited backward. Hegel distinguishes between three forms of absolute reflection: positioning reflection, external reflection, and determining reflection. This triad forms the fundamental dialectic matrix of Hegel's philosophy. A reference to religion can serve as a good example. Let us take the pagan universe as the *positioning reflection*, whose inner harmony is "cut off" or disturbed by the emergence of Judaism (*external reflection*), where God has the status of the transcendental. The *determinate reflection* is Christianity, in which God is not alien to men, but he "becomes man" with the figure of Jesus Christ. Another example of this dialectical matrix is the constitution or formation of nations, as a process of "reviving or returning to their lost roots."

It is in this sense that Žižek reads the *absolute recoil*: there is nothing prior to the loss *to which we should return*. Therefore, dialectic is

> an inconsistent mess (first phase, the starting point) which is negated and, through negation, the Origin is projected or posited backwards, so that a tension is created between the present and the lost Origin (second phase). In the third phase, the Origin is perceived as inaccessible, relativized—we are in external reflection, that is, our reflection is external to the posited Origin which is experienced as a transcendent presupposition. In the fourth phase of absolute reflection, our external reflexive movement is transposed back into the Origin itself, as its own self-withdrawal or decentering. (*AR*, 149)

In this sense, retroactivity is the name of the dialectic: the dialectical process determines or rather constitutes its own presuppositions or its own past. To put this in the form of a proposition: a dialectical process retroactively creates its own conditions of possibility. In Žižek's own terms, what retroactively comes into existence is not the previously existing form of a thing or a matter, but the thing/matter which, even though articulated in the Old, emerges as the New, altered from the form of the present. With the rise of the latter, "the previous form is (mis)perceived as 'hitherto formless matter'; that is, the 'formlessness' itself is a retroactive effect, a violent erasure of the previous form" (*LN*, 272).

Žižek's dialectic is always-already a dialectic that works retroactively. The dialectical relation between the Old and the New is not a teleological narrative in which the New is already inscribed in the Old and the social formation arises from the Old in a successive or linear line. Every social formation creates (positions) its past. Therefore, "Hegel's dialectic is the science of the gap between the Old and the New, of accounting for this gap" (*LN*, 273). But in Žižek's understanding, it is not only the gap between the Old and the New but also its "self-reflective redoubling," which is to say the cut between the two, that is elaborated. It "simultaneously describes the gap, within the Old itself; between the Old 'in-itself' (as it was before the New) and the Old retroactively posited by the New" (*LN*, 273). The retroactive positioning of presuppositions is the exact opposite of teleology. Missing the retroactive positioning of presuppositions means that one is already in the ideological field of what Žižek refers to as evolutionary teleology: "an ideological narrative thus emerges in which previous epochs are conceived as progressive stages or steps towards the present 'civilized' epoch" (*LN*, 272). The process of retroactively positing the presuppositions is for Žižek the materialist substitute for "teleology"—an accusation which Hegel often received.

An important question persists here: Why does Žižek need the Hegelian concept of *absolute recoil*? Prior to *Less Than Nothing* and *Absolute Recoil*, Žižek's "big book" was *The Parallax View*. According to him, the parallax (a term he borrows from Kojin Karatani) is the "apparent displacement of an object (the shift of its position against a background), caused by a change in observational position that provides a new line of sight" (*PV*, 17). For example, we can take Marx's work with regard to the relation between the critique of political economy and the political novelty. Or as Žižek argues, the ultimate Marxian parallax is constituted by the critique of political economy and politics. The parallax dimension relies on the fact that one is not reducible to the other. This is the Žižekian lesson: Marx's critique of political economy is not only a critique of the classical political economy (Smith, Ricardo), but it is also a form of critique, a transcendental one, that allows us to articulate the elementary forms of social edifice under capitalism itself. And this "transcendental" framework cannot be anything else but philosophical. In fact, this is exactly what Marx said in the famous letter to Lassalle.[3]

Karatani takes the example of the mirror and the image we see. This shift between the mirror and what I see is the "pronounced parallax between the mirror and the photographic image."[4] When we look in the mirror, we see ourselves *plus* something we cannot see without the reflective surface: we see the world *with us in it*. Another way of putting it is that we see the world "without our absence"—that is, without that blind spot which marks our indelible immersion in it. The famous figure of "the double," once popular in fantastic literature, and which Freud and Lacan later associated with the anguishing experience of the uncanny,[5] concerns precisely this "missing absence": What if the reflected image were suddenly to start moving while I remained in the same position? The anguishing effect of the double—of someone other than me who is nonetheless me—is not that he is a poor copy of me who fools other people into believing his authenticity. The problem is that the double is effectively *more me than myself*: the blind spot from which I gaze at the mirror, this *absent* standpoint which at the same time marks my embedding in the world and divides me from it, is *absent* in the double: as I gaze at him, *I see myself fully embedded in the world*—more so than myself (insofar as I include this absent standpoint from which I see the double). My being in the world is marked by an alienation from this grasping at once my own being, as I am deprived of the capacity of seeing myself "from the outside," but the double is constituted through the *alienation of this alienation*, the embedding of my image in the image of the world in a fit more perfect than the one I experience within my own skin. And we find this same operation—through which an alienation is first marked as the presence of an absence, and then, through a redoubling, becomes a more fully constituted being—in the way Marx conceives the shift from social to religious alienation.

However, the Hegelian twist to be added here, according to Žižek, is that "the observed difference is not simply 'subjective,' due to the fact that the same object which exists 'out there' is seen from two different stances, or points of view" (*PV*, 17). In this regard, the concept of "absolute recoil" is Hegel's term for what Žižek used as a parallax—the withdrawal that creates the object it withdraws from. This is the definition of the parallax in his *The Parallax View*. In other words, it is Žižek's way of not having a Hegelianism that depends on a Kantian concept, since parallax *is a Kantian idea*. The *parallax* move of Hegel consists in the Kantian distinction between *phenomenal* and *noumenal* worlds. Kant famously declared that he reduced the field of knowledge in order to make room for religious belief; our access to noumenal world would deprive us of our freedom. Freedom is possible only in the field of phenomenal domain. Hegel's answer to the Kantian problematic is not to prove or show that one can go beyond the phenomenal domain and thus reach the noumenal level. He is not concerned with overcoming the Kantian gap, and gaining access to Absolute Knowledge, as it is claimed all too often. Hegel is essentially a superficial thinker: his entire philosophy is dedicated to emptying out the "beyond" of any substance, doing away with all essentialist dualisms. In other words, Hegel is not concerned with showing that we can reach beyond phenomena, without getting caught in antinomies, but that there is no outside the phenomenal world.

His answer to Kant is that "this very gap is the solution: Being itself is incomplete" (*SFA*, 70). Therefore, "the task is to think this impossibility not as a limit, but as a positive fact—and this, perhaps, is what at his most radical Hegel does" (*LN*, 239). Impossibility is an ontological fact, argues Žižek. In this sense, Hegel is the most radical thinker of *parallax*, where the gaps in knowledge are gaps in being as being. In other words, every idea of objective reality is constituted through transcendental subjectivity.

But where does Marxism, or more precisely, dialectical materialism, come to form the philosophical base of Žižek's work, so to speak? And more concretely, how should we understand Žižek's dialectical materialism? Žižek himself elaborates that his work should be understood as an exercise in, and not on, dialectical materialism; that is to say, dialectical materialism is not the topic but is practised in the work itself. In doing so, Žižek's solution is to elevate Hegel's speculative notion of *absolute recoil* to a universal principle of ontological import. Drawing on traditions that are already known, he maintains that dialectical materialism is the only "true philosophical inheritor of what Hegel designates as the speculative attitude of the thought towards objectivity." This is the core of Žižek's argument: dialectical materialism concerns the most radical attempt to ground subjectivity *qua* subjectivity in objectivity—not merely to find the hidden "objective reality" of thought, but he uses Lacan and Hegel to ground subjectivity *in its negative character* in the Real.

Healing the Wounds

Having all this in mind, why is Hegel (together with Lacan) the foundation of Žižek's philosophical system? Žižek does not simply return to Hegel. His return has the form of *repetition*—not a repetition which is not repeating of the same, but rather a repetition of the Hegelian gesture. Why does Žižek need to repeat Hegel in order to rethink dialectical materialism? Or, to put it in other words, why does every materialism worthy of its name return to (and repeat) Hegel? The "return to Hegel" is necessary for the field of possibility for thinking. With the return to the Hegelian dialectic, we are able to think the unconscious, class struggle, scientific creativity, political radicalism, and so on.

The question, then, is, how is it possible to make a monster of Hegelian philosophy and take it for granted in order to legitimize the philosophical and political position? The Hegelian monster has a name and it is Absolute Knowing, which is understood as the position in which *spirit heals all wounds*, that is to say, an ideal, complete, and closed society without excesses and contradictions. But is this really the Hegelian Absolute? The standard approach to the Absolute is that it reconciles all antagonisms. Hegel famously claimed: "the wounds of Spirit heal and leave no scars behind."[6] We can read this statement either as a sign of a totalizing unification (idealism) or as a sign of the very groundlessness of the dialectical movement. The movement of Spirit leaves no scars (leaves nothing behind) because it is the healing that *produces* the wound. Spirit leaves behind not a trail of scars—it does not "stick" to what was already there—but a trail of fantasmatic wounds (losses that were never present to begin with, losses that only had any being in so far as they were lost) which, precisely because they are not events in the sense of reality (of identifiable interruptions in the continuum of time), make no "marks" in history (scars). The "wounds of Spirit leave no scar" because Spirit does not work through ruptures in the fabric of history: it works by positing the presupposed loss (what "would have been" before the rupture or event) and not by presupposing the posited (the wound that the scar would have healed). This strange process, through which we only lose what we never had, allows us to get to the most difficult point in Hegelian thinking and hence the actual reason why it is a thought so prone to misreading: if the proof of contingency is the lack of "marks," then there are no marks of contingency. In this sense, teleological determinism is indistinguishable from historical contingency: if there are only retroactive events demarcated by what we lost after them (but never directly had access to before them), then there is no transcendental structure to guarantee not only that an event has taken place but also that there are events in the Hegelian system to begin with. To formulate this in dense but nonetheless coherent terms: the proof of contingency is the very appearance of necessity, the illusion of the one—totality, the very (lack of the) mark of the multiple without totalization. Hegelian history is the history of the impossible, later defined by Lacan as "that which does not cease to write itself," just like the logic of the Hegelian Spirit, which does not cease *not* to leave a scar behind.

This analysis of the dialectical movement from the standpoint of loss allows us to return to the discussion concerning ground and the *absolute recoil*. Have we not seen how the passage from the contingent to the necessary is mediated by the impossible (the work of Spirit is mediated by scars that "do not cease not to write" themselves)? The work of the impossible in Hegel is precisely what the figure of "recoil" names: the operation of withdrawal which creates that which it subtracts from, a form of wound which only appears after it has been healed. The absolute recoil is therefore truly the operation that clarifies the core of the Hegelian dialectic, which allows us to reintroduce contingency—and therefore materialism—into the dialectic, without letting go of the fundamental Hegelian insights concerning retroaction, contradiction, and the logic of self-difference. Equally fundamental is the role of this conceptual operation in clarifying the "misreadings" of Hegel. If "recoiling" names the standpoint from which we can discern how the appearance of necessity is the only "scar" of contingency, how the affirmation of identity is ultimately the proof of nonidentity, then we can assume that a reading of Hegel that cannot count on such standpoint will lack the resources to distinguish materialism from idealism, the affirmation that ideas are born from the senseless and temporal "healing" of a nonexistent wound, from the affirmation that time and sense are finally gathered at the necessity of an idea to realize itself.

Žižek and Christianity

We come, thus, to the perplexing situation of recognizing in religion a condition for the critique of ideology and ideological mystifications. But how could it be that the critique of beliefs necessarily passes through belief itself? This is precisely the thesis argued by Žižek. The premise of the *Puppet and the Dwarf* (and of his entire "Christian materialist" project) is the following:

> What we are getting today is a kind of "suspended" belief, a belief that can thrive only as not fully (publicly) admitted, as a private obscene secret. Against this attitude, one should insist even more emphatically that the "vulgar" question "Do you really believe or not?" matters—more than ever, perhaps. My claim here is not merely that I am a materialist through and through, and that the subversive kernel of Christianity is accessible also to a materialist approach; my thesis is much stronger: this kernel is accessible only to a materialist approach—and vice versa: to become a true dialectical materialist, one should go through the Christian experience. (*PD*, 6)

The structure of this proposal is deceptively simple, for in fact it proposes two contradictory movements: to produce a materialist reading of Christianity (i.e., to produce a materialist theory of belief that doesn't coincide with its immediate notion) and to reform dialectical materialism itself through the consideration of Christianity (i.e., to demonstrate that the Christian religious experience poses a challenge to materialism that calls for its reinvention). These are seemingly circular tasks and therefore impossible: How can we produce a materialist reading of Christianity if this reading itself is supposed to change what we mean by "materialist," and therefore affect the way we read Christianity, to begin with?

The way out of this circularity was already well known to Hegel, a philosopher who was troubled by the question of foundations and beginnings in all matters speculative. For Hegel, there is a twist in this circular relation between rational thinking and the religious experience, an asymmetry that is in fact what characterizes Christianity to begin with, namely, the way Christianity stages the limit of belief within its own faith. The title of "revealed" religion is merited for Christianity not because it reveals "a" religious truth, but rather because it stages the truth of religion *as such,* showing us that the suspension of belief has the structure of a belief—a "barren belief," so to speak. This is why, already in his *Faith and Knowledge*, Hegel proposes a strange continuity between the "Historical Good Friday"—the death of

God within Christian faith—and the "Speculative Good Friday"—the doing away with God in rational thinking:

> But the pure concept or infinity as the abyss of nothingness in which all being is engulfed, must signify the infinite grief [of the finite] purely as a moment of the supreme Idea, and no more than a moment. Formerly, the infinite grief only existed historically in the formative process of culture. It existed as the feeling that "God Himself is dead," upon which the religion of more recent times rests; the same feeling that Pascal expressed in so to speak sheerly empirical form: "la nature est telle qu'elle marque partout un Dieu perdu et dans l'homme et hors de l'homme." [Nature is such that it signifies everywhere a lost God both within and outside man.] By marking this feeling as a moment of the supreme Idea, the pure concept must give philosophical existence to what used to be either the moral precept that we must sacrifice the empirical being (Wesen), or the concept of formal abstraction [e.g., the categorical imperative]. Thereby it must re-establish for philosophy the Idea of absolute freedom and along with it the absolute Passion, the speculative Good Friday in place of the historic Good Friday. Good Friday must be speculatively re-established in the whole truth and harshness of its God-forsakenness. Since the [more] serene, less well grounded, and more individual style of the dogmatic philosophies and of the natural religions must vanish, the highest totality can and must achieve its resurrection solely from this harsh consciousness of loss, encompassing everything, and ascending in all its earnestness and out of its deepest ground to the most serene freedom of its shape.[7]

Hegel provides us an entry point into the Žižekian encounter between materialism and religion: while the religious or idealist undertones of materialism cannot be directly accessed by materialism itself, the materialist core of the religious experience is itself thematized within Christianity, and, in particular, in the special role the death of God takes in it. We could venture that the death of God is the point at which the two sides of a circle cross, as in a Möebius strip, and the materialist kernel of religion motivates a reformed dialectical materialism in which the other side of this same "twist" can now be found, since it is a materialism which can now account for the general theory of barren beliefs, that is, for the effective structure of belief's separation from the believer in general.

Therefore, in his return to Hegel, Žižek is also recuperating a view of religion which in fact recognizes within Marxism an "underlying current" that was already dormant in it, namely, the understanding that the space of representation—of the discourse that models the world—is itself inconsistent and passes over into that which it models. This, in fact, is one of Hegel's most important ideas in the *Phenomenology of Spirit*, and the true turning point of the passage between Christianity and speculative thinking. Hegel is essentially a superficial thinker: all his philosophy is dedicated to emptying out the "beyond" of any substance, doing away with all essentialist dualisms—or, as mentioned in the quote earlier, a thinker who tries to carry out the task of accepting "the whole truth and harshness" of the world's "God-forsakenness." But if this is the case, then Hegel cannot criticize mystifications from the standpoint of the de-mystified, or representations from the standpoint of the underlying reality. He has himself willingly thrown away the philosopher's main tool of critique and therefore should accept the title that has been given to him by most of his commentators—Marx included—of being a great idealist, committed to the all-encompassing surface of ideas. But this understanding of Hegel leaves out the other side of his gesture, for the emptying out of the world's "depth" is correlate with the recognition that its superficiality is "bent" or "twisted": it contains sites where what is becomes its own negation. And so another way out of religious thinking opens up: not "beyond," "beside," or "behind" it but through its own immanent inconsistency, the site where representation undermines itself, becoming its other. For Hegel this is precisely what happens with the passion of Christ—and in a double sense—since it is both the first religious experience of the inner limit of religion *and* the first nonreligious thinking of the existence of such contradictory sites within representation in general. The Passion therefore does not only locate the point where representation touches on its other—were this its limit, Christianity would be an ode to the "unrepresentable"—but it also empties out the substance of this otherness by rendering it coextensive with rational thinking:

> in the Christian Revelation, no one comes towards us, nothing comes out of this manifestation, it does not *show* anything. Nothing, except that now the relations "referred/referrend," "signifier/signified" do not have a continuation. God does not *become* manifest: he *is*, side by side, *fuür sich seiende Manifestation.* What is unveiled, if one still wants to use this term, is only that there was the necessity of appearing in Him, in the very strict sense of being-for-an-Other, the impossibility of being totally "Him" in the case of remaining solely "in Himself" (. . .) On the other hand, if one no longer imagines God as an objectifiable content, one also does not incur on the risk of splitting him between His *essence* and his *appearance*, His *before* and His *after*.[8]

Returning to Žižek's materialist theory of religion, we can now understand why he explicitly says: "since Hegel was the philosopher of Christianity, it is no wonder that a Hegelian approach to Christ's death brings out a radical emancipatory potential" (*LN*, 6). At the beginning of *The Fear of Four Words*, after quoting Chesterton at length, Žižek puts forward the axiom of his Hegelian reading of Christianity:

The axiom of this essay is that there is only one philosophy which thought the implications of the four words ["He Was Made Man"] through to the end: Hegel's idealism—which is why almost all philosophers are also no less frightened of Hegel's idealism. (MC, 26)

In his Seminar VII, Lacan opposes the thesis of the "death of God," arguing that God was dead from the very beginning, but only in Christianity he is self-aware of that. He refers to Hegel when he speaks about a "certain atheistic message in Christianity itself." But which God dies and what are the consequences? Žižek argues that God has to die twice: in Judaism "in itself," whereas in Christianity God dies "for itself." And this is the true atheistic dimension of "Christianity as the 'religion of atheism': God cannot be directly negated, it is the subsequent erasure of the individual that sets the Holy Spirit free from its embodiments, that sublates God into a virtual fiction sustained only by the collective of believers" (AR, 261–2).

It is at this point that the relevance of a "return to Hegel" makes itself felt, because, from the standpoint of his Hegelian-inspired Marxist theory of belief, the critique of belief does *not* take the form of an increasing passivity or a retreat from those practices that are structured by beliefs—rather, the critique of the belief in God *has the form of a collective practice*. It is the immediate, passive engagement with reality which appears, from Žižek's standpoint, as the idealist—secretively social—commitment to fantasies, ideals, and mystifications, while the active, collective engagement with practices that are explicitly mediated by abstractions that have the potential, in emptying out the substance of this mediation, to produce true critical effects. Rather than turn from religion to "social practice," as the orthodox Marxist analysis suggests, Žižek's Marxism transposes the full Hegelian passage between religion and speculative thinking into the relation between religious practice and materialism: just as Reason generalizes and radicalizes the "infinite grief" of the "historical Good Friday" by emptying out every "beyond" of its substance, so would materialism preserve and radicalize religious collective practice by emptying out every belief of its substantial mediator.

In the *Phenomenology of Spirit*, Hegel writes:

> The death of the Mediator [that is, Christ] is the death not only of his natural aspect or of his particular being-for-self, not only of the already dead husk stripped of its essential Being, but also of the *abstraction* of the divine Being. For the Mediator, in so far as his death has not yet completed the reconciliation, is the one-sidedness which takes as *essential* Being the simple element of thought in contrast to actuality: this one-sided extreme of the Self does not as yet have equal worth with essential Being; this it first has as Spirit. The death of this picture-thought contains, therefore, at the same time the death of the *abstraction of the divine Being* which is not posited as Self.[9]

However, in the *Philosophy of History*, he gives a slightly distinctive presentation:

> The followers of Christ, united in this sense and living in the spiritual life, form a community which is the Kingdom of God. "Where two or three are gathered together in my name," (that is, in the determination of that which I am)—says Christ—"there am I in the midst of them." The community is the real and present life in the Spirit of Christ.[10]

The conclusion to be drawn from this is that God emerges only through his loss (the dialectic of supposing and presupposing that Hegel relies on) and this loss is fully consummated in the Holy Spirit (*AR*, 261). The Holy Spirit is kept alive only through the interaction of individuals; it is a virtual Substance (which should not be confused with Hegel's "objective spirit" *qua* virtual substance) which exists when people recognize themselves in it (the Communist Party, psychoanalytic institutions/societies, amorous couples, et cetera). In short, this is the most radical form of atheism: one doesn't proclaim the inexistence of God, but it is God himself who proclaims it, who makes us believe in his inexistence. It is at this point that the truly materialist dimension of Christianity emerges, a materialism which is concerned with the form of the life of the collectivities.

This Hegelian-Žižekian view of religion as a self-sublating process, out of which atheism is born, allows us to imagine a different sort of critique of fundamentalisms—one that doesn't attack fundamentalism by referring back to the "fundaments" or "foundations" (Grund), since that is exactly what fundamentalisms already do. Instead, Hegel provides us with an alternative form of critique, one which seeks in the rational kernel of religious thinking an ally against mystification and obscurantism in both religious and secular forms.

* * *

In his short text *How to Begin from the Beginning*, Žižek quotes Lenin's even shorter text *On Ascending a High Mountain*, in which Lenin tries to make sense of retreats in the revolutionary process, as happened with the New Economic Policy, and he writes against those communists who are doomed to imagine a revolutionary process thus creating a socialist economy "without making mistakes, without retreats, without numerous alterations to what is unfinished or wrongly done." For Lenin, mistakes are part of the revolutionary process itself: "communists who have no illusions, who do not give way to despondency, and who preserve their strength and flexibility 'to begin from the beginning' over and over again in approaching an extremely difficult task, are not doomed (and in all probability will not perish)."[11] The crucial task of every emancipatory movement or revolutionary process is not (only) to preserve the achieved success or progress but also to go back to the point of departure. In this regard, "a revolutionary process is not a gradual progress, but a repetitive movement, a movement of *repeating the beginning* again and again" (*IC*, 210). To begin from the beginning does not mean to go back to where we were stopped, that is to say, to the twentieth-century socialist projects in all their varieties, but to go back to their starting point and begin anew.

To "begin from the beginning" is an excellent example showing how the idea of what we "lost" with "bureaucratic socialism" (all forms of "democratic" socialist experiments in the last century, such as the Soviets) was only retroactively posited as a loss. It was never in actuality a possibility, but it is only now, from the standpoint of the "healing" of the Stalinist wound, that we see the Soviets as a "pure democratic tool" that we lost. Žižek's position is that the dialectical procedure is not (as Bertolt Brecht suggested) to account for the agent who carried out the revolution that later became an obstacle to it. This logic should be rejected, and it should instead be argued that "in the dialectical analysis of history, on the contrary, each new stage 'rewrites the past' and retroactively delegitimizes the previous one" (*AR*, 18). This retroactive delegitimization "makes 'vanishing mediators' of past phenomena: although a past phenomenon can be a necessary moment in the emergence of a new form, its role becomes invisible once the New has arrived" (*AR*, 18).

This is where we should look for the liberatory potential of the wound. The Fall is something that creates good out of its own fall, which means that there is no situation or level in which the goodness resides and from which we fall. In this sense, the new incarnation of the idea of communism will have to let go of the previous century's socialist experiments and cease to consider that phantom as something that happened but was "hurt" or *wounded* by Stalinism. Rather, as the loss that was never positive, it only appeared as a lost democratic tool *after* it was lost.

Our first task, therefore, is not to fight the "dominance" in the current historical structured whole, the dominance that makes itself responsible for what we have lost, for the contingencies that never became part of the actual whole. In making itself responsible for the fantasmatic status of "true communism," this instance also makes itself an indispensable part of our identity as "democrat" socialists, as militants "betrayed" by the course of the socialist experiments of the twentieth century, alleviating our guilt and failures. Our first task is rather to let go of the identity sustained by this loss itself, *to lose the loss*, which means both to let it go and to recuperate it as being constitutively a ghost, as something that "is neither being, nor non-being, but the unrealized."[12] In other words, our task is to operate a *withdrawal* which itself constitutes the opening for a new field of experimentations in what Marx used to call "possible communism."

Notes

1. G. W. F. Hegel, *Science of Logic* (New York: Prometheus House, 1991), 441.
2. Hegel, *Science*, 400.
3. In a letter to Ferdinand Lassalle in early 1858, Marx declared, "The work I am presently concerned with is a Critique of Economic Categories or, if you like, a critical exposé of the system of the bourgeois economy. It is at once an exposé and, by the same token, a critique of the system."
4. Kojin Karatani, *Transcritique: On Kant and Marx* (Cambridge, MA: MIT Press, 2003), 2.
5. Sigmund Freud, *The Uncanny* (London: Penguin, 2003).
6. G. W. F. Hegel, *Phenomenology of Spirit* (Oxford: Oxford University Press, 1977), 407.
7. G. W. F. Hegel, *Faith and Knowledge* (New York: State University of New York Press, 1977), 190–1.
8. Gérard Lebrun, *La patience du concept: essai sur le discours hégélien* (Paris: Gallimard, 1972), 39.
9. Hegel, *Phenomenology*, 476.
10. G. W. F. Hegel, *Philosophy of History* (New York: Dover, 1991), 328.
11. V. I. Lenin, "On Ascending a High Mountain," available online: https://www.marxists.org/archive/lenin/works/1922/feb/x01.htm.
12. Jacques Lacan, *The Four Fundamental Concepts of Psychoanalysis* (New York: W.W. Norton & Company, 1998), 30.

3

Žižek and the (Chinese Dialectic of the) Revolution

Frank Ruda

The Great Proletarian Cultural Revolution was unique in attacking the key point: not just the takeover of state power, but the new economic organization and reorganization of daily life. Its failure was precisely the failure to create a new form of everyday life. (CH, 77)

1

This is not a text on Žižek and China. Neither is it a text on Žižek reception in China, of which I know very little, nor it is a text on Žižek's reception of China, even though the following remarks deal with issues that pertain to the contemporary status of China from Žižek's point of view. This is also not a text on Žižek and the concept of the revolution in general or what a revolution à la Žižek would look like, even though his often-repeated claim that the day after the revolution is de facto more important than the day of the revolution itself certainly plays a crucial role in the following. The present text turns to a debate that is crucial for Žižek's own theoretical-systematic endeavor which also has to do with something that happened in China. The latter is the Chinese Cultural Revolution, which in 2017, depending on the count, celebrated its fiftieth anniversary. It depends on the count because even the exact dating of the end and beginning of what one addresses as the Chinese Cultural Revolution is an object of some dispute: one option is that it begins in

1966 and ends in 1976 with Mao's death and with the taking of power of Deng Xiaoping; another option—and because there are many, this here is not an exhaustive list—is that it begins in mid-1966 and already ends in autumn 1967 and thereby is only one stage in a series of events. The present text will disappoint any reader who is interested in these questions as political questions, since it will not address any of these intricate issues. It will solely examine the relation of Žižek's thought to the Chinese Cultural Revolution.[1] But thereby it will neither attempt to speak from a sovereignly distant position of philosophical reflection which would ignore historically specific developments, conjunctures, and events and only concentrate on Žižek's comments on China nor will it, for that matter, begin its discussion by offering a philosophical reading of one of Mao's works and then compare it to what Žižek has to say about the latter.[2]

2

What follows is an attempt to side with and to think from the position generated by Žižek. It is an attempt to see in what precise way one is, from this very position, able to assess and critically engage with the Chinese Cultural Revolution. Yet, whatever the specific position is from which one starts, it is certainly impossible to say anything about this particular revolution if one does not relate it to another major political event, namely the Russian Revolution—an event of which Žižek is certainly one of the most refined theoretical analysts in contemporary philosophy. In line with Mao's repeated remarks that one should oppose all mechanical application of historical experiences to contexts and conjunctures foreign to them, because this will lead—practically as well as theoretically—to situational blindness and to a transcendentalization or de-historicization of singular political experiences and practices, one must be specific. Because every revolution is not only determined by its specific historical situation—a point already hammered home by Lenin's famous insistence on the "concrete analysis of concrete situations," which must accompany and ground all revolutionary action—but any real revolution also revolutionizes what we mean by revolution.

3

One should remember here, and to paraphrase Marx, that all history of the writing of the history of revolution is part of the history of struggles about (the) history (of emancipation). Why is this the case? Recall how François Furet, for example, read the French Revolution as a legal summoning of the general estates and therefore ultimately not as a revolution but as a coup whose very possibility was inscribed into the previous constitution of the French monarchical state. For him, in this sense, there was and is no true revolutionary dimension in the French Revolution, as Žižek has pointed out clearly (*LN*, 805–58). In this context, it is also rather easy to recall how the history of revolutions is often and solely represented as a history composed of crimes and acts of terror that they ultimately amount to nothing but gigantic blood-thirsty criminal sequences. Even though terror almost always was a crucial component of any historical revolution,[3] to see in revolutionary events only a manifestation and an excess of terrorist violence is obviously missing their point. It often amounts even to denying the revolutionary agents and events their own rationality. This certainly happens when both are explained by recourse to groundless resentment, seductive propaganda, or plain and simple aberrance.

4

Writing history in this way is writing history from the perspective of the end of the revolution. The question is not, how did this happen, but how did it happen that people did not see that this (end) will happen? In this way, one in advance (even though post festum) determines the failure of the revolution, its revolutionary end as its inherent and natural telos. One Aristotelianizes the revolution. Such a writing of history is not only a writing of history from the perspective of its end but also one that looks at the events from the outside. To be able to separate reason and terror, one started to write the history of the revolutions from the perspective of their end, from a supposedly neutral point of view on what then has had (unavoidably) become a great crime. Yet and obviously, one can write revolutionary history differently. One may think of Hegel and his account of the French Revolution, of which one knows that he did not only follow it with enthusiasm but whose anniversary he celebrated each year till the end of his days—without ever denying its failure. Rather its celebration allowed for an appropriate and even harsh and remorseless analysis of the implications of the terror it produced.[4] But Hegel does not reconstruct the French Revolution from the perspective of the spectator—as, for example, Kant did[5]—but from an immanent perspective and precisely thereby shows that the revolutionary terror was more than just a mere mistake, which could have been avoided. Rather the terror was inscribed into the very conceptual set-up of the French Revolution. But in Hegel's diagnosis, this can be stated without thereby arguing that the revolution was nothing but terroristic or that terror is the only (negative) outcome of the revolution. Hegel's critique is therefore not simply considering the objective course of historical events but rather, to put it with Badiou, how they were "subjectivated."[6]

5

We can thus distinguish between different modes of writing history. One mode writes history from the end and thus from an external point of view, which makes the very history it constructs unintelligible and makes its agents easily appear pathological. Another form of writing history deals with its object immanently and assumes in Hegel's spirit—and is there any other?—that there is reason in history, even when it appears as or on a slaughter bench.[7] But we can also add a further distinction, on the side of the immanent writings of history which insist on the rationality of historical events. Since there can also be an immanent contradiction between immanent ways of writing history. We then encounter a contradiction, or some agony, in the midst of the people's writings of history. There are thus different ways of delineating and understanding the inner rationality of the failure(s) of a revolution. Both ways agree on the revolutionary character of the event(s) and are also in agreement, different from external assessments, about the possibility to think through specific failures without pathologizing revolutionary action tout court. But both locate the failure of the revolution elsewhere, in a different point, in another reason.

6

The following remarks will attempt to contribute to an immanent reconstruction of how two different immanent accounts that agree about the revolutionary character of the Chinese Cultural Revolution came to disagree on how to draw its balance sheet. This discussion was a discussion among comrades: between Slavoj Žižek and the French philosopher Alain Badiou. The publicly accessible material of this debate was published in part as text accompanying a selection of Mao's writings, which Žižek edited and published in 2007 (*PC*), which then was translated a year later into French (*ZPM*) and the French version of the book was adjoined by a letter from Badiou and a reply to this very letter by Žižek. These two editions will provide the basis for the following remarks.

7

Žižek begins his reflections on Mao with a decisive point, namely by remarking that "[o]ne of the most devious traps which lurks in wait for Marxists is the search for the moment of the Fall, when things took the wrong turn in the history of Marxism" (*PC*, 1). The reason as to why this trap is a trap is that one can be enticed to believe one can neatly separate the (good) from the (bad) elements when identifying a moment at which it all turned wrong. This moment is then as if an intruder, an enemy, or the ruin coming from the outside which spoils the previously unproblematic phase of revolutionary practice. Conceiving of revolutionary failure in this manner, we fall prey to a strange kind of purism—the belief in the possibility of pure unproblematic emancipatory practice, which then is externally disturbed and hindered by some alien or foreign element that produces a pure kind of problem. But if we talk in this manner about a failure of a revolution, it is never really the failure of this very revolution. It is never the failure of the thing itself. One thus here encounters a process that operates as an internalized and inverted version of the externally discrediting of revolutionary practice. If the failure here remains ultimately external to the practice which failed (it is due to intruders or enemies or external obstacles), (part of) the practice itself is kept clean of its very failure. But this implies that one ultimately cannot understand how and why it failed. One seeks to account for it, by keeping it away from the thing with which it is entangled. What is thus produced is an impossibility of any self-criticism.

8

Žižek's point is that the first step to accept and subjectivize any failure of a political practice and movement consists in creating the process of harsh self-critique, a critique that is harsher than any external critique could ever be. It means to accept that the revolution has failed. In the concrete case, Žižek does not speak about Mao and the Cultural Revolution as if its failure would simply be external to the Marxist vision or to the project of emancipation and this is to say, to a certain extent, to his own project. For Žižek, the failure of the Cultural Revolution has become a condition for his own thought. To think through the Cultural Revolution from such a perspective means to think that failure is immanent to (the history of) Marxism. How to account for failure from within this history? Žižek argues that one has to take into account that the history of Marxism consists of a series of displacements: there is a first displacement that happens in the transition from Marx to Lenin and a second one in the transition from Lenin to Mao. First a displacement from one of the most progressive countries in the world (England or Germany) to a relatively underdeveloped one (Russia); then a further displacement from the worker to the peasants as revolutionary agents. These displacements are not at all betrayals of any originally pure doctrine, rather the doctrine of Marxism constitutes itself only through these displacements. For Žižek, there is thus no pure Marxist doctrine (of emancipation). He makes this point in the following way: "This is the movement of concrete universality; this radical transubstantiation through which the original theory has to reinvent itself in a new context: only by way of surviving this transplant can it emerge as effectively universal" (*PC*, 4). The first Marxist revolution, for this reason, did not happen in Germany but in Russia. It was produced through Lenin's "betrayal" of Marx's original critique of political economy. The thing itself does not get lost in these transfers. Rather—similar to what Walter Benjamin saw as the task of the translator[8]—the real thing emerged only through its translations, transfers, displacements, and betrayals. The thing is generated through the betrayals of the thing.

9

In this sense, it would be in advance inappropriate and ill-conceived to understand Mao's version of Marxism as theoretically inadequate. But it would be equally inappropriate to identify in it nothing but an application of Marxism in a different context. And to lose track of the violent rupture with certain elements of Marx's and Lenin's thought. Mao breaks, but he breaks faithfully with Marx and Lenin and precisely this constitutes Chinese Marxism. The Chinese dialectic arose from and out of a failure of (Marxist and Leninist) dialectic materialism.

10

For Žižek, Mao's displacement and rupture with Lenin concern mainly the relationship between working class and peasantry. Lenin's and even more so Stalin's untrusting and suspicious view of the reactionary attitude of peasantry was linked to the assumption that the possession of land (and thus basic means of production) leads any peasant to think conservatively. Mao transforms this mistrust into a political form of trust. This transformation is far-reaching, since he does not only transform the evaluation of the peasantry, but he thereby also transforms the proletarian position within Marxism. Mao transforms the position of the revolutionary agents, whose revolutionary action always was also supposed to create the conditions of possibility of their own existence. Mao does for Žižek generate a renewed concept of the proletariat, which is no longer that of a substanceless and substance-deprived subject. But this is no simple substitution. Rather it is—as Žižek shows in his reading of Mao's text on contradiction—linked to a dialectical volte-face of Mao. It is directed against "the dogmatic Marxists" (PC, 6) and consists in interpreting the concept of contradiction—that is differentiated into principal or universal and particular forms—in such a way that the universality of contradiction, the actual contradiction that decides a situation, can lie in what appears to be a mere particular contradiction and thus not in the predominant contradiction. The universal dimension of a situation does not always and automatically derive from the universally determining contradiction, but from a particular contradiction which gains in a situation a specific significance (and which Hegel would have addressed in terms of concrete universality). Without taking into account the singular particularity of the situation as well as of the decisive type of contradiction within it, the universal dimension of contradiction and thus of one's revolutionary and politicizing practice that seeks to mobilize the force of contradiction can easily be missed or remain practically ineffective

11

We sometimes therefore do not see the universal significance if we look for it in distance from the sphere of particularity or singularity. Looking for universal meaning beyond the particular does sometimes not allow for the production of any universal significance whatsoever. In this vein, Žižek argues that there can be situations, as was for example the case for China during the Japanese occupation, where "any direct focusing on class struggle . . . goes against class struggle itself" (*PC*, 6). If one were to constantly and only refer to the principal contradiction of a situation, this can easily and directly lead into forms of dogmatic opportunism, which will unavoidably make one miss the constitutive contradictions of a situation.

12

Mao performs an analogous reversal in Žižek's reading in relation to the productive forces and the relations of production. This becomes manifest when Mao remarks that the principal contradiction is located on the level of the relations of production, but that in certain situations the productive forces can also become the most relevant and most decisive factor. Mao thereby indicates for Žižek that emancipatory politics is never only about (re-)organizing the economy; political struggle manifests also and maybe always also in the attempts that determine what can count as politics at all. The question is thus always: which precise particular contradiction can be concretely politicized in such a way that it can attain a universal significance?

13

It is here that Žižek indicates that Mao's overall orientation has a contemporary significance. He takes up the problem of defending democracy under all conditions as sole thinkable political form (*PC*, 7). Such a defense of democracy at all costs can in certain situations lead to a straightforward weakening and disorientation of anticapitalist movements.[9] When even the establishment is against the establishment, it might not be the most effective gesture to be against the establishment— or one is only against the establishment by attacking something that the establishment would not attack, especially when it attacks the establishment. For Žižek, Mao's actuality is embodied in the insight that one always needs a concrete and ideology-critical analysis of the position from which one articulates one's analysis of the most significant contradictions. This necessitates to analytically determine which aspects of existing contradictions are primary and which are determinant for and within a specific historical situation and conjuncture. Mao's greatness lies in rejecting all too easy claims for a synthetic and unified perspective. This derives from the fact that he always insisted on the primacy of struggle (even between the primary and secondary contradictions within the same conjuncture or the struggle within one and the same political position, say the communists).

14

But it is precisely here that problems emerge. Since for Žižek, Mao's insistence on the priority of struggle, which also implies a primacy of division over synthesis and unity, leads him to endorse a problematic form of generalization. Mao's generalization is problematic because it turns from an insistence on dialectical complexities into a "cosmology-ontology of the 'eternal struggle of opposites'" (PC, 9). Mao, Žižek claims, overgeneralizes and turns into a principle the idea that struggling and splitting have the general (onto-)logical priority over unity and synthesis. It is this overgeneralization with which Mao betrays his own previous dialectical genius. Every split produces further splitting—even on the level of the atoms that were for long considered indivisible, as one of Mao's own examples goes (PC, 9)—no unity will ever remain stable and one always divides into two. But in this way instability and splitting are reified, for Žižek, into a stable form of dialectical dynamics. Mao in this reading ends up in and with a logic of bad infinity whose practical truth is gruesome: "If one is to believe Mao's latest biography, he caused the greatest famine in history by exporting food to Russia to buy nuclear and arms industries . . . in 1958–1961. Mao knew exactly what was happening, saying: 'half of China may well have to die'" (PC, 10). The problem with this is not only that we appear to encounter a cosmological justification of millions of deaths as dialectically unavoidable. The real conceptual problem that we encounter here is that Mao is led to such claims, in Žižek's reading, because he repeatedly rejects the negation of negation as universal dialectical law and thereby cannot avoid a far-reaching structural inconsistency.

15

Žižek's own elaboration of the negation of negation allows to grasp this critical point more clearly: "First the old order is negated within its own ideological-political form; then, this form itself has to be negated" (PC, 16). This means, for example, that one encounters the negation of negation when the language of an enemy changes and the latter can no longer formulate her attack in the ways in which she previously employed (comparable to when "the church starts to defend itself in the language of science" (PC, 17)). The victory over the enemy depends on the enemy (unconsciously) avowing her own defeat. But this means that one (sometimes) needs the obstacle to a victory to be able to be victorious. This is not a problem that is only encountered with Mao but already with Marx. Because Marx seemed for Žižek to have assumed that a capitalist process of production might be able to generate a productive potential that could provide the material conditions for the highest realization of society. But, and here one can see how Žižek argues that the failure is inscribed into the very kernel of Marxism, one should never miss that what appears to be an obstacle to liberation also serves as the productive condition of possibility for liberation. Since what makes capitalism work is precisely what appears as an obstacle to the full realization of the productive potentials of the productive forces. But the obstacle is an enabling obstacle, that is, it is what creates these potentials in the first place (certain inventions are only made because something did not work smoothly or because something went wrong). The condition of impossibility of the full realization of the productive forces is therefore the very condition of possibility of its existence. This is the "logic of the obstacle as positive condition" (*PC*, 18). Mao knew this, since "Marxism could be the product only of capitalist society" (*PC*, 56); any origin is impure, any beginning is a deviation. Only in capitalism does one start to dream of communism. This is (not only) a problem, but immediately introduces the necessity of an auto-critique (of the ways in which we dream). If the obstacle is a positive condition, one must be careful to not naively (as for Žižek Marx did) dream of a world without obstacles.

16

For Žižek, Mao perpetuates Marx's mistake because he does not see that only the negation of negation truly is a negation. One does not negate if one repeatedly negates specific enemies, insists again and again on the splitting of the unity of one's organization. One does not negate if one only negates determinately. Because in this way, one never negates the way in which one negates. Thereby one never negates the framework of determinations (*PC*, 19). This happens in Mao, according to Žižek, because one point remains persistently untouched that stabilizes Mao's entire badly infinite dynamic of order, namely his own position (in the political process). Even though he takes the step from a determinate transgression of the law to the law of transgression, from crime against the law to law as the successfully performed crime, his own position remains unaffected by all strategic and dialectical reversals. This is why Žižek refers to the great chairman as the lord of misrule—a figure from the Middle Ages who in bigger households was selected to preside during carnivalesque festivities and whose function was to chair during the time of carnivalesque reversals and burlesques reenactments of the common order (*PC*, 20).

17

Žižek's argument is not that the Cultural Revolution was a bloody carnival and Mao its prince. Any carnival is a temporarily limited exception from the order. But Mao turned limited exception into a permanent one and turned the exception into the new order. This is precisely how the problem of avoiding the negation of negation manifests in the form of establishing an order of and as exception: "all temporary stabilizations of the revolution amounted to so many restorations of the old Order, so that the only way to keep the revolution" (*PC*, 21) was to not let it ever end. Each new determination was just another determination that had to be negated; each new element of order was identified as repetition of the old order and hence had to be negated anew. The problem with this was that Mao's rejection of the negation of negation led him to only negate in an abstract manner: he negates whatever determination in a therefore endless process of repeatedly producing new determinations (this is why one can here identify the logic of the fury of destruction that Hegel already identified as underlying the violent and destructive outburst characteristic to the French Revolution). For Žižek, Mao had the right project, namely that of a cultural revolution which even revolutionizes its own foundations and which thus seeks to even revolutionize what we mean by revolution. But without any stable formation of a new—symbolic—order, that is, of new habits, of new ways in which one dreams and desires, this revolution of the revolution manifested in the form of repeated acts of destroying any new element of stability and thereby came dangerously close to and even anticipated or mimicked capitalism's own destructive tendency. Mao's revolution repeatedly negates any determination without being able to negate this compulsion to negate. It therefore could not be also, again repeatedly, turn against itself, stuck in the negation of order as new order.

18

Mao's politics in this reading leads to a destructive compulsion of a permanently self-revolutionizing order, which does not want to be and implement any order at all. This diagnosis allows to explain, according to Žižek, how one can read the transition from Mao's China to present-day China: the permanent self-revolutionizing movement, which evaporates everything stable into thin air is ultimately structurally analogous to the reproductive movement, which is the inherent dynamic of capitalism itself. Against its will "the final result of Mao's Cultural Revolution [. . . is therefore] today's unprecedented explosion of capitalist dynamics in China" (*PC*, 25). The lord of misrule is the one who implemented (an authoritarian) capitalism with Asian values, as Žižek has it. As consequence of the Cultural Revolution allowed its victory turned out to be its defeat. When the enemy commences to redetermine the very ways in which one's victory is played out and the very means and forms in which one seeks to overcome her, she has won in advance. Because this is what historically manifested and this is the true failure of the Cultural Revolution—and here one can see the truly radical critique Žižek articulates—it is only from an immanent perspective that one can actually see that one—and here he is explicitly addressing Alain Badiou—that the latter "should have been consistent and denied the evental status of the Cultural Revolution" (*PC*, 25). The historical Chinese Cultural Revolution was no event, but a strange and temporarily limited transitory moment, a vanishing mediator for the development of contemporary authoritarian capitalism. Yet, what is needed is a real Cultural Revolution.

19

One year after this far-reaching critique, the French translation of Žižek's text is published. In an additional commentary, Badiou praises Žižek's reflections, because the latter saw Mao's novelty (even though evaluating it critically) and raised the crucial question of how to conceive of the concatenation between dialectics and politics which concerns the fate of both. Badiou also praises Žižek's noticing that Mao did not endorse the negation of negation. But the former immediately remarks that the latter is also problematically fighting on two fronts (*ZPM*, 285): on the one side, he attacks those who see in Mao only a criminal, but he also criticizes those who defend Mao. For Badiou, Mao had anticipated this very problem, namely that his defenders will become (his) enemies—this is the famous remark about the location of the bourgeoisie within the Communist Party. Because of this anticipation and even against Mao's own explicit statements, one can, for Badiou, therefore identify a "politics of negation of negation" (*ZPM*, 285) in Mao's thought.

20

This politics unfolds from the insight into the fact that the political process which tried to abolish the old world, created a new form of the negation of itself, notably one that manifested therefore as re*form*ism and as renegadism. Neither did previously exist and both will try to criminalize the very political process from which they originated. Badiou does thus confirm that Žižek is neither a renegade nor a Maoist.

21

This is a crucial point since one cannot debate and disagree with renegades. Renegades do not see failures, they only can see crimes in real political processes. But it is decisive to have a real debate, for Badiou, among those who agree that capitalism and its political forms are intolerable and thus to properly think (through) the failures of the attempts to abolish it. The debate about political failure must be a discussion among those who see in such a failure also their own failure, that is to say, a failure from which they must learn. Badiou does therefore indicate concrete points of disagreement and of agreement with Žižek's assessment (whose more detailed elaboration I leave for another time and place).[10] I will only focus on the main point he puts forward: "What I mainly want to make you understand is that you do not define rigorously enough the points in which there can be a question of Mao's universality" (*ZPM*, 288). This is pertinent since Žižek's point is that this very universality is in question.

22

How to formulate the (potential) universality of Mao's position? Badiou must argue for the existence of it—against the renegades and in distance from Žižek's account. He approaches this issue by raising a question, namely "the first question is . . . necessarily: which problems do we today share with Mao? Wherein is reading his texts something else than a nostalgic exercise or purely critical?" (*ZPM*, 289). And he answers that what we share with Mao and that which therefore constitutes Mao's universality lies less in the concrete problems within the Chinese conjuncture he was facing but rather in the way in which he was tackling the problems that are still ours. What we share with Mao is thus a shared set of problems. What are those? They originate in the failure of the revolution in Russia.

23

Badiou sees in Lenin's political stance which led to the victorious revolution of 1917 not only a taking over of state power but structurally the solution to a historical problem that was generated by the Paris Commune. This problem was how to organize emancipation in a stable and defensible manner since the Commune only lasted for seventy-two days. But if emancipation is supposed to be universal it has to last and ought to be translatable into new and different contexts. Lenin's solution to the question of how to expand and make emancipation permanent was to create a solidly and militarily organized, disciplined party. When this party became the dominant political force in the Russian state, holding power, it actually solved the problem of the Paris Commune. The party-solution of the Commune problem was for Badiou so effectively realized in Russia that it was, and for this very reason, also used in China, Vietnam, Cambodia, and Albania. But the party taking over the state(-solution) created problems of its own. Not only was the original aim of the emancipatory Marxist project to abolish state power conceptually irreconcilable with taking and maintaining power, but also the implementation of the revolutionary party as new agent of power furthermore produced a new form of authority, a type of terrorist authoritarianism that emerged precisely in the linkage of state power and party (which is why bureaucracy plays a crucial role here). Mao's universality lies for Badiou in his attempt to find a solution to this newly emerging problem, to a problem that only emerges because Lenin solved the previous historical problem of the Paris Commune in a particular manner.

24

What to do or how to break the emancipation-deadening cycle of replacing bourgeois state power with a state power held by the Communist

Party which thereby structurally reproduces the very thing it wanted to overcome? Mao's answer, for Badiou, is the Cultural Revolution—and this is where his universality must be situated. The Cultural Revolution is what Badiou describes, and here mimicking Marx's comments about the Paris Commune, as the finally found political form, the finally found political form of the "dictatorship of the proletariat" (*ZPM*, 292). By pointedly repeating Marx's formulation within the coordinates of Mao's claim, the Cultural Revolution appears as if the history of emancipation went full circle: the Paris Commune created a problem (how to make emancipation last against its enemies and how to find a form that is expandable), the Leninist party sought to solve it by means of a military form of organization that sought to overtake state power which then led into state terrorism and bureaucracy (Stalinism) that then was attempted be overturned again by reintroducing the masses (and their self-organized movement) into the political picture (the Chinese Cultural Revolution). This attempt even led inter alia to the (literal and historical) recreation of the Commune (in the Commune of Shanghai) (*ZPM*, 294) as a crucial component of the Cultural Revolution.[11] This is a repetition of the immediate as a result, in Hegelian terms: a politics of negation of negation.

25

But, and this is the far-reaching problem: the Cultural Revolution and with it, Mao failed. This is why the problem to which he sought to propose a solution—the return to the Commune after its immediate problem of organizational duration had been solved—is for Badiou still with us. This is why there is a universality in Mao's failure. As Badiou insinuates: the Cultural Revolution was, for the epoch of the socialist one-party states (this is: for everyone alive today), what the Paris Commune was for Marx and Lenin. It forces us to think how to precisely solve the problem it encountered and thereby brought to the fore, notably: how to organize emancipation in a lasting manner without establishing an authoritarian state that leads into the deadlocks that come with any purely military and bureaucratically terrorist apparatus. The contemporaneity of this question indicates Mao's universality. What is needed—one can thus contend—is another, a new Lenin(ist solution).

26

Žižek replies. He insists that this is a debate among those who are most affected by the failure of the revolution. He thus agrees that the failure is more radical than any anti-emancipatory or anticommunist critique would be able to assert or comprehend. The Cultural Revolution had the precisely right target: it did not only "take state-power, but [sought] to economically reorganize daily live" (*ZPM*, 301), but it led into a strange paradox. The paradox was that the revivification of the revolutionary movement through the intervention of the mobilization of the masses did itself not come from the masses. Against the state-ification of the revolution (the problem of the revolutionary party becoming an agent of power that does not want to lose power), the Chinese attempt led to a (state-ordained) reintegration and reactivation of the mass movement for the sake of the revolution. But because this re-revolutionizing did not come from the masses but was coordinated from the top of the state, it led to a situation where "a leader effectuates an uncontrolled upheaval while looking to exercise total personal power" (*ZPM*, 302). This indicates for Žižek that whatever happened in the course of the Cultural Revolution was not a simple execution of a plan but followed a paradoxical logic, that created "a dynamic of its own" (*ZPM*, 302).

27

The dynamic in question must be properly analyzed. The paradigm of such an analysis Žižek finds in Hegel's "cold" (*ZPM*, 305) analysis of the French Revolution. Why is it this the paradigm? Because it confronts the ultimate problem: it seems that the practical success or failure of a revolution does not only evaluate the idea of revolution but also brings out the consistency—or inner contradictoriness and divisiveness—of a conceptual thought of the revolution. A revolution must withstand the test of its being put to practice. Put differently, "the failure of reality to fully actualize an idea is at the same time the failure (the limit) of the idea itself" (*ZPM*, 306). What happens thus in the aftermath of the Cultural Revolution—the capitalist explosion in China—ought to be read in a similar vein to what happened in the aftermath of the French Revolution: the failure of the Jacobin utopian ends produced as their symptom the bourgeois utilitarian society. If the consequence of the revolution does less lie in its terroristic nature, but in the fact that the bourgeois utilitarian society created by the (French) Revolution is haunted by what it was produced by, namely the (Jacobin) terror of undoing all determinations; the Cultural Revolution repeats this very problem and the truth of the failure of the Cultural Revolution is thus for Žižek literally embodied by the capitalist development in China. The latter is not an accidental aftermath but a product within which its internal contradiction, problem, or inconsistency is enacted in another way. Similar to how bourgeois society transforms terror into an everyday form of living, contemporary China transforms revolutionary terror into the very mode of its reproduction and hence into something nonrevolutionary. For Žižek, this insight can orient us. It can orient us not by making us aim for a revolution without failure(s) but by learning from previous failures and by therefore reaching another level of synthesis, by synthesizing failure better. We ought to learn from the aftermath of the French Revolution for what we make of China.

28

The reference to Hegel's analysis of the revolution does elucidate how Žižek's harshly critical account of the Cultural Revolution does not amount to being a simple dismissal. Hegel did never shy away from defending the position that the French Revolution was a world-historical event that was absolutely constitutive for modernity. It was historically conditioned by the Lutheran Reformation. The latter affirmatively emphasized the purely subjective grounding of any form of (religious or civil) faith. This allowed to do away with any objective and external institution or all kinds of external rituals of belief as necessary for the constitution of a community of believers. With this act—"I only believe what I believe on the basis of my own conviction"— the subject itself became the decisive guarantor for any understanding of faith and provided the ground for any form of collective. The French Revolution created a new dimension of this very idea and realized it in a more far-reaching and radical manner. It did so by demonstrating that there is no pre-given objectivity that any subjective community with regard to its own constitution would rely on, except the act of constituting itself on its own (and in its own image). This implied that any community can undo (almost) any objectively given feature, except itself. But if this is the case, any collective form of organization is able to create a (and its own and singular) form of objectivity. The French Revolution demonstrated this, but it also— as inter alia Marx perspicaciously analyzed—did not find the appropriate form of organization of this very potential of the political collective. This was the problem bequeathed to modernity by the French Revolution for Hegel. Žižek's account of the Cultural Revolution brings to the fore how his understanding of modernity is that modernity is determined by the history of an unsolved problem. This problem is the problem of how to transform our ways of life, of how to change our everyday life, and thereby of how to perform a real cultural revolution. To solve this problem, it is imperative to break with the problematic dynamic of an order that is suspended and whose supposed suspension creates a far more radical return to order. One must rupture the badly infinite dialectic of order and exception (as order, that is: carnival) and thus raise the question of the Cultural Revolution, namely, how do we transform life in such a way that we create a new collective everyday life which does overcome the status of a permanent exception and allows for the creation of new collective habits? This is the question modernity still has to tackle.

Notes

1 There are people far more qualified to elucidate these sequencing issues and the details of this conjuncture, especially regarding their more general outlook and impact. Here one cannot but refer to the majestic: Alessandro Russo,

Cultural Revolution and Revolutionary Culture (Durham: Duke University Press 2020).

2 Even though it is rather tempting to return to the famous text on contradiction or to the one on practice. But both are from 1937, which clearly predates the Cultural Revolution.

3 For this, see also Alain Badiou, *Logics of Worlds, Being and Event, 2* (London: Continuum, 2009), 20–8.

4 G. W. F. Hegel, *The Phenomenology of Spirit* (Cambridge: Cambridge University Press, 2018), 339–47.

5 Cf. Alain Badiou, *Metapolitics* (New York: Verso 2005), 10–26.

6 Alain Badiou, *The Century* (London: Polity Press, 2007), 5.

7 G. W. F. Hegel, *The Philosophy of History* (Ontario: Kitchener, 2001), 35.

8 Walter Benjamin, "The Task of the Translator," in *Selected Writings*, vol. 1, ed. Marcus Bullock and Michael W. Jennings (Cambridge: The Belknap Press, 2002), 253–63.

9 For this also cf. Frank Ruda, *For Badiou. Idealism without Idealism* (Evanston: Northwestern University Press 2015).

10 They concern inter alia Mao's exchange of food against weapons with the USSR, which produced a famine, but was for Badiou also politically necessary, since China was since the 1950s in war with the United States in Korea and then helped the Vietnamese. The project of the "Great Leap Forward," which for Badiou allowed to break with the Russians, was therefore itself a revolutionary necessity, but came with an economic vengeance. Finally, and most interestingly, Badiou remarks that of Mao's designated enemies—and in clear difference to Stalin's regime—only Liu Shaoqi (who was from 1959 till 1968 the second president of the People's Republic of China) and, probably, Lin Biao lost their life, even at the most violent times of the Cultural Revolution. Deng Xiaoping later even became head of state—which indicates that there were no purges comparable to those under Stalin.

11 It is crucial to note that already Lenin saw in the Soviet state a state that was created according to the standards established by the Paris Commune.

4

Being Sexed

Žižek's Modern Ontology

James Penney

As a quintessentially psychoanalytic thinker, Slavoj Žižek has been concerned since his earliest work with the epistemological implications of Freud's theory of sexuality, including its formalization by Lacan, for how we conceive of the limits of knowledge. Lately, however, alongside intellectual allies like Joan Copjec and Alenka Zupančič, the focus has shifted from sex conceived as a fault or inconsistency in the forms of knowledge to sex as a disruption or torsion in the very fabric, so to speak, of being. Staging a critical encounter with the most modern postmillennial discourses, from so-called object-oriented ontology and speculative realism to quantum physics and queer theory, Žižek has reintroduced the subject of the unconscious into the interrogation of being, insisting with great consequence that this being, or more precisely its failure or inconsistency, is not one—that it is necessarily, in other words, *sexed*. In what follows I will trace the relinking of being and sex in Žižek's recent work, situating it within a broader intellectual project premised on the contention that the development of the consequences of psychoanalysis for ontology has only just begun. I will take stock of the general significance of these consequences for philosophy and contemporary sexuality theory and then explore how they echo across Žižek's provocative and controversial engagement with MeToo discourse and queer theory.

Two fundamental insights inform Žižek's intervention into the problem of ontology, the one psychoanalytic and the other, though inspired by Lacan's work, primarily philosophical. The first sees Žižek draw out the ontological consequences of Freud's idea of primal repression, which he links to his own underlying premise concerning what he calls the less-than-zero, in other words, the idea that being is intrinsically thwarted or incomplete. Though Žižek does not do so himself, instead basing his own development on his influential reading of Lacan's teaching, there is much to be gained by tracing the psychoanalytic origins of the idea of a lack in being back to Freud's own writing. In the essay "Repression" (1915), we find Freud's most concise formulation of his key concept:

> We have reason to assume that there is a primal repression, a first phase of repression, which consists in the psychical (ideational) representative of the instinct being denied entrance into the conscious. With this a fixation is established; the representative in question persists unaltered from then onwards and the instinct remains attached to it.[1]

Freud has already argued by this point in the essay that repression operates not on the libido or drive itself but rather on its representations (*Vorstellungsrepräsentanzen*). Primal repression assumes the presence of such a representation in the unconscious, whose force of attraction then pulls down the conscious and preconscious ideas that feature associative links with it, thereby forming symptoms. When the unconscious discerns a homophony, for example, between a conscious or preconscious representation and the object of primal repression, the former may then be repressed as a means of protecting the ego from unpleasant or excess affect. The primally repressed representation—I will call these representations signifiers for convenience's sake—together with its associated cathexis (affective energy or libidinal investment), is the agency thanks to which what Freud calls repression proper, sometimes referred to as secondary repression, will occur. To be noted here is how Freud's description takes for granted the always-already quality of the primally repressed signifier, which he assumes is present in the unconscious—or more precisely absent from consciousness from the outset. Garden-variety repression, the kind that creates everyday neurotic symptoms, can be explained only if we assume the presence in the unconscious of a signifier that has already been repressed. For Freud, primal repression involves an actually existing instinctual representative which has been "denied entrance into the conscious." A difficulty emerges, however, when we note that this prior repression, together with the libidinal energy attached to its signifier, remains unaccounted for on this level of Freud's analysis.

In the essay "The Unconscious" published the same year, Freud grapples more explicitly with the problem of how the drive's primary signifier comes to be repressed into the unconscious. Here is where Freud's speculations have recourse to a negative value akin to, and generative of, the one Žižek mobilizes in his ontological speculations. On what he calls the economic level of his discussion, Freud assumes that repression involves the withdrawal of preconscious libido from the signifier that is subject to its force. Indeed, all forms of repression for Freud involve "a withdrawal of the cathexis of energy (or of libido)."[2] However, since he has based his formulation of ordinary repression on the assumption that the affect attached to the primally repressed signifier is the force that fuels the action of that repression, Freud cannot explain how this latter signifier came to be repressed. In short, Freud's schema cannot account for the cathexis of the primally unconscious signifier, since the libido here concerned should have been lost on the occasion when it was (presumably) originally repressed. Freud writes,

> When it comes to describing *primal* repression, the mechanism . . . of withdrawal of preconscious cathexis would fail to meet the case; for here we are dealing with an unconscious idea which has as yet received no cathexis from the *Pcs.* [preconscious] and therefore cannot have that cathexis withdrawn from it.[3]

The logical difficulty forces Freud to assume the existence of what he calls an anticathexis, a purely negative energetic value. This negative quantum of affect allows the preconscious to defend itself against the libidinally invested unconscious signifier, which would otherwise attempt to gain access to the preconscious, where it becomes potentially available to consciousness. The notion of anticathexis allows Freud to maintain his definition of repression as an energetic withdrawal: the libidinal subtraction at work in primal repression leaves behind a deficit in the preconscious which can then account for the permanency of its unconscious confinement. In the strange world of Freudian economics, in other words, the field of psychical energy is cut through by a negativity that has to be assumed in order to account for primal repression, even if affect as such is only ever encountered experientially as a positive value, most notably in the form of the symptom. Indeed, Freud argues that even the passive drives actively exert their force; affect is by definition a positive quantum. Nevertheless, the Freudian psychical economy must assume the existence of a negative magnitude in the preconscious-consciousness system in order to account for the phenomenon of primal repression. To be sure, Freud nowhere explicitly accounts for the *event* of primal repression; it is only ever assumed already to have taken place. The implication, never properly spelled out, is the existence of a kind of energetic-libidinal vortex that breaks the continuity of consciousness, grounding this consciousness in the peculiar quality of its inherent incompleteness.

With salutary effects of clarification, Lacan reconceptualizes Freud's somewhat confusingly formulated idea of negative cathexis as a missing *signifier*. Here the idea is that the unconscious emerges as an effect of the absence of a signifier adequate to (maternal) desire; this is what requires the intervention of the phallic signifier whose function is to hold the place, problematically, of the missing one. The Lacanian unconscious is strictly correlative to the Symbolic Order's incompletion; we are subjected to an order of signifiers from which one signifier is constitutively missing. In the Freudian presentation, the psyche is posited rather as a field of positive libidinal energy cut through by a kind of black hole whose gravitational pull prevents the network of forces from fully actualizing themselves. For Freud, on what we might call the ontological plane of the *Trieb* (drive), there is only the positivity of the libido, except for the fact that a portion of this positivity is defective, thwarted, or fails to come to be. The notion of being as compromised, as achieving its existence by virtue of an inherent misfire or failure-to-become, is thus already palpable in the Freudian formulation.

The second, more properly philosophical, insight that Žižek brings to his ontological speculations departs from this originally Freudian premise of the (partially) thwarted formation of being to the conclusion that the notion of the external limit or opposite is illegitimate. Žižek locates the jump from one view to the other in the shift from Kant's critical epistemology to Hegel's dialectical materialism. Kant's doctrine of the transcendental constitution of subjectivity installs knowledge of the thing-in-itself beyond the reach of human reason. The corollary is that philosophy should be confined to the task of acquainting itself with the means and mechanisms of this constitution, leaving aside the problem of the object's being as unsolvable. Hegel's philosophy for Žižek makes two epochal leaps. First, it commutes the limit of human knowledge onto the object itself, arguing that what appears to us as a lack in our knowledge of the object is merely a reflection of this same object's inherent inconsistency or self-contradiction. Second, Hegel's philosophy muddles the traditional distinction between epistemology and ontology with the idea that if our knowledge is inherently limited or imperfect, this is not because there is some positive attribute of being that escapes our powers of intellection. Rather, the fault in our knowledge, the antinomial destiny of ratiocination, is a proper consequence of the problematic nature of being itself. "Kant admits antinomies," sums up Žižek, "but only at the epistemological level, not as immanent features of the unreachable Thing-in-itself." By contrast, "Hegel transposes epistemological antinomies into the ontological sphere and thereby undermines every ontology" (*SFA*, 120).

In Žižek's Hegelian-Lacanian view, any possible manifestation of being becomes actual by paradoxical virtue of an inherent failure to realize itself. Actuality comes served, as it were, with thwarted virtualities already baked in. In consequence, any possible object in our reality achieves its existence only because it fails to secure identity with itself, in this sense never managing to become properly real. This explains why no amount of knowledge that we might collect about a given object can satisfy us as to its exhaustiveness. Complete knowledge could only be gained about a reality that had fully come to be, whose existence had been definitively consummated. For Žižek, Hegel's absolute knowledge rests on the speculative conviction that no such reality can exist.

If being is always compromised, however, it does not follow that the nature of the compromise is always the same. Anticipatory, though unwitting, excogitations of the psychoanalytic doctrine of sexual difference are there to be found in the philosophical tradition. Witness, for instance, Joan Copjec's justly famous tracing of the logical structure of Lacan's formulas of sexuation, product of an idiosyncratic appropriation of predicate logic, back to Kant's antinomies of pure reason.[4] But it is not until the invention of Freudian psychoanalysis that we find a deliberate attempt to think through the two different ways in which subjects can attempt, and of course fail, to negotiate the intrinsic deficit of being. As Žižek's work helps to show, the great stumbling block that has thwarted the sceptical, half-hearted efforts of Anglo-American gender and queer theories (as well as the more recently developed trans discourses) to come to terms with sexual difference as psychoanalysis has struggled to define it is an inauspicious, at times plainly obtuse, misconstrual of the properties of the difference concerned.

Lacan's decisive intervention makes two interrelated moves. First, sexual difference is no longer, as it was in the premodern sexual cosmologies (yin-yang, sun-moon, Mars-Venus, etc.), a difference between positive, fully pre-constituted entities. Rather, with Lacan, sexual difference becomes a pure, properly transcendental (in the sense of *a priori*) difference that cuts through both sexuated, that is to say *failed*, attempts at compensating for being's indwelling defect. Though the sexes are only two in number, they do not form a binary. This is so because a binary implies a (logical) relation, which Lacan strictly forbids with his famous axiom *Il n'y a pas de rapport sexuel*. To stress the conceptual gap separating psychoanalysis from contemporary gender ideology, we can express the same idea this way: *each of the two sexes is nonbinary*. Masculinity and femininity are two distinct, but botched, expressions of the struggle to manage the trauma of the constitutively missing signifier; or, ontologically put, the underlying deficiency in being.

Second, and just as crucially, the exotic-looking and counterintuitive logical abstractions with which Lacan articulates sexual difference are designed to do precisely what they appear to do: they stop us reducing sexual difference to either intuition (sense perception) or substance. For psychoanalysis, sexual difference is abstract in the precise sense that it is based neither on the empirical, predicative qualities of the subject, in other words all that can be said about it in discourse, nor on the subject's own intuitions regarding itself, including most significantly what we now call its gender identification. Sexual difference has no positive existence, no empirically verifiable substantive reality in biology, genetics, hormones, appearance, self-apprehension, or even performance, in the Butlerian sense of the term. It stands to reason that it took a discourse premised exclusively on a praxis of listening to discern that sexual difference finally concerns two distinct ways in which speech stumbles over itself, encountering over and over again the Real that subverts all pretensions to ontological continuity.

In the wake of Copjec's pioneering essay, Žižek revisits in his recent work the strong implication in Lacan's teaching that femininity harbours over masculinity what we can only call an ontological priority. In short, this priority is a feature of femininity's capacity more directly to tarry with being's indwelling fault. Though it has frequently been done elsewhere, a concise rehearsal of the basics of the Lacanian formulas is helpful here. Lacan grounds the universality of masculine castration ($\forall x \Phi x$) on the existence of a logically prior constitutive exception ($\exists x \overline{\Phi x}$). For its part, femininity is formalized first as the negation of the existence of an exception to castration ($\overline{\exists x \Phi x}$) and then as a negation—unconventional in predicate logic—not of the phallic function itself, but rather of the universal quantifier, in other words the all ($\overline{\forall x} \Phi x$). This latter proposition concerning the not-all quality of the phallic function is the rationale for the contention that femininity has privileged access to the inconsistency of being.

As one might expect, Žižek gives Lacan's formalization of femininity as *pas-toute* a Hegelian gloss, going as far as to argue that the shift from the Kantian to the Hegelian systems also implies a transition from a masculine to a feminine logic. The Kantian *Ding-as-sich* is akin to the masculine exception to castration in its exemption from, or exteriority to, the transcendental constitution of subjectivity. Kant's thing is the external, nonsensuous, indeed quasi-ontological guarantee for the unity of transcendental apperception; it is the essence, in other words, that conditions the unification or totalization of the world of appearances. By contrast, Hegel's formulation of the passage from substance to subject asserts that self-consciousness recognizes how essence is finally just another appearance, with the result that the idea of a reality behind the façade of the sensible is emptied out, but not *eliminated* as such. For Žižek, Hegel's subject is feminine in the precise sense that it is equivalent to this nothing, this acknowledged or registered void, not beyond but *immanent to* the phenomenal world. Feminine being generates a world of appearances that cannot be totalized; this world remains unamenable to assemblage into a knowable, seamless whole.

The original, and still ambient, complaint voiced against Lacan's formalization of sexual difference in the late 1960s and early 1970s (and by extension against the original Freudian theory of femininity) was developed most consequentially in the work of Luce Irigaray, beginning with her influential text translated as *Speculum: Of the Other Woman*. Irigaray's project was premised on the view that the lack of an equivalent signifier to the phallus for women is a product of the history of patriarchy since the Platonic consolidation of the origins of the Western philosophical tradition. In consequence, feminism must set itself the task of constructing the opposing binary term for the phallus which the dominance of male discourse, so it was argued, would have suppressed. The resulting doctrinal incompatibility, which led to Irigaray's controversial ouster from the fledgling (Lacanian) Department of Psychoanalysis in the University of Paris, repeated Freud's gesture of exclusion aimed at such "feminist" figures as Karen Horney, for example.[5] The orthodox argument concerning sexual difference, however, is precisely that femininity is theoretically incomprehensible in the absence of the premise that it proceeds in consequence of the nonexistence—the primary repression in Freudian terms—of the feminine binary signifier. Moreover, this nonexistence is not (at least straightforwardly) historical in nature. Not only is there no necessary causal link between the absence of a signifier for femininity and women's historical subordination but, for Žižek and his allies, Lacan's work lends to femininity an advantage on the very level of its being. This advantage lies in femininity's immunity to the illusion of the exceptional ontological prop, the obscenely enjoying primal father, which fuels, as Freud already saw, the traumatic fires of the (masculine) superego. Simply put, feminine subjectivity, in its capacity to resist the temptation of the hysterical position and its reintroduction of a figure of exceptionality, is inherently better equipped to engage with the fundamental ontological deficit, with the cut in being related to the unfigurable quality of (maternal) desire.

Žižek articulates what amounts to a theory of patriarchy when he suggests that masculine subjectivity activates a reactive and ordinarily misogynistic (though necessarily frustrated) attempt to ground and totalize the feminine inconsistency of being. Here Žižek outlines two sets of consequences that stem from what I began to discuss as Freudian primal repression and am now figuring as the absence, or more strongly the *missing* quality, of the binary or "secondary" signifier:

> In the first version, the binary signifier, the symmetric counterpart of S_1, is "primordially repressed," and it is in order to supplement the void of this repression that the chain of S_2 emerges, i.e. the original fact is the couple of S_1 and the Void at the place of its counterpart, and the chain of S_2 is secondary; in the second version, in the account of the emergence of S_1 as the "enigmatic term," the empty signifier, the primordial fact is, on the contrary, S_2, the signifying chain in its incompleteness, and it is in order to fill in the void of this incompleteness that S_1 intervenes. (*SFA*, 144)

There is a logical, as opposed to temporal, order defining the relation between the two phases. As Žižek puts it, "the 'feminine' version . . . comes first, it accounts for the very emergence of multiplicity, of the non-totalizable series whose lack is then filled in by the reflexive Master-signifier, the signifier of the lack of the signifier" (*SFA*, 144). At the logically inaugural or prior moment, femininity acknowledges primary repression in its construction of an ontology without the guarantee of an S_1 (master or phallic signifier). It is only then, at a subsequent (logical) moment, that masculine discourse intervenes to generate an S_1 whose function is deceptively to iron out the incompleteness and inconsistency that feminine being will leave exposed.

The Freudian equivalent of Žižek's Lacan-inspired iteration of femininity's ontological priority is the girl's spontaneous apprehension of her lack at the very outset of her version of the Oedipus narrative. For Freud, the feminine subject is always-already castrated. "A little girl behaves differently," he writes. Making her judgment "in a flash," she "shows that she is without it and wants to have it."[6] In the Lacanian theory of femininity, it is precisely the element that has most rankled generations of feminists and gender theorists—the notorious *Penisneid*, that is—that is recast as the rationale for the feminine subject's ontological privilege. Psychically speaking, the Freudian girl, and by extension the Lacanian subject sexuated in the feminine way (s/he is not always biologically female), experiences *lack without loss*. This is the difference that makes the feminine subject less vulnerable to gauzily reactive nostalgic fantasies of past better times. Here the most obvious and seemingly reductive example is the best: the well-documented popularity among white heterosexual men of Trump's quite ridiculous MAGA theme, together with all the parallel versions offered by the world's growing number of (male) authoritarian right-wing populists. With castration, the feminine subject loses not the phallus but rather the assumption in fantasy that there is something to be lost. For Žižek, this is the factor that grants femininity closer proximity to the generic, most fundamental level of subjectivity. "This radical loss of a loss defines woman's basic subjectivity," Žižek concludes. "The loss shifts here from transitive to intransitive, i.e. woman is not without the object, woman is just without, and the name of this 'just without' is $, the (barred) subject" (*SFA*, 145).

Relatedly, Žižek makes his most explicit overtures to queer theory and transgender discourse by linking the missing signifier of femininity, in other words the nonbinary nature of sexual difference, to the contemporary proliferation of sexualities and sexual identities. In conformity with Lacanian orthodoxy, Žižek insists that masculinity and femininity are not merely two among many more, or possibly even an infinite number of, possibilities for sexual identification; indeed, sex is anathema to the very notion of identification for psychoanalysis. The complication arises when we shift the understanding of sexual difference from the difference between two distinct, established sexes to an absolute difference that "cuts across every sexual identity" (*SFA*, 132), undermining each from within. Žižek will even go so far as to claim that "there are three sexes": "masculine, feminine and the difference itself" (*SFA*, 133).

The point is not to conjure out of thin air a third category of sex with the same ontological status as the other two. The intention is rather to capture the irreducibility of the difference that is sexual to the binary form: there is always a leftover, an excess, a constituency of the *Unbehagen* in the realm of sex populated by subjects who sit especially uncomfortably on either side of the divide. This being said, sexual identity is *always* problematic and finally unachievable from the perspective of psychoanalysis, no matter how seemingly normative a subject's gender performance appears to be. Further, the question of sexual identity is necessarily *intersubjective*: we depend on the Other for our sexual identity and this Other always in some measure fails to provide the desired assurance. Indeed, this insight relates to those aspects of trans discourse—the certainty with which the subject tends to experience its lived sexual identity as different from its biological sex and the ensuing demand that it be recognized without fail by the Other—which have rightfully raised questions in analytic circles. In this restricted, very precise sense, the Real of sexual difference is literally transphobic: hostile to the discursive confirmation or sanction of any sexual identity whatsoever.[7]

Cannily, Žižek anticipates the queer/trans rejoinder to the orthodox argument. By creating this category of "others," he would simply reinforce the problematic (phallocentric, patriarchal, heterosexist, cis-centric) and exhaustively dismantled logic of the hegemonic norm and its abject deviations. For psychoanalysis, however, the problem with this counterargument is that the allegedly normative forms of masculinity and femininity are already failed in their pretension to establish a sexual binary. In other words, these others, in their inability to conform to an already failed norm, become a kind of symptomatic truth of the sexual relation *in its nonexistence*, in its very impossibility. Thus, it is not the either-or, masculine or feminine, element of sexual difference that is universal, that admits of no exception. What is universal is rather the difference itself, the properly transcendental difference that precedes the sexual division, thereby impeding the achievement of sexual identity *tout court*. As Žižek puts it,

> This difference is the universal as such—universal not as a neutral frame elevated above its two species, but as their constitutive antagonism, and the third element [in the present context figured by queer/trans] stands for the difference as such, for the "pure" difference/antagonism which precedes the differentiated terms . . . This third element is not the mark of an empirical remainder that escapes the class classification, but *the materialization of their antagonistic difference itself*. (SFA, 133)

The quotation's last sentence signals a shift in an implicit comparison of sexual difference with class antagonism in the Marxist tradition. But the point stands: because the binary between masculinity and femininity or the bourgeoisie and the proletariat fails—never manages to function as a proper binary, that is—there is always a supplemental element which, though not a third category, functions to figure the failure. Though Žižek himself does not do so, I would argue that the psychoanalytic theory of sexual difference grants a kind of ontological priority to this supplemental element in the same way that it grants ontological priority to femininity over masculinity. Indeed, with its proximity to the ontological deficit, to sex's allergy to realized identity, queer/trans (as figured in Žižek's discussion, rather than in any of its specific iterations) can be viewed as a kind of annex of femininity, the manifestations of which are properly inexhaustible. The final paradox is surely that this view of the limitless proliferation of gender and sex-identity phenomena under the sign of femininity depends on the exclusionary force of the psychoanalytic premise of sexual difference. That is, the special ontological importance of both femininity and queer/trans *is lost* under the hegemonic and more intuitively persuasive assumption that masculinity and femininity are merely two possibilities among many for sexuated subjectivity.

Despite his willingness to relate trans and queer concerns to the Lacanian theory of sexual difference, not to mention the tremendous value of his subtle commentary on this theory's counterintuitive irreducibility to the premises of dominant gender theories, there is another area of Žižek's discourse on sexuality that raises important questions and can be approached in a more critical light. Particularly questionable, however insightful and provocative, is the analysis of the MeToo movement. A careful consideration of Žižek's engagement with its discourse provides an illuminating context within which to gauge the difficulty posed by the "application" of the thesis of ontological inconsistency to concrete political situations.

It will first prove helpful, however, to consider how Žižek illustrates the dialectical reversals and contradictions inherent in the concept of sexuality as psychoanalysis theorizes it with the example of so-called incel (involuntary celibate) discourse. This discourse has inspired, among other unfortunate events, a sidewalk van attack that killed ten people in Toronto in April, 2018.[8] Shrewdly, Žižek teases out the inconsistency marking incel discourse's rationalizations. Proponents share the implicit, classically patriarchal assumption that men are owed sex by women, in other words that one of their duties as women is to take care of men's sexual needs. At the same time, however, the envious sense of injustice directed at sexually successful men requires an argument in favor of what Žižek calls "an egalitarian redistribution of sex." Though men are expected sexually to dominate women from a position of social superiority, all men must be placed on the same level playing field with respect to their sexual access to the opposite sex. Conclusion: "incel [discourse] is the point of exception at which advocates of hierarchy who opposed egalitarian human rights demand the most brutal egalitarian redistribution" (*SFA*, 201). The contradiction lies in the sexist juxtaposition of the idea of male sexual superiority over women with a notion of equality (of sexual access to women) between men.

But Žižek's response to this inconsistency is not, as one might expect, to extend the egalitarianism between men to relations between the sexes. This is what might be expected of the standard liberal feminist response: genuine equality between men is only possible in a situation where women have equal rights. Instead, enlisting psychoanalysis, Žižek avers that sexuality is the arena where universal human rights cannot apply. If sexuality is the domain of human experience where what we say and what we do are most at odds, then the application of the rationalist framework of rights can have perversely antifeminist unintended consequences. Provocatively choosing sexual realism over a banal and illusory political correctness, Žižek insists that what must "be accepted in all its brutality is the ultimate incompatibility of sexuality and human rights" (*SFA*, 201).

The example of the use of (verbal) contracts in sexual relations is offered in support of this seemingly outrageous claim. This is where Žižek begins to broach MeToo discourse and, unsurprisingly perhaps, where the argument encounters a degree of difficulty. The initial context is a theoretical *rapprochement* of a recent Australian sexual rights law with Marx's materialist critique of the liberal approach to labor contracts. As Žižek relates, the state of New South Wales passed a law stating that "if you want to have sex you must ask for it clearly, and then hear a verbal 'yes' back" (*SFA*, 201). The absence of the partner's uttered response exposes the instigator to legal sanction. Quoting Marx's critique of the falsely symmetrical freedom with which capitalist and worker agree to specific terms for work, Žižek then suggests that the premise of formal equality fails to account for how apparently free decisions can be forced by impersonal macroeconomic factors which transcend the situation as contractually defined. The perspective from which the laborer appears to be free to take the job or not remains blind to the fact that he has no choice but to sell his labor power on the (in this sense unfree) market. In situations of high unemployment, for example, the worker may depend on the job for survival. For Marx as for Žižek, these are the properly structural ("systemic," as one now says) elements that make rights discourse an ineffective conceptual framework within which to address the inequalities that capitalism never fails to nurture.

But how does Žižek relate these structurally determinative aspects of capitalism to the sphere of sexuality? Like the liberalism that Marx attacks, contractual sex assumes a neutral relational background of equally distributed power against which participants negotiate their engagement with one another. In reality, however, "the form of the free contract can conceal coercion and violence" (*SFA*, 202). Indeed, it is hardly difficult to imagine a Harvey Weinstein-type figure equipping himself with a legal department-composed nondisclosure agreement for those occasions when he invites his ingenues up to his hotel suite to give them what he claims will be professional advice. Though it may work to clarify the terms of the exchange, this hypothetical document does nothing to redress the stark inequality in power that separates superstar producer from struggling wannabe actor.

Žižek goes beyond this familiar argument, however, when he offers a rationale to explain the difficulty of creating genuine equality in the realm of sex. Sexual encounters never take place against a neutral or equitable background because they are always distorted by enjoyment (*jouissance*) which, writes Žižek, "introduces asymmetry, surplus, envy into the balance of the exchange of pleasures" (*SFA*, 202). In this view, eroticization requires some level of inequality or ambiguity when it comes to conventional binaries of pleasure and pain, dominance and submission, love and lust, for example. Enjoyment can be an enemy of progressivism in sexuality on the level of its hostility to the assumption concerning self-interest that animates rights rhetoric in liberal discourses. Here it's not simply a question of acknowledging the power differentials that complicate sexual relations in patriarchal society. For Žižek, we must also recognize how these inequalities function as inherent elements of erotic life, working even to eroticize situations that would otherwise, for us, lack sexual appeal.

Žižek goes on explicitly to valorize, at least in part, the post-MeToo discourse of unambiguous sexual consent for its mediation and mitigation of the power imbalances that complicate sexual relations as he, in tandem with psychoanalysis more broadly, conceives them. Citing the sort of dialectical reversal figured topologically on a Möbius strip, Žižek claims that the most stringent application of contractual constraints can create conditions of emancipation for women in heterosexual relationships. The example here is Kant's notorious hyper-rationalist definition of marriage as a formal contract that defines the mutual access of man and wife to the other's genital regions, and more specifically the (possibly not entirely serious) corollary that the Prussian philosopher draws from it: a woman has the right to demand the return of her wayward husband on the grounds that he has absconded with something, that is, his penis, that is rightfully her property. "The only way to reach emancipation," Žižek concludes, "is to progress to the end of the path of . . . self-objectification" (*SFA*, 204). Paradoxically, the woman's relative power in a traditionally conceived marriage can increase to the extent that its particular psychological and situational features are supplanted in favor of a redefinition of the relationship in purely abstract, instrumental, and legalistic terms.

Unexpectedly, Žižek insists on seeing value even in the radical 1980s feminism of figures such as Andrea Dworkin and Catherine MacKinnon, who became notorious within academic feminism during this period for their allegedly extreme—sex-negative, according to their critics— positions on sexual violence and pornography. Cannily, Žižek discerns a line of continuity extending from Marx's critique of liberal labor law to the radical feminist view of the impossibility of authentic, egalitarian heterosexual relations under patriarchy. He spells out the structural reasoning according to which, "if by 'rape' we understand an enforced sexual exchange, then every (hetero)sexual act is ultimately a case of rape" (*SFA*, 206). The premise of structural determination makes visible the specific details of a situation that expose its distortion by systemic power imbalances.

On the level of its underlying assumptions, the conclusion is abundantly clear: "MeToo privileges structural weakness at the expense of objective weakness." But Žižek's own position on this privilege is rather less so. Indeed, he goes on to make some quite astonishing claims, including for example that the ultimate goal of the MeToo movement "is to keep men, independently of their qualities, formally reduced to oppressors," constantly under threat "of being publicly outed as sexual predators" (*SFA*, 206). Apparently, the power of structural or systemic determination as a tool for concrete social analysis is to be celebrated as long as its impact and consequences remain somewhat far from home. Referencing his own (unspecified) experience in an academic debate, Žižek complains that he cannot respond to the critical remarks on his work by "say, a black lesbian," without being "more or less automatically suspected at least of acting as a white homophobic supremacist" (*SFA*, 206).

What begins as a nuanced, insightful, and properly dialectical investigation into the difficulties psychoanalytic theory poses for certain strands of feminist and queer discourse and activism threatens to regress into a reactive lament by a figure whose various symbolic identities (male, European, white, straight) put him at a disadvantage in discourses that have been gaining ground, for better *and* for worse, in academic as well as in broader social settings over the past several decades. In my view, the problem stems from Žižek's surprisingly uncritical reliance on a distinction between so-called structural and objective weaknesses, more specifically a particular iteration of the distinction borrowed from a lecture by Jean-Claude Milner. We can return to the example of contracts in labor and sex to work this out. Even though, in the objective sense, the worker comes to the agreement of his own volition, the contract is nevertheless unjust in the structural sense because the worker, or more specifically his labor power, is a commodity in the capitalist system of exchange, and therefore a generator of a surplus value which is appropriated by the capitalist. Similarly, a man and a woman can come to an explicitly articulated agreement setting the terms for their sexual engagement with one another. But this way of framing the relation ignores the structural level on which women are a kind of sexual commodity that circulates between men even in situations where the woman, objectively speaking, has more economic or social power. Again, the background against which the contract is negotiated is always structurally distorted in a fashion that privileges some subjects over others. The premise of formal equality is an ideological screen that functions to obfuscate the deeper systemic inequality.

Within the broader philosophical outlines of his thought, however, Žižek rejects the availability of the so-called objective knowledge with which a person's relative level of power in a given social situation could be accurately assessed. In a brilliant analysis of the notion of the subkulak deployed in the third volume of *Capital*, for example, Žižek argues that Marx's inability exhaustively to enumerate the sociological identities of the groups belonging to the classes of modern capitalist society demonstrates the necessity with which "objective social analysis breaks down and subjective political attitude directly inscribes itself into the 'objective' order" (*SFA*, 247). In other words, the subkulak category is a symptom of the failure of Marx's purely materialist-sociological method, which abstracts the dominant ideologies of social groups from their members' properly subjective, in the sense of necessarily distorted, perception of their location within the social formation.

This is the implication for the discussion of sexuality: no putatively complete catalogue of the facts surrounding an encounter from which stems an accusation of harassment or abuse, as could be gleaned from CCTV footage for example, can provide a neutral account of what actually took place. This is so because, among other reasons, any viewer of the hypothetical footage will inscribe their own subjective investment onto the camera's seemingly objective representation. There is a further corollary, however. Žižek's own account can offer no disinterested take on the diverse, complex, and not unproblematic discourses surrounding the MeToo phenomenon. Indeed, the qualities of the reaction to the criticisms directed at him reveal Žižek's identification with the objective descriptors in the crosshairs of the kind of liberal-progressive, identity-predicated, politically correct cultural currents that his work, not without justification, aims to call into question.

To be sure, Žižek is too subtle and astute a thinker not to be aware of this complexity on another level of his analysis. He is generous enough to grant his critics their point concerning how "one should not read statements [by a transgender subject or a woman] only with regard to their objective content since the subjective position from which they are spoken is part of their truth-value" (*SFA*, 258). In this salutary statement, Žižek brings to bear the fundamental psychoanalytic insight concerning the irreducibility of the subject of the unconscious to the content of its enunciations. He is most assuredly correct to insist that the premise of the subject of enunciation must not be held to imply that "MeToo and LGBT+ statements" are "automatically authentic," since the subject who makes them can be "haunted by moralist self-victimization or by aggressive rage" (*SFA*, 258), for instance. I would insist that Žižek cannot be disqualified from making these arguments because of his position of exteriority with respect to the signifiers of marginality and oppression of concern here. In making them, however, he should perhaps be expected to steel himself to the inevitability of the criticisms he laments, and to resist the temptation to reduce the MeToo and LGBT+ discourses, as his analysis sometimes will do, to their more hysterical and moralistic exemplars. The psychoanalytic lesson on the impossibility of sexual identity is too important, and lately discursively too fragile, to be marred by descent to the level of self-victimization and disavowed aggression that Žižek justly decries.

Notes

1 Sigmund Freud, "Repression," in *The Standard Edition of the Complete Psychological Works of Sigmund Freud*, ed. and trans. James Strachey, vol. 14 (London: Vintage, 2001 [1957]), 148.

2 Sigmund Freud, "The Unconscious," in *The Standard Edition*, vol. 14, 154–5.

3 Freud, "Unconscious," 181.

4 See Joan Copjec, "Sex and the Euthanasia of Reason," in *Read My Desire: Lacan Against the Historicists* (Cambridge, MA: MIT Press, 1994), 201–36, as well as the more recent "The Fable of the Stork and Other False Sexual Theories," *Differences: A Journal of Feminist Cultural Studies* 21, no. 1 (2010): 63–73.

5 For the history of the debate between Freud and his critics within the psychoanalytic movement during his lifetime, see in particular Juliet Mitchell, "Introduction—I," and Octave Mannoni, "Feminine Sexuality in Psychoanalytic Doctrine," in *Feminine Sexuality: Jacques Lacan and the école freudienne*, ed. Juliet Mitchell and Jacqueline Rose (London: Norton, 1982), 1–26 and 123–36.

6 Sigmund Freud, "Some Psychical Consequences of the Anatomical Distinction Between the Sexes," (1925), in *The Standard Edition*, trans. and ed. James Strachey, vol. 19 (London: Vintage, 2001 [1961)], 252.

7 In response to the anonymous reader's claim that this contention ventures "pretty close to an open apparent hostility to trans identities," I would only reiterate the general psychoanalytic view in the process of articulation in this essay concerning the nonexistence and impossibility of fully constituted, infallibly recognized sexual identities, no matter the type. Psychoanalysis, in other words, is to some degree "hostile" to identity *tout court*. Further, the claim being made clearly concerns trans discourse and only aspects or certain tendencies of it, not trans persons as individuals. In my own view, this theoretical position does not imply any particular *a priori* response to the demand for hormonal or surgical interventions, for example. For Lacanians, "trans" is not a clinical structure, and there should be no assumption of a unitary or consistent correspondence between trans discourse and concepts such as neurosis, psychosis, or perversion, though Žižek does of course link the trans phenomenon to femininity conceived in the Lacanian manner. Though the track record of psychoanalysis broadly speaking on trans issues is in many ways problematic, it is also true that the significant hostility that trans discourse has directed toward psychoanalysis is closely linked to a fundamental tenet of analytic method: a certain austere reticence symbolically to endorse any subject's plea for the recognition of its identity, of the way it desires to be viewed by the Other, for the reason that such an endorsement blocks the emergence of clinical evidence of the unconscious. It should also be noted in response to the reader's accusation that my own argument goes on to suggest an

ontological priority for queer/trans in the same way Žižek's does for femininity. For an instance of the polemic between Lacanian and trans discourses on sex, compare Žižek's "The Sexual Is Political," *The Philosophical Salon*, August 1, 2016, to Che Gossett, "Žižek's Trans/Gender Trouble," *Los Angeles Review of Books*, September 13, 2016. For a recent example of hegemonic queer theory's objections to Žižek's work on sexuality, see Chris Coffman, "Queering Žižek," *Postmodern Culture* 23, no. 1 (2012).

8 See, for example, Leyland Cecco, "Toronto Van Attack Suspect Says He Was 'Radicalized' Online by 'Incels,'" *The Guardian*, September 27, 2019.

5

Nil Actum Credens, Si Quid Superesset Agendum

Or, Slavoj, Can't You See I'm Burning? Žižek *avec* the Clusterfuck of 2020

Clint Burnham

I argue in this chapter what may seem a paradoxical or ahistorical claim: that Slavoj Žižek's approach to such modernist authors and thinkers as Edith Wharton, Henry James, or Sigmund Freud can help us to think about 2020's global clusterfuck of climate crisis, Covid-19, and state violence. That is, Žižek's literary criticism, from the bringing out of a retroactive melancholy in Countess Olenska's love affair in Wharton's *The Age of Innocence* (*ARDM*, 215, 235; *DSST*, 146) to his argument that James's Kate Soper in *The Wings of the Dove* is the novel's true ethical hero (*PV*, 129–44) helps us to understand the spatio-temporal conundrum that is the present moment, which can be thought of simply as to whether pain or troubles stack: whether misfortune arrives singly or piles up willy-nilly.[1] Žižek's methodology I derive from an offhand remark in the notes to a minor, introductory text, *How to Read Lacan*, where he proposes "combining this dream ['of the father who doesn't know he is dead'] with the dream . . . about the dead son who appears to the father with the terrible appeal 'Father, can't you see I'm burning?'" (*HRL*, 123, n. 43). In what follows, that is, I want to read those two dreams (*avec* Freud's essay "a child is being beaten") both for how they can help us to understand today's global crises and for how the question of reading them together ("combining this dream," as Žižek puts it) in turn provides a model for seeing how the crises themselves are combined. Or, rather, for asking whether the crises do combine in ways that create new crises in turn (which would be a matter of dialectics) or whether, as computer jargon has it, they "stack" or "queue," so we can only think of one and then another. That first option—a dialectics of crises—then derives in turn from Žižek's method, where combining two dreams leads to a new insight.

A Child Is Being Beaten: Earth or Negro?

I begin, however, *not* with either of Freud's dream but rather by working through some of the logic of the *earth as child* via Freud's analysis of the fantasy "a child is being beaten."[2] Remarking how often his patients "confess to having indulged in the phantasy: 'A child is being beaten,'" Freud lists a variety of permutations: from a boy being beaten by the father, to a boy being beaten by the mother, to a girl being beaten by the father. Moreover, Freud wants us to attend to disavowed enjoyment. To attend to our climate crisis, we ask: What does this mean for the environmentalist subject? What are the unconscious anxieties and fantasies that subvent contemporary environmentalism? How can such a politics be confronted in terms of its enjoyment, its *jouissance*, in order to understand better why, and how, we oppose resource extraction? That is, thinking of the environment as mother or child—or, rather, pointing out that our conflicted cathexes in family dynamics underlie our attitudes toward nature and the climate crisis—suggests a certain psychoanalytic universality. We all, presumably, have mothers, and are or were children.

Then, attending to another crisis, state violence, what if we add to the fantasy that the earth is being beaten—a Black man is being beaten? As various Lacanian commentators have pointed out, the structure of fantasy entails a position of the viewer: put simply, "a child"—or a Negro—can only be beaten when there is someone watching. Indeed, this is the conundrum that media theorists, who believe that all news is good news, run up against. Contrary to what we think, the more visible police and state violence, the more it continues. And so, writing on the theatricalization of fantasy, Andrew Bielski notes:

> In his *Ethics* seminar Lacan expresses the extimate or ex-centric relation of the subject to the other by stating that the other "is something strange to me, although it is at the heart of me." The uncanny opening of the curtain, through which the viewer is suddenly thrown into a relation with all that

the stage discloses—above all the fact that something unbearably near to him is concealed there, lurking in the décor—allows Lacan to present the paradoxical structure according to which the spectator of fantasy is always present onstage as an actor as well, even if in veiled form. Roberto Harari, in exploring this problematic, which Lacan himself derives from Freud's classic study, "A Child is Being Beaten," describes how fantasy induces a subject that looks from the perspective of a spectator at what is transpiring on the stage, and also looks from some point on the stage—which is seldom an eye—at the very place where the subject sits in the auditorium.[3]

Roberto Harari elaborates:

[T]he subject is usually present as an actor but at the same time is the spectator. *Hence, phantasies activate a subject that looks as a spectator at what is developing before it, and also looks at where it is.* This is how the scopic appears as the inexorable floor of the phantasy. Some fragment of the subject is, in the phantasy, something that gazes at it from the stage, which is not necessarily an eye.[4]

What this means is that the "earth is being beaten" or "the Black man is being beaten" functions as a fantasy qua not only structuring our desire but constituting our subjectivity as viewer. This is certainly what Jamieson Webster describes in her brief article "The Coronavirus Delirium Factory," with a series of "scenes" starting with "A Patient is Being Intubated—I Can't Breathe" to "A World Is Being Beaten—Black Lives Matter."[5] Noting the string of signifiers "Corona, Crown, Trump, Law, Police," Webster brings it back to Freud, noting that he writes of "the beating fantasy that it is 'not clearly sexual, not in itself sadistic, but yet the stuff from which both will later come.'"

But that is not exactly it. For what various scholars all agree, including Jamieson Webster, Tavia Nyong'o, Darian Leader, Derek Hook,[6] and Luz Calvo, is the importance of a transition or alternation between grammatical transitive and intransitive modalities, the voyeurism of the speaking subject, and the alternatives of remembered or viewed events and fantasized or imagined events. In the canonical example in Freud, we have "a child is being beaten" as representing a sibling versus a series of children being beaten, and underlying, as a kind of vanishing mediator, is "I am being beaten." And "I am being beaten" is fantasized, it is not remembered, it is only wished for. Mark this point, please, for it is significant in my discussion here: the distinction between what is remembered and what is fantasized.

And the reverse is also true: what is *not* remembered, seldom commented upon, an important aspect of Freud's case studies: "In my patient's milieu it was almost always the same books whose contents gave a new stimulus to the beating-phantasies: those accessible to young people such as the so-called *'Bibliothèque rose,' Uncle Tom's Cabin*, etc."[7] That is, European subjects' fascination with scenes of racial violence is foundational to psychoanalytic theory. The logic of this substratum, although not commented upon, as far as I know, by Fanon, nonetheless lends its support to his exegesis of white fantasies *of/desires for* the Negro qua rapist:

> Here is my own view of the matter. First the little girl sees a sibling rival beaten by the father, a libidinal aggressive. At this stage ... the father, who is now the pole of her libido, refuses in a way to take up the aggression that the little girl's unconscious demands of him. At this point, lacking support, this free-floating aggression requires an investment. Since the girl is at the age in which *the child begins to enter the folklore and the culture along roads that we know*, the Negro becomes the predestined depositary of this aggression. If we go farther into the labyrinth, we discover that when a woman lives the fantasy of rape by a Negro, it is in some way the fulfillment of a private dream, of an inner wish. Accomplishing the phenomenon of turning against self, it is the woman who rapes herself.[8]

Fanon's logic, if remorseless, and dipping not a little into some distasteful characterizations of feminine desire, cannot be gainsaid. In witnessing a child being beaten, the child in turn wishes to be beaten and then, *because of the signifiers available, the signifiers of children's literature*, inserts into place the Negro. Again, we have to remember the distinction between what is remembered and what is fantasized. But if a Negro is beating me, or raping me, shouldn't he be punished? Discussing scenes of children and adults alike being beaten in *Uncle Tom's Cabin*, Tavia Nyong'o and Luz Calvo have remarked on how those scenes then function both to carry narratives of Black subjugation (and not only in an American context but also in a properly transnational one) *and* to situate the reader as the viewer.[9] This bears repeating and elaborating: *Uncle Tom's Cabin* interpellates the reader, *the complicit, enjoying reader*. And Calvo then makes an audacious argument that "there may exist another fantasy—"a Black man is being beaten" that functions as a transitional fantasy between Freud's "a child is being beaten" and Fanon's "a Negro is raping me" fantasy.[10] The causality here is properly Lacanian, or like a Möbius strip: Fanon shows that the child transfers its aggressive and masochistic desires onto the black man because of folklore. But culture's contribution to fantasies (or the role of signifiers) does not flow in a linear or unidirectional fashion. Nor do they stack— hence the Möbius. Can we not say that the spectacle of George Floyd being beaten functions both as a scene of punishment and "a new stimulus to the beating-phantasies" (Freud), as it "begins to enter the folklore and the culture along roads that we know" (Fanon)?

Don't You See I'm Burning?

I want to turn to the first of our two dreams that, via Freud, have entered the psychoanalytic canon and in turn been woven together by Žižek. A man has hired an old man to keep watch over his recently deceased son's corpse while the father sleeps in the next room. Candles fall over—the watchman has in turn fallen asleep—and the delinquent parent dreams his son is trying to awaken him with the words "Father don't you see I'm burning?"[11] Consider Lacan's commentary in *Seminar XI*, where he argues that the function of dreams is to keep us sleeping,[12] that the dream contains more of the Real than the dreamer's waking life, harkening back as it does to the child's fever (*that* is the burning: even forest fires are metaphors, meta-forests as my colleague Hilda Fernandez-Alvarez argues in a fine paper on Japan's suicide forest, Aokigahara),[13] which stages or acts as an homage to the missed encounter. We only miss forests when they are gone. And Lacan's interpretation is also a warning against being satisfied with our knowledge. Consider where he goes, as he corrects Freud—"the terrible vision of the dead son taking the father by the arm designates a beyond that makes itself heard in the dream. . . . It is only," he adds, "in the dream that this truly unique encounter can occur." But then the most remarkable conclusion: "no one can say what the death of a child is, except the father *qua* father, that is to say, no conscious being. For the true formula of atheism is not *God is dead* . . . the true formula of atheism is *God is unconscious.*"[14]

Lacan's argument here is that no, of course the father cannot see that the child is burning—of course we cannot see that the planet is burning—for the father is unconscious. Our knowledge of the dead child, the beaten Negro, the beaten planet, is doomed to be unconscious. Which is the only place where knowledge can function.

Žižek's gloss on Lacan's reading is well known: "It is not the intrusion from external reality that awakened the unfortunate father, but the unbearably traumatic character of what he encountered in the dream—in so far as 'dreaming' means fantasizing to avoid confronting the Real, the father woke up so that he could go on dreaming" (*HRL*, 58). Ellie Ragland adds: "Freud fails to see what the dream really shows the father: the son's form as a horribly gruesome burning body that takes his father by the arm, touching him."[15] To understand what these readings add to Lacan and then Freud, consider first of all that signs of climate emergency (bedraggled polar bears in northern Canada), or systemic racism (burning down a police precinct house), of the spreading virus (big-screen televisions across America showing CNN infographics) are themselves in the Imaginary, and like the father's solicitude toward his son, only maintain our narcissistic self-image. *We* care about the environment, *we* are woke, *we* wear masks.

Didn't Know He Was Dead

There is another dream of Freud's, also starring a father, that is germane to the current moment. In a 1911 paper on the "two principles of mental functioning" (i.e., the pleasure principle and the reality principle), Freud describes a dream a patient repeatedly had after his father died following a long illness: "*his father was alive once more and . . . he was talking to him in his usual way. But he felt it exceedingly painful that his father had really died, only without knowing it.*"[16] Freud remarks that the only way to understand

> this apparently nonsensical dream is by adding "as the dreamer wished" or "in consequence of his wish" after the words "that his father had really died," and by further adding "that he [the dreamer] wished it" to the last words. The dream-thought then runs: it was a painful memory for him that he had been obliged to wish for his father's death (as a release) while he was still alive, and how terrible it would have been if his father had had any suspicion of it!

(Freud also makes the delightful comment that "one is bound to use the currency that is in use in the country one is exploring—in our case a neurotic currency.")[17]

In his *Seminar VI*, Lacan devotes two lessons to this dream.[18] In the first session, he discusses how in Freud's comments he adds those phrases (that he [the dreamer] had wished for his father's death, etc.), which means not only that the dream had subtracted those signifiers, and that this was repression in its purest form, but also that this was not actually anything the dreamer would not have already known.[19] For what is subtracted is what we know—we *know* the earth/Negro is dead—knowledge isn't the problem, but racism or environmental despoilation gives us too much enjoyment; also it's a matter of self-image—we do not know or refuse to know that this means we are racists or polluters (again enjoyment: being deplorables, giletjaunes)—that is, what Eduardo Bonilla-Silva calls "racism without racists." This split between knowing and enjoying Lacan begins to articulate in his early forms of the graph of desire, where "he did not know" lies at the level of the ego (the *sujet de l'énoncé*), and "he was dead" at the level of the Symbolic qua unconscious (the *sujet de l'enunciation*).[20]

Bring Them Together

But let us return to the example set for us by Žižek. That is, what can we learn from bringing these dreams or signifying chains into conversation with each other, into non-relation? I propose the following: that *he did not know he had died* is a vanishing mediator or necessary link between *a child is being beaten* and *father can't you see I'm burning*. Consider the two arguments, from my reading of *a child is being beaten,* first, that what is assumed or fantasized but never enunciated is that I am being beaten (this is fantasized and never remembered, only wished for—a certain masochism); second, that in the racialized tropes brought in via Fanon and Luz Calvo, "a Black man is being beaten" functions as a transitional fantasy between Freud's "a child is being beaten" and Fanon's "a Negro is raping me" fantasy.[21] In the canonical reading, masochism: but in the racialized reading, the Negro is punished *for our very fantasy.* So *a child is being beaten* qua treasure trove of signifiers means, successively, that the spectacle of the destruction of the earth is a picture marked by our desire, our desire for our own destruction, and out of guilt for our desire, we desire first our own death, accomplished via Covid-19, and then punish Black bodies. We turn to the father, appealing to the big Other—can't you see I'm burning, can't you see I'm burning up with fever, with Covid-19, with forest fires (with metaforest fires). But just as that utterance is a reproach to those who cannot see, who refuse knowledge (of Covid-19, of systemic racism and white supremacy, of climate disaster), or rather *before* (the temporality here is of Lacan's "Logical Time"), before we can make that utterance, we have the dream of the father who did not know he had died. "Father, can't you see you are dead?" indeed! It is worth remembering that Lacan's two readings of Freud's dream of the father who did not know he had died, in *Seminar VI* (1958–59) and *Seminar XI* (1961–62), themselves straddle his theory of the "between two deaths," worked out in *Seminar VII* (1959–60), denoting the zone between one's symbolic death and one's physical death.[22] And then to bring this back to racialized state violence, if the no-knock warrant police murder of Breonna Taylor can be read as—father can't you see I'm sleeping—again, it is the utterance, as Lacan says "Is it not the missed reality that caused the death of the child expressed in these words?,"[23] a missed encounter with the Real, a "missed reality" qua treasure trove of signifiers that caused the death (... of Breonna Taylor, of the earth, of the Covid-19 patient, not only the cop, pollution, virus . . .) but expressed in those words. Then, the gap between Breonna Taylor's death in March 2020 and that of George Floyd in May 2020 surely this gap is the gap "between two deaths": Breonna died physically in March, but her symbolic death then was utterable once the George Floyd uprising began.

A Three Way

If I have been calling the triangulation of Covid-19, climate crisis, and state violence a clusterfuck, it bears speculating first, whether or not such incidents, to use a bureaucratic appropriation of Benjamin Bratton, "stack" or they replace each other.[24] "Misfortunes never come singly," so says Tolstoy (and Marx); but, in Camus's *La Peste*, a character inquires, "have you ever heard of a man with cancer being killed in an auto smash?"

The dream of the father who did not know he was dead obviously has much to teach us about knowledge and the unconscious and helps to explain, say, why the father can't see that the child is burning (or, variously, why anti-maskers continue in their delusions, why racism isn't apprehended and wiped out, why climate denial continues apace). This is not to argue that such lack of knowledge does not have its political economy: Todd McGowan has argued forcefully for why the right often resist masks: "the mask covers the face, which functions as a fetish." That is, the face is more of a mask than the mask proper, for, as fetish, it covers up our lack. Then, he continues, the mask is a sign of collectivity, since when we wear a mask we explicitly signal our concerns for others: "I can no longer think of myself in isolation once I recognize the necessity of wearing the mask."[25] But we must explain such disavowals not simply in terms of a satisfying finger-pointing at climate deniers: for Lacan's reading is also that we have to learn to dispense with the subject supposed to know:

> The impotence of the Other to respond is due to an impasse and this impasse—as we know—is called the limitation of his knowledge. "He did not know that he had died," that he has come to this absoluteness of the Other only by a death not accepted but undergone, and undergone because of the desire of the subject; this the subject knows, as I might say: that the Other must not to know it, that the Other demands not to know it, this is the privileged part in these two not-to-be-confused demands: that of the subject and that of the Other.[26]

The dream of the father who did not know he had died is also the realization that there is no big Other, that science cannot be appealed to, it is *not*, as the kids like to say, real. As Žižek argues, "if what we experience as 'reality' is structured by fantasy, and if fantasy serves as the screen that protects us from being directly overwhelmed by the raw Real, then *reality itself can function as an escape from encountering the Real*" (HRL, 57). So too we can do that via this *triangulation*, or better yet *trifecta* of Freud's three dreams, or his three phraseologies, utterances, signifying chains: *a child is being beaten, father can't you see I'm burning*, and *he did not know he had died*. Reading Freud in this Žižekian way helps us to think about questions of whether pain, or misfortune, or indeed lack, stacks. Consider two jokes, one well known (the borrowed kettle) and the other less so (one of Freud's marriage-broker jokes). The borrowed kettle joke, which Freud initially drew on to illustrate the resistance of dream logic to contradiction, is the story of the neighbor who returns a damaged kettle, and when confronted with the broken vessel, first says that he did not borrow the kettle, then that it was already damaged, and finally that it was in fine shape when it was returned.

The other joke runs as follows:

> The would-be bridegroom complained that the bride had one leg shorter than the other and limped. The *Schadchen* contradicted him: "You're wrong. Suppose you marry a woman with healthy, straight limbs! What do you gain from it? You never have a day's security that she won't fall down, break a leg and afterwards be lame all her life. And think of the suffering then, the agitation, and the doctor's bill! But if you take *this* one, that can't happen to you. Here you have a *fait accompli*." The appearance of logic is very thin in this case, and no one will be ready to prefer an already "accomplished misfortune" to one that is merely a possibility.²⁷

In both jokes we have a case of whether misfortunes cancel each other out or can be added to each other: that is, a question of their ontology. Another way of thinking of this comes to us from the Roman poet Lucan: *nil actum credens, si quid superesset agendum*, or "believing that nothing was done as long as anything remained to be done" [Don't let perfect be the enemy of good—Voltaire]. Quoted in Kant's second preface to his *Critique of Pure Reason* the tag is of a piece with Lacan and Camus but not Tolstoy, Marx, and the Freud of our jokes.²⁸

Here a final stacking or combination can be found in Žižek's use of Freud's "kettle logic" in his 2004 book *Iraq: The Borrowed Kettle*, in which he suffered the justifications for the 2003 invasion of Iraq to the same analysis. The justifications were as follows: first, Iraq has weapons of mass destruction; second, if not (since we cannot find them), he was responsible for 9/11; third, since even George Bush admitted there was no evidence of Saddam Hussein's culpability for 9/11, his is a murderous dictatorial regime and should be removed for reasons of stability in the region (*I*, 1–2). Žižek argues that what "conferred a semblance of consistency on this multitude of reasons was, of course, ideology," but the usefulness of Freud to Žižekian ideology critique should not be comforting to liberals or the left. In a footnote to this passage, he argues that the same inconsistency (or unconscious logic, the logic of the dream) can be found in left opposition to the invasion, with reasons ranging from *it's really about oil and hegemony* to *it will merely boost anti-American terrorism* and finally *it will cost too much money* (*I*, 180).

In the introduction to this chapter, I mentioned Žižek's criticism of such modernists as Edith Wharton; by way of conclusion, I want to turn to two readings of Henry James's novels made possible by the psychoanalytic argument proposed earlier. Consider another application of the "father can't you see I'm burning?" dream, in Sigi Jöttkandt's essay on Henry James's *The*

Wings of the Dove. Jöttkandt argues that in the novel, the death of Milly Theale (whose fortune is bequeathed to Kate Croy's lover Merton Densher)

recalls, albeit inversely, the dream Freud recounts of the father whose child cries out that he is burning. In the Freudian dream, the father wakes up, *in order to continue dreaming,* that is, in order to avoid the "real" of his dream . . . Milly, in reverse, dies to avoid waking up; she dies in order to maintain the fantasy whose promise of complete satisfaction is, paradoxically, the guarantee against completing the field of representation. Milly's death is thus, in a very precise sense, a desiring death, a death died in accordance with desire.[29]

Žižek argues against Jöttkandt's interpretation, agreeing with her description of "Milly's sacrificial gesture as a hysterical solution," but adding that he is "tempted to propose the opposite ethical solution" (*PV*, 131).[30] This counterexample of my method, read again with Žižek, will, I hope, help us to understand better the contemporary moment. That is, an "opposite ethical solution" can be seen in another of James's novels that deal with romantic rivalry, *The Bostonians.* There Olive Chancellor, a women's rights advocate, is worried that Southern conservative Basil Ransom will steal away her *protégée,* Verena Tarrant, and so she mulls over encouraging another suitor, whom she suspects she can manipulate easier.

"By this time she had also definitely reasoned it out that Basil Ransom and Henry Burrage could not both capture Miss Tarrant, that therefore there could not be two dangers, but only one; that this was a good deal gained, and that it behoved her to determine which peril had most reality, in order that she might deal with that one only."[31] Two dangers or one? Or rather, which peril (climate crisis, the pandemic, or state violence) has most reality?

Notes

1 Please see for a richer discussion of Žižek's contributions to literary criticism, *Everything You Always Wanted to Know about Literature but Were Afraid to Ask Žižek*, ed. Russell Sbriglia (Durham: Duke University Press, 2017).

2 Sigmund Freud, "A Child Is Being Beaten: A Contribution to the Study of the Origin of Sexual Perversions," in *The Standard Edition of the Complete Psychological Works of Sigmund Freud, Volume XVII (1917–1919): An Infantile Neurosis and Other Works*, trans. James Strachey (London: Hogarth Press and the Institute of Psychoanalysis, 1955), 175–204.

3 Andrew Bielski, "Actes Manquants: Theatre and the Psychoanalytic Act," *The Journal of Culture and the Unconscious* IX, no. 1 (2013–2014): 51.

4 Roberto Harari, *Lacan's Seminar on Anxiety: An Introduction*, trans. Jane C. Lamb-Ruiz (New York: Other Press, 2001), 213. Harari distinguishes between

phantasy and *fantasy*, denoting by the former an almost exclusively sexual nature and the latter "the activity of daily imagination." In the book's previous chapter, Harari develops an analysis of Lacan's graphs of desire, referring to the role of floors (or forms) "*in the constitution of the [objet] a*," 188 (Italics Harari's).

5 https://www.psychoanalysis.today/en-GB/PT-Articles/Webster-157560/The-Coronavirus-Delirium-Factory.aspx (accessed February 22, 2021).

6 Thus Hook (discussing Leader as well): "the crucial formulation 'I am being beaten by my father'. . . pinpoints the unconscious fantasy," "Apartheid's Lost Attachments," in *(Post)Apartheid Conditions: Psychoanalysis and Social Formation* (London: Palgrave, 2013), 132.

7 Freud, "A Child," 180.

8 Frantz Fanon, *Black Skin, White Masks*, trans. Charles Lam Markmann (London: Pluto, 2008), 138. Emphasis mine.

9 Tavia Nyong'o, "Racial Kitsch and Black Performance," *The Yale Journal of Criticism* 15, no. 2 (2002): 376.

10 Luz Calvo, "Racial Fantasies and the Primal Scene of Miscegenation," *International Journal of Psychoanalysis* 89 (2008): 64.

11 Sigmund Freud, "The Interpretation of Dreams," in *The Standard Edition of the Complete Psychological Works of Sigmund Freud, Volume V (1900–1901): The Interpretation of Dreams* (Second Part) and *On Dreams*, trans. James Strachey (London: Hogarth Press and the Institute of Psychoanalysis, 1955), 509–11. As always with the status of dreams in Freud's corpus, the framing or introduction matters. Consider how the dream is indexed in the *Standard Edition*: "Burning Child (Unknown Father—Freud's Patient)"—that is, the dreamer was an "unknown father," and the dream was reported to Freud by a patient (717). The dream, it turns out, was mentioned in a lecture that the patient (a woman) attended—nonetheless Freud does not hesitate to devote some space to its analysis—and the dream was evidently so powerful that the patient in turn incorporated it into her own dreams.

12 This is also Freud's conclusion: or, rather, that the dream both allows the father to imagine his son is still alive *and* to catch a bit more sleep. Freud, *The Interpretation of Dreams*, 510, 571.

13 Hilda Fernandez-Alvarez, "Aokigahara Forest: An Aesthetic Space of Residual Surplus," in *Lacan and the Environment*, ed. C. Burnham and P. Kingsbury (New York: Palgrave, 2021), 182.

14 Jacques Lacan, *The Seminar: XI, 1964–1965. Four Fundamental Concepts of Psychoanalysis*, trans. Alan Sheridan (New York: Norton, 1998), 59.

15 Ellie Ragland, "The Relation between the Voice and the Gaze," in *Reading Seminar XI Lacan's Four Fundamental Concepts of Psychoanalysis*, ed. Richard Feldstein, Bruce Fink, and Maire Jaanus (Albany: State University of New York Press, 1995), 194.

16 Freud talks about it in two places, in *The Interpretation of Dreams*, but first, in the 1911 paper "Formulations on the Two Principles of Mental

Functioning," which offered one of the first, if highly condensed, discussions of the pleasure principle versus reality principle (this was written while he was working on the Schreber essay). His discussion of the dream was then added to the 1911 edition of the *Interpretation*.

17 Sigmund Freud, "Formulations on the Two Principles of Mental Functioning," in *The Standard Edition of the Complete Psychological Works of Sigmund Freud, Volume XII (1911–1913): The Case of Schreber, Papers on Technique, and Other Works*, trans. James Strachey (London: Hogarth Press and the Institute of Psychoanalysis, 1955), 225.

18 Jacques Lacan, *The Seminar: VI, 1958–59: Desire and Its Interpretation*, trans. Bruce Fink (Cambridge: Polity, 2019). Lessons of November 26, 1958 (43–59) and December 10, 1958 (78–94).

19 Lacan, *The Seminar: VI*, 55.

20 Lacan, *The Seminar: VI*, 88–9.

21 Calvo, "Racial Fantasies," 64.

22 There is a debate on two fronts with respect to this phrase. On the one hand, did Lacan coin it, or is it, as he notes in *Seminar VII*, "Someone among you has baptized the topology that I have sketched out for you this year with the apt and somewhat humorous phrase, the zone between-two-deaths. Your Vacation time will give you the time to consider whether its rigor seems to you to be especially effective. I ask you to think it over." *The Ethics of Psychoanalysis*, trans. Dennis Porter (New York: Norton, 1997), 320. See also Marc de Kesel, *Eros and Ethics*, trans. Sigi Jöttkandt (Albany: State University of New York Press, 2009), 238 and 322n49. On the other hand, are we talking about Antigone's two deaths, her symbolic death (when she can no longer live in the community because she has violated Creon's prohibition, but has not yet committed suicide) versus her physical death, or Polynieces's two deaths, first his physical death, followed by, when Antigone scatters dust on his body, his symbolic death.

23 Lacan, *XI*, 58.

24 Benjamin Bratton, *The Stack: On Software and Sovereignty* (Cambridge, MA: MIT Press, 2016).

25 YouTube lecture July 26, 2020.

26 Jacques Lacan, *The Seminar: IX, 1961–62: On Identification*, trans. Cormac Gallagher, available online: www.lacaninireland.com, 143.

27 Both jokes—the borrowed kettle and the marriage broker—are to be found in Sigmund Freud, "Jokes and the Relation to the Unconscious," in *The Standard Edition of the Complete Psychological Works of Sigmund Freud, Volume VIII (1905)*, trans. James Strachey (London: Hogarth Press and the Institute of Psychoanalysis, 1955), 62–3. The borrowed kettle is first discussed in *The Interpretation of Dreams* when analyzing his "specimen dream" of Irma's injection and again later in *Jokes* (205).

28 Immanuel Kant, *Critique of Pure Reason*, trans. Werner S. Pluhar (Indianapolis: Hackett, 1996), 27 [Bxxiv].

29 Sigi Jöttkandt, *Acting Beautifully: Henry James and the Ethical Aesthetic* (Albany: State University of New York Press, 2005), 86.
30 Žižek quotes from a 2002 conference paper by Jöttkandt, in which she used the term "hysterical solution," which is not to be found in the 2005 book quoted earlier.
31 Henry James, *The Bostonians* (Harmondsworth: Penguin, 1987), 310.

6

What's Wrong with Being Happy?

Žižek's Critique of Happiness

Jeffrey R. Di Leo

Big happiness is large and growing larger by the day. Science and industry are working day and night so that happiness pursues us wherever we go. More and more data is being collected that will make the science of happiness as predictive as the laws of physics. All of this is wonderful news for the scientists and industries devoted to the study of happiness. But what if there is no such thing as happiness? Or what if the early Greeks like Solon were right when they said that a man *is* happy only when he is dead? "Until he is dead," says Solon, "keep the 'happy' in reserve." "Till then," he continues, "he is not happy, but only lucky."[1] For someone like Aristotle, who believed that happiness was an activity, this view is clearly absurd.[2] But there are also those in the philosophical tradition who are critical or even fearful of happiness. Arguably, the rejection of happiness and its pursuit is a cornerstone of the modern condition and modernity.

This chapter examines Slavoj Žižek's argument for saying "No Thanks!" to happiness both within the philosophical and psychological traditions as well as its importance as an act of public philosophy, particularly via arenas such as YouTube.[3] As an important public advocate of a modern— and highly unpopular—"tragic" view of happiness,[4] Žižek stands squarely against the celebration of happiness in American society. This chapter asks what is the price of pursuing happiness under late capitalism? Is it one worth taking? Or should we follow Žižek and reject happiness? For Žižek, as we shall see, the answer here is clear, but is his argument convincing enough to convince more than the tragic few? We'll begin by reviewing the typically modern position on happiness found in the writings of Sigmund Freud, and their further development in Jacques Lacan, before turning to Žižek's psychoanalytic critique of happiness.

Happiness and Its Discontents

Very early in his career, while working with Josef Breuer on their jointly published *Studies on Hysteria*, Freud writes of a common objection to his treatment by patients:

> "Why, you tell me yourself that my illness is probably connected with my circumstances and the events of my life. You cannot alter these in any way. How do you propose to help me, then?"[5]

To which Freud replies:

> No doubt fate would find it easier than I do to relieve you of your illness. But you will be able to convince yourself that much will be gained if we succeed in transforming your hysterical misery into uncommon unhappiness. With a mental life that has been restored to health you will be better armed against that unhappiness.[6]

It is important to note that in the last line in the earlier passage "mental life" appeared as "nervous system" in German editions of Freud's work prior to 1925.[7] It has been said "in 1895 Freud was at the half-way stage in the process of moving from physiological to psychological explanations of psychopathological states."[8] If so, he was also halfway in the process of moving from physiological to psychological explanations of happiness—and unhappiness. But it is really with the introduction of the "destructive instinct" or the death drive that Freud places something other than happiness as the goal of life.

In *Beyond the Pleasure Principle*, which was first published in 1920, twenty-five years after his work with Breuer, Freud introduces the death instinct. "If we are to take it as a truth that knows no exception that everything living dies for *internal* reasons—becomes inorganic once again—then we shall be compelled to say that 'the goal of all life is death,'" writes Freud, "and, looking backwards, that 'what was inanimate existed before what is living.'"[9] He would later formally link the "love instinct" (Eros) to the "death instinct" (Thanatos). Together, they are the only basic instincts. "The aim of the first of these basic instincts is to establish even greater unities and to preserve them thus—in short, to bind together; the aim of the second, on the contrary, is to undo connections and so to destroy things."[10] For Freud, "the final aim of the destructive instinct is to reduce living things to an inorganic state."[11] Along with these two primal forces is the "pleasure principle," which Freud describes as "a tendency operating in the service of a function whose business it is to free the mental apparatus from excitation or to keep the amount of excitation in it constant or to keep it as low as possible."[12] As to whether the pleasure principle "requires a reduction, or perhaps ultimately the extinction, of the tension of the instinctual needs (that is, a state of *Nirvana*) leads to problems that are still unexamined in the relations between the pleasure principle and the two primal forces, Eros and the death instinct."[13] So, while we have the unexamined potential for Nirvana in Freud, what about happiness?

In *Civilization and Its Discontents*, first published in 1930, Freud leaves no doubt as to his position on happiness. While it can hardly be doubted that people "seek happiness, they want to become happy and to remain so,"[14] this conflicts with both our basic instincts and the world. According to Freud,

> the pleasure-principle draws up the programme of life's purpose. This principle dominates the operation of the mental apparatus from the very beginning; there can be no doubt about its efficiency, and yet its programme is in conflict with the whole world, with the macrocosm as much as with the microcosm. It simply cannot be put into execution, the whole constitution of things runs counter to it; one might say the intention that man should be "happy" is not included in the scheme of "Creation." What is called happiness in its narrowest sense comes from the satisfaction—most often instantaneous—of pent-up needs which have reached great intensity, and by its very nature can only be a transitory experience. When any condition desired by the pleasure-principle is protracted, it results in a feeling only of mild comfort; we are so constituted that we can only intensely enjoy contrasts, much less intensely states themselves. Our possibilities of happiness are thus limited from the start by our very constitution. It is much less difficult to be unhappy.[15]

For Freud, not only does the present state of civilization "inadequately provid[e] us with what we require to make us happy in life,"[16] but so too does "the scheme of 'Creation.'" Thus, while unhappiness is readily attainable, happiness is not. To expect otherwise goes against the fundamental tenets of psychoanalysis.

In psychoanalysis, Jacques Lacan would continue to develop in novel ways the critique of happiness that Freud initiated. For Lacan, "Freud leaves no doubt, any more than Aristotle, that what man is seeking, his goal, is happiness."[17] However, referring to the passage earlier by Freud about the conflict between happiness and the world, writes Lacan, "I prefer to read in *Civilization and Its Discontents* the idea Freud expresses there concerning happiness, namely, that absolutely nothing is prepared for it, either in macrocosm or microcosm."[18] For Lacan, this is the "completely new" point Freud makes about a very old topic.

Lacan makes a major point about the limits of happiness by turning to the story of Oedipus. But unlike Freud, who uses the story to establish the Oedipus complex, a cornerstone of his psychoanalysis, Lacan says that "in a sense Oedipus did not suffer from the Oedipus complex."[19] "He simply killed a man," continues Lacan, "whom he didn't know was his father."[20] However, rather than abandoning the myth in his psychoanalysis, Lacan reinterprets it to show the conflict between happiness and knowledge:

> [Oedipus] doesn't know that in achieving happiness, both conjugal happiness and that of his job as king, of being the guide to the happiness of the state, he is sleeping with his mother. One might therefore ask what the treatment he inflicts on himself means. Which treatment? He gives up the very thing that captivated him. In fact, he has been duped, tricked by reason of the fact that he achieved happiness. Beyond the sphere of the service of goods and in spite of the complete success of this service, he enters into the zone in which he pursues his desire.[21]

For Lacan, the tragedy of Oedipus is not the desire for his mother, but rather his desire to know. Happiness then leads Oedipus to pursue the desire to know to its end, which then leaves him "to deal with the consequence of that desire that led him to go beyond the limit, namely the desire to know."[22] "He has learned," comments Lacan, "and still wants to learn something more."[23]

Nevertheless, writes Lacan, in our own time "happiness has become a political matter."[24] And because of this,

> the question of happiness is not susceptible to an Aristotelian solution, that the prerequisite [for happiness] is situated at the level of the needs of all men. Whereas Aristotle chooses between the different forms of the good that he offers the master, and tells him that only certain of these are worthy of his devotion—namely, contemplation—the dialectic of the master has, I insist, been discredited in our eyes for historical reasons that have to do with the period of history in which we find ourselves. Those reasons are expressed in politics by the following formula: "There is no satisfaction for the individual outside of the satisfaction of all."[25]

For Lacan, this is the context of analysis circa mid-twentieth century. It is also the context "that the analyst sets himself up to receive, a demand for happiness."[26] "To refocus analysis on the dialectic makes evident the fact that the goal is indefinitely postponed," writes Lacan. "It's not the fault of analysis if the question of happiness cannot be articulated in any other way at the present time."²⁷ Moreover, whereas for Aristotle, there *was* a discipline of happiness, for Lacan, at the present moment in history, we are "far from any formulation of a discipline of happiness."²⁸ For him, happiness is a "bourgeois dream" and the analyst that guarantees "the possibility that a subject will in some way be able to find happiness even in analysis is a form of fraud."²⁹ Nevertheless, "we do not disclaim our competence to promise happiness in a period in which the question of its extent has become so complicated" as a political factor.³⁰ "To be fair," says Lacan to his colleagues, "the progress of humanism from Aristotle to St Francis (of Sales) did not fill the aporias of happiness either."³¹ In short, in spite of these pragmatic remarks to his colleagues regarding happiness in psychoanalysis, Lacan finds himself at odds with American psychology on this topic.

In his report to the Rome Congress in 1953, Lacan says that the behaviorism of American psychology is "at the antipodes of the psychoanalytic experience."³² He contends that behaviorism "so dominates the notion of psychology in America that it has now completely obscured the inspiration of Freud in psychoanalysis itself."³³ His description of psychoanalysis in the United States to his colleagues in Rome is that it has

> inclined towards the adaptation of the individual to the social environment, towards the quest for behaviour patterns, and towards all the objectification implied in the notion of "human relations." And the indigenous [American] term "human engineering" strongly implies a privileged position of exclusion in relation to the human object.³⁴

A few years later, he expands on this thought in a lecture in Vienna:

> But its practice in the American sphere has been so summarily reduced to a means of obtaining "success" and to a mode of demanding "happiness" that it should be pointed out that this constitutes a repudiation of psychoanalysis, a repudiation that occurs among too may of its adherents from the simple, basic fact, that they have never wished to know anything about the Freudian discovery, and that they will never know anything about it, even by way of repression.³⁵

For Lacan, the American way of life revolves around signifiers such as adaptation, human relations, human engineering, brain trust, success, basic personality, pattern, happy ending, and happiness. These signifiers mark the ideology of American free enterprise and are antithetical to the form of psychoanalysis he develops. "A team of egos," writes Lacan, "no doubt less equal than autonomous (but by what stamp of origin do they recognize each other in the sufficiency of their autonomy?), offers itself to Americans to guide them toward happiness," comments Lacan, "without upsetting the autonomies, whether egoistic or not, that pave with their nonconflictual spheres the American way of getting there."[36]

An Unethical Category

Following in the psychoanalytic footsteps of Freud and Lacan, Žižek argues that if the goal of life is happiness, then we are in for problems—*big* problems. It is an argument that he has consistently made for the past thirty years, along the way adding to it additional layers of political and cultural evidence. Though heavily steeped in Lacanian psychoanalysis, his argument is not just directed to fellow analysts and philosophers but rather to anyone who will listen to him. And he draws our attention to his position on happiness by swimming against the strong American current in celebration and pursuit of happiness.[37]

A recent example is the sold-out debate he had with the psychologist Jordan Peterson on the topic of happiness. Called the "duel of the century," Žižek defends a Marxist position on happiness, whereas Peterson takes the capitalist side. But Žižek finds it ironic that the participants in this duel "are both marginalized by the official academic community."[38] He says that though he is "supposed to defend here the left, liberal line against the neo-conservatives," he is most often attacked by left liberals. The politics of his position on happiness get even more complicated when one takes into account that he follows Lacan (who in turn followed Saint-Just) in regarding happiness as a "political factor."[39]

In an early work, *For They Know Not What They Do: Enjoyment as a Political Factor* (1991), he says, "What Saint-Just meant by 'happiness' has of course little to do with enjoyment: it implies revolutionary Virtue, a radical renunciation of the decadent pleasures of the *ancient régime*" (253–4). Ten years later he writes in *On Belief* that "liberalism tries to avoid (or, rather, cover up)" a paradox at the center of this line of thought, namely, the idea that "'totalitarianism' imposes on the subject his or her own good, even if it is against his will—recall King Charles' (in)famous statement: 'If any shall be so foolishly unnatural as to oppose their king, their country and their own good, we will make them happy, by God's blessing—even against their wills'" (*OB*, 119). Liberals avoid the paradox of happiness as a political factor by "clinging to the end to the fiction of the subject's immediate free self-perception ('I don't claim to know better than you what you want—just look deep into yourself and decide freely what you want!')" (*OB*, 119). In short, like Lacan, Žižek's announcement of happiness as a political factor or matter both signals a split from the Aristotelian approach to happiness and is also expressed in politics by the same formula noted earlier: "There is no satisfaction for the individual outside of the satisfaction of all."

Most appropriately, Žižek chooses the example of China in his debate with Peterson to illustrate the coming together of the three notions from the title of the debate: happiness, communism, and capitalism. It also allows him to show how the left in the twentieth century defined itself through opposition to two "fundamental tendencies of modernity: the reign of capital with its aggressive market competition, [and] the authoritarian bureaucratic state power." For Žižek, China combines these two features of modernity "on behalf of the majority of the people" in an extreme form: a "strong totalitarian state" and "state-wide capitalist dynamics." He then asks: "Are the Chinese any happier for all that?" The answer here is of course "No," which Žižek says is determined by psychoanalysis, not philosophy or economics.

Psychoanalysis shows us that "humans are very creative in sabotaging our pursuit of happiness," says Žižek. He continues by telling the audience,

Happiness is a confused notion, basically it relies on the subject's inability or unreadiness to fully confront the consequences of his/her/their desire. In our daily lives, we pretend to desire things, which we do not really desire, so that ultimately the worst thing that can happen is to get what we officially desire.

Elsewhere, in a YouTube video that has been viewed 1.6 million times, he repeats this line of thought and illustrates it through what he calls the "traditional male chauvinist scenario": a married man is in a cold relationship so takes on a mistress. He dreams all the time that if my wife were to disappear it would open up a new life for me with the mistress. But, says Žižek, "every psychoanalyst will tell you what quite often happens" is that when the wife goes away, you also lose the mistress. You thought this is all you wanted but it turns out that what you really wanted is not to live with the mistress, but "to keep her at a distance as an object of desire about which you dream." This, for Žižek, is how things function: "we don't really want what we think we desire." Ultimately, for him, happiness is an "unethical category."[40]

While Žižek rails against happiness from many different directions and contexts, the core tenets of his approach remain consistent: psychoanalysis establishes happiness as "the betrayal of desire" (*WDR*, 58). As psychoanalysis, at least for Žižek, "is a kind of anti-ethics" (*LC*, 16), happiness is regarded by him as an "unethical category" both in the sense that he doubts its veracity as a mere category *and* that he does not see it as constitutive of morality like for example Aristotle, Bentham, and Mill.[41] For Žižek, happiness is "not a category of truth, but a category of mere Being, and, as such, confused, indeterminate, inconsistent" (*WDR*, 59).[42] It is also a term used everywhere. Thus, it is hard for Žižek not to hit something or someone every time he swings his argument against happiness.

His targets not just include the philosophical tradition regarding the pursuit of happiness (e.g. Aristotle, Locke, Mill), but also revered religious figures like the Dalai Lama, who he says "has had much success recently preaching the gospel of happiness around the world, and no wonder he is finding the greatest response precisely in the USA, the ultimate empire of the (pursuit of) happiness" (*WDR*, 59). Other major targets include fundamental Christian beliefs such as the idea of living "happily ever after," which he says is "a Christianized version of paganism" (*WDR*, 59). Happiness is "a *pagan* concept," writes Žižek, noting that pagans believe happiness is the goal of life and "religious experience and political activity are considered the highest forms of happiness (see Aristotle)" (*WDR*, 59). "In short," concludes Žižek, "'happiness' belongs to the pleasure principle, and what undermines it is the insistence of a Beyond of the pleasure principle" (*WDR*, 59). The politics, though, of his position on happiness defy easy left/right classification.

For example, of conservatives, he says they are "fully justified in legitimating their opposition to radical knowledge in terms of happiness: knowledge ultimately makes us unhappy" (*WDR*, 61). For Žižek, there "is deep within each of us a *Wissenstrieb*, a drive to know" (*WDR*, 61). However, he notes, "Lacan claims that the spontaneous attitude of a human being is that of 'I don't want to know about it'" (*WDR*, 61). As one Lacan commentator bluntly summarizes this position, "happiness amounts to the stupidity of 'not wanting to know' the truth about symbolic castration, the inconsistency of the Other, and the actual lack of the Other."[43] As a consequence of our "stupidity," happiness not only becomes, as noted earlier, a political factor and can mean only that "everybody is identical with everyone else," but also that "it is only the phallus which is happy and not its bearer."[44] Thus, by *fully justifying* the conservative argument for stupidity and grounding it in their pursuit of happiness, Žižek appears as siding against liberals who *fully reject* this argument because they believe that knowledge leads to happiness.

If conservatives find an ally in Žižek's assault on happiness, then liberals find an enemy. For example, one of the casualties of Žižek's assault on happiness is Jürgen Habermas. Žižek identifies Habermas as "the great representative of the Enlightenment tradition" (*WDR*, 63). However, Žižek finds hidden in Habermas's argument advocating biogenetic manipulation the underlying premise "that the ultimate ethical duty is that of protecting the Other from pain," which would include in some cases keeping the Other "in protective ignorance" (*WDR*, 63). Žižek says that keeping knowledge away from the Other is not about "autonomy" and "freedom" as Habermas would have us believe, but it is really about "happiness" (*WDR*, 63), which thus places this "great representative of the Enlightenment tradition" on "the same side as conservative advocates of blessed ignorance" (*WDR*, 64). In short, both conservatives *and* liberals become targets through Žižek's critique of happiness because "the opposition between Rightist populism and liberal tolerance is a false one" (*WDR*, 82). For Žižek, they are "two sides of the same coin" (*WDR*,

82). What then should we be striving for if not happiness conservative- or liberal-style? Žižek's answer here is clear: "not the Fascist with a human face, but the freedom fighter with an inhuman face" (*WDR*, 82).

To go along with this "inhuman face," he also calls for, following Alain Badiou, an "'inhuman' ethics, an ethics addressing an inhuman subject" (*LC*, 16). This direction for ethics is part of his critique of the humanist ethics of the Western philosophical tradition predicated on its use of "Man" and "human person," which for Žižek "is a mask that conceals the pure subjectivity of the Neighbor" (*LC*, 16). So, Žižek's anti-ethics, which serves as a base for his rejection of happiness, is also a rejection of humanism *and* the majority of Western ethics dating back to the Greeks.

So if taking on humanism, ethics, and the conservative and the liberal political establishment were not enough, Žižek's critique of happiness also takes on the institution of psychology. Here he is directly following in the footsteps of his mentor, Lacan, in rejecting behavioral psychology and its contemporary instantiations, such as the new discipline of "happiness studies." For Žižek, we live in "era of spiritualized hedonism" (*FT*, 54), where happiness is regarded "as the supreme duty" (*LC*, 22). "No wonder," he says, "over the last decade the study of happiness emerged as a scientific discipline of its own: there are now 'professors of happiness' at universities, 'quality of life' institutes attached to them, and numerous research papers; there is even the *Journal of Happiness Studies*" (*LC*, 44). Since he said this in 2008, the study of happiness has not only grown exponentially, but has increasingly expanded into, as Tamsin Shaw calls it, "The New Military-Industrial Complex of Big Data Psy-Ops."[45] The latter includes the defense industry, British and American intelligence agencies, and companies like Cambridge Analytica, a company which Žižek says "makes it clear how cold manipulation and the care for love and human welfare are two sides of the same coin" (*LTD*, 244). Žižek then calls for us to expand the critique of the happiness industry:

> The predominant critique proceeds in the way of demystification: beneath the innocent-sounding research into happiness and welfare, it discerns a dark, hidden, gigantic complex of social control and manipulation exerted by the combined forces of private corporations and state agencies. But what is urgently needed is also the opposite move: instead of just asking what dark content is hidden beneath the form of scientific research into happiness, we should focus on the form itself. Is the topic of scientific research into human welfare and happiness (at least the way it is practiced today) really so innocent, or is it already itself permeated by the stance of control and manipulation? (*LTD*, 246–7).

From Lacan's complaints about the rise of behavioral psychology in America to Žižek's identification of the happiness research at the core of the military-industrial complex today, there is good reason to be suspicious about the pursuit of happiness. But Žižek makes an even more important point about the rise of the happiness industry, one that should not get lost in the shuffle of his theoretical arguments against happiness: though we live in an era wherein "the goal of life is directly defined as happiness," we still see an explosion in "the number of people suffering from anxiety and depression" (*FT*, 54–5). "It is the enigma of this self-sabotaging of happiness and pleasure," comments Žižek of this rise in cases of anxiety and depression in an age devoted to happiness, that "makes Freud's message more *pertinent* than ever" (*FT*, 55; my emphasis).[46] He repeats this last line in his 2020 essay, "Happiness? No, thanks!" changing the word *pertinent* to *actual* (*LTD*, 247). All modesty aside and with due respect to Freud, it is Žižek's message about happiness that needs to be touted as not only actual and pertinent but also vital in dark times.

Conclusion

Žižek's arguments against happiness are among his most important contributions to our understanding of modernity today. If Freud's work on modern unhappiness announced one of the more important theoretical dimensions of modernity, then Žižek via Lacan can be seen as an extension and development of the project of modernity. Žižek's call to reject happiness and humanism though is not mere philosophical pessimism or antagonism in the face of a world gone "happy," but rather a diagnosis for a world that is sick but chooses "happiness" over knowledge nevertheless.

Still, we have only scratched the surface of the damage that the pursuit of happiness continues to inflict upon our world. Žižek explains, for example, how the kingdom of Bhutan "decided to focus on Gross National Happiness (GNH) rather than Gross National Product (GNP)" (*LTD*, 247),[47] further extending, for example, the legacies of the work of Jeremy Bentham, Gustav Theodor Fechner, and William Stanley Jevons to connect happiness to economics in the sociopolitical sphere.[48] In the United States, Žižek's critique of happiness goes to the very core of our Declaration of Independence and founding principles that link the pursuit of happiness to the pursuit of humans as property, that is to say, slavery.

According to Žižek, the Declaration of Independence is where the "US defines itself as the land of the 'pursuit of happiness'" (*LDS*, 253) and is a "key element of the 'American (ideological) dream'" (*LC*, 466, n. 43). He also reminds us that the phrase "pursuit of happiness" was negotiated into the Declaration "*as a way to negate the black slaves' right to property*" (*LC*, 466, n. 43; his emphasis). What "the pursuit of happiness" in the US Declaration of Independence "stands for is not a direct promise of happiness—as a US citizen, I am guaranteed the freedom to pursue happiness, not happiness itself, and it depends on me whether I will achieve it or not" (*LDS*, 253). However, "since authentic desire is never a desire for happiness," this "amounts to something like 'a desire for no-desire, a desire to compromise one's desire,'" which for Žižek is nothing less than an "abomination" (*LDS*, 253). As Black Lives Matter forges a new American Revolution today, Žižek's thoughts on the contribution of the pursuit of happiness to racial injustice take on added significance.

Ultimately though, Žižek's critique of happiness is a work of theory. And like Jacques Derrida's critique of logocentrism, which turned the metaphysics of Western philosophy on its head, so too does Žižek's critique of happiness have the potential to turn Western philosophy's ethical and sociopolitical traditions regarding the pursuit of happiness on their heads. While we see in figures like Immanuel Kant a resistance to the pursuit of happiness in preference to the pursuit of duty,[49] these thoughts tend to be marginalized in the broader context where happiness is regarded "as the supreme duty." As Žižek says, in Kant "ethical duty functions like a foreign traumatic intruder that from the outside disturbs the subject's homeostatic balance, its unbearable pressure forcing the subject to act 'beyond the pleasure principle,' ignoring the pursuit of pleasures" (*LC*, 45). Žižek contends that the same description of how ethical duty functions also holds for *desire* in Lacan, "which is why enjoyment is not something that comes naturally to the subject, as a realization of her inner potential, but is the content of a traumatic superego injunction" (*LC*, 45).

Given the rise of fascism with a human face in America, Žižek's freedom fighter with an inhuman face and ethics looks to be an increasingly better alternative. So too does giving up the pursuit of happiness if it only amounts to a "desire for no-desire." But what of all those people who still believe in the pursuit of happiness? For Žižek, like Lacan, happiness is also a "bourgeois dream"—one that is firmly embedded in neoliberal America and its spiritualized hedonism. As a public philosopher, Žižek's critique of happiness extends to a wide audience an updated version of one of the key aspects of the modern condition of civilization touted by Freud a century ago. Žižek's analysis brilliantly reveals how the devolving conditions of neoliberal capital in the new millennium underwrite unprecedented levels of social control and manipulation under the guise of the pursuit of happiness. In sum, much of what's wrong with happiness is the same as what's wrong with neoliberal capitalism.

Notes

1   Herodotus, *The Histories*, Book 1, trans. Aubrey de Sélincourt, rev. A. R. Burn (New York: Penguin Books, 1972), 53.
2   Aristotle, *Nicomachean Ethics*, in *The Basic Works of Aristotle*, trans. W. D. Ross, ed. Richard McKeon (New York: Random House, 1941), 946.

3 His work on happiness on YouTube includes the following: his debate with Jordan Peterson, "Happiness: Capitalism vs. Marxism," *YouTube Video*, 2:37:47, April 20, 2019, available online: https://www.youtube.com/watch?v=pT1vutd4Gnk; "'Liberal Tolerant Hedonism' and 'Happiness,' 'Immoral Ethics,' and 'Western Buddhism,'" *YouTube Video*, 4:04, March 23, 2020, available online: https://www.youtube.com/watch?v=xb4jh306OGg; "Why Be Happy When You Could Be Interesting?—Big Think," *YouTube Video*, 2:01, June 25, 2012, available online: https://www.youtube.com/watch?v=U88jj6PSD7w; and "The Price of Happiness and Desire," *YouTube Video*, 0:57, March 13, 2007, available online: https://www.youtube.com/watch?v=bqhWiohr_gQ.

4 Though I do not argue for the use of "tragic" as a description of Žižek's view of happiness in this chapter, it is based on the important use of Greek tragedy in establishing his position. This comes directly through Žižek's various comments on Sophocles's *Antigone* and *Oedipus the King*, and indirectly through Lacan's comments on the same (Lacan's comments on *Oedipus the King* and happiness are discussed later in this chapter). See, for example, Slavoj Žižek, *Antigone* (New York: Bloomsbury, 2016) and "Wither Oedipus?" in *The Ticklish Subject: The Absent Center of Political Ontology* (New York and London: Verso, 1999), 313–400.

5 Sigmund Freud, "Psychotherapy of Hysteria [1895]," in Sigmund Freud and Joseph Breuer, *Studies on Hysteria* [1895], ed. and trans. James Strachey (New York: Avon Books, 1966), 351.

6 Freud, "Psychotherapy of Hysteria [1895]," 351.

7 Freud, "Psychotherapy of Hysteria [1895]," 351, n. 1.

8 James Strachey, "Editor's Introduction," in Sigmund Freud and Joseph Breuer, *Studies on Hysteria* [1895], ed. and trans. James Strachey (New York: Avon Books, 1966), xxv.

9 Sigmund Freud, *Beyond the Pleasure Principle* [1920], trans. James Strachey (New York: Liveright Publishing Corporation, 1950), 50.

10 Sigmund Freud, *An Outline of Psychoanalysis* [1940], trans. James Strachey (New York: W. W. Norton & Company, 1949), 20.

11 Freud, *An Outline*, 20.

12 Freud, *Beyond*, 86.

13 Freud, *An Outline*, 109.

14 Sigmund Freud, *Civilization and Its Discontents* [1929], trans. Joan Riviere (London: The Hogarth Press, 1955), 27.

15 Freud, *Civilization*, 27–8.

16 Freud, *Civilization*, 92.

17 Jacques Lacan, *The Seminar of Jacques Lacan, Book VII: The Ethics of Psychoanalysis 1959–1960*, trans. Dennis Porter (New York: W. W. Norton & Company, 1997), 13.

18 Lacan, *VII*, 13.

19 Lacan, *VII*, 304.

20 Lacan, *VII*, 304.
21 Lacan, *VII*, 304.
22 Lacan, *VII*, 305.
23 Lacan, *VII*, 305.
24 Lacan, *VII*, 292.
25 Lacan, *VII*, 292.
26 Lacan, *VII*, 292.
27 Lacan, *VII*, 292.
28 Lacan, *VII*, 292.
29 Lacan, *VII*, 303.
30 Jacques Lacan, "The Direction of the Treatment and the Principles of Its Power," in *Écrits: A Selection*, trans. Alan Sheridan (New York: W. W. Norton & Company Inc., 1977), 252. This is a report to the Colloque de Royaumont on July 10–13, 1958.
31 Lacan, *The Direction*, 252.
32 Jacques Lacan, "Function and Field of Speech and Language," in *Écrits: A Selection*, trans. Alan Sheridan (New York: W. W. Norton & Company Inc., 1977), 37–8. This is a report to the Rome Congress held at the Istituto di Psicologia della Università de Roma on July 26–67, 1953.
33 Lacan, "Function and Field of Speech and Language," 38.
34 Lacan, "Function and Field of Speech and Language," 38.
35 Jacques Lacan, "The Freudian Thing, or the Meaning of the Return to Freud in Psychoanalysis," in *Écrits: A Selection*, trans. Alan Sheridan (New York: W. W. Norton & Company Inc., 1977), 127–8. This is an expanded version of a lecture given at the Neuro-psychiatric Clinic in Vienna on November 7, 1955.
36 Lacan, *The Direction*, 231.
37 For a survey of the American celebration of happiness, see Daniel Horowitz, *Happier? The History of a Cultural Movement that Aspired to Transform America* (New York: Oxford University Press, 2018).
38 Jordan Peterson and Slavoj Žižek, "Happiness: Capitalism vs. Marxism."
39 Saint-Just said "Happiness Is a New Idea in Europe"/"Le bonheur est une idée neuve en Europe," in *Oeuvres completes*, ed. Louis Antoine de Saint-Just (Paris: Gérard Lebovici, 1984), 715.
40 Žižek, "Why Be Happy When You Could Be Interesting?—Big Think."
41 See Aristotle, *Nicomachean Ethics*; Jeremy Bentham, *An Introduction to the Principles of Morals and Legislation* [1780] (Oxford: At the Clarendon Press, 1879); and John Stuart Mill, *Utilitarianism*, 3rd ed. (London: Longmans, Green, Reader, and Dyer, 1867).
42 Žižek says here that he is putting this in Alain Badiou's terms. However, when this passage is revised for his article, "Happiness? No. Thanks!" in *A Left that Dares Speak Its Name: Untimely Interventions* (Medford: Polity, 2020) it is changed to "as Hegel would have put it" (248). Why the change? Presumably

because Badiou's *Métaphysique du Bonheur reel* (Paris: Presses Universitaires de France, 2015), argues that we should not give up on the aspiration to be happy. All philosophy is a metaphysics of happiness, and that in order to be truly happy, we need philosophy. Badiou's position here is thus clearly at odds with Žižek's, which concludes that we must give up on the aspiration to be happy.

43   Lorenzo Chiesa, "Lacan with Artaud: *j'ouïs-sens, jouis-sens, jouis-sans*," in *Lacan: The Silent Partners*, ed. Slavoj Žižek (New York: Verso, 2006), 360, n. 17 and 361, n. 18. Chiesa is referencing here Jacques Lacan, *Le séminaire livre XVII* (Paris: Seuil, 1991), 83–4, 150, 56.

44   Chiesa, "Lacan with Artaud," 361, n. 18.

45   Tamsin Shaw, "The New Military-Industrial Complex of Big Data Psy-Ops," *The New York Review of Books*, March 21, 2018, available online: https://www.nybooks.com/daily/2018/03/21/the-digital-military-industrial-complex/

46   Freud's "death drive" might be regarded as a mediation of Friedrich Nietzsche's affirmation of the will and Arthur Schopenhauer's negation of it. Žižek, however, argues that the death drive should not be confused with the return to the inorganic absence of any life-tension or with the craving for self-annihilation. For Žižek, "the death drive, on the contrary, is *the very opposite of dying*, it is a name for the 'undead' eternal life itself, for the horrible fate of being caught in the endless repetitive cycle of wandering around in guilt and pain" (*TS*, 292). See also Žižek, "Slavoj Žižek on Death Drive—Why Todestrieb Is a Philosophical Concept,'" *YouTube Video*, 1:29;43, March 6, 2009, available online: https://www.youtube.com/watch?v=uBd2r4YeQxls.

47   The term "Gross National Happiness" was coined in 1972 by Sicco Mansholt, one of the founders of the European Union and the fourth president of the European Commission. It was popularized though in the 1990s by Bhutan's fourth king, Jigme Singye Wangchuck. In 2011, the UN General Assembly passed a resolution encouraging member nations to measure happiness and well-being (UN General Assembly 2011). For a study of the politics of Gross National Happiness, see Kent Schroeder, *Politics of Gross National Happiness: Governance and Development in Bhutan* (Cham: Palgrave Macmillan, 2018).

48   For a survey of the respective efforts of Bentham, Fechner, and Jevons to connect happiness to economics, see William Davies, *The Happiness Industry: How the Government and Big Business Sold Us Well-Being* (London: Verso, 2015).

49   "To secure one's own happiness is at least indirectly a duty," argues Kant, "for discontent with one's condition under a pressure of many cares and amidst unsatisfied wants could easily become a great temptation to transgress duties" (*Foundations of the Metaphysics of Morals*, in *Critique of Practical Reason and Other Writings in Moral Philosophy*, trans. and ed. Lewis White Beck (Chicago: The University of Chicago Press, 1949), 60 [IV, 399]. "But," continues Kant, "without any view to duty, all men have the strongest and deepest inclination to happiness, because in this idea all inclinations are summed up" (60 [IV, 399]). As such, duty and happiness are at odds with each other in Kant.

PART II

A Leftist Plea for Modernism

7

Žižek *avec* Montaigne

Zahi Zalloua

Both Jacques Lacan and Slavoj Žižek turn to early modern philosophers as a way to recast the subject of philosophy. If Žižek, not unlike the late Lacan, rehabilitates René Descartes's subject, rejecting an all-too-quick postmodern dismissal of his thought,[1] Lacan finds in Michel de Montaigne a memorable instance of the *aphanisis* of the subject, prefiguring the split subject of psychoanalysis. In Žižek's idiosyncratic reading of Descartes, it is first and foremost the emptiness of the Cartesian subject—and not the positivity of the *cogito* (the thinking substance)—that captures his interest. Indeed, as Žižek stresses, the Cartesian subject is paradoxically "*a subject bereft of subjectivity.*"[2] I argue that this Žižekian view of the subject better describes or, at least, is already anticipated by Montaigne. The Montaignian subject is defined by its ontological incompleteness and hermeneutic slipperiness. It is beyond comprehension, mastery, and control. As Montaigne observes: "But we are, I know not how, double within ourselves, with the result that we do not believe what we believe, and we cannot rid ourselves of what we condemn."[3] Lacan credits Montaigne for his keen disclosure of the provisional character of the subject, in what he names the "*aphanisis* of the subject." Surprisingly, Žižek never comments on Lacan's praise of Montaigne. There is in fact, to my knowledge, no trace of Montaigne in Žižek's massive corpus; perhaps it was the favorable postmodern reception the essayist received that is to blame, making him unappealing for this decidedly anti-postmodernist philosopher.[4] In reading Žižek *avec* Montaigne, this chapter recasts Montaigne's singular skepticism—embodied in his motto "What do I know?" (393)—as an engine of negativity that not only troubles the ego by inducing moments of *aphanisis* but also provides modern philosophy with a theoretical jolt, a dangerous psychoanalytic supplement to its cognitive norms and procedures. Of particular interest, then, is philosophy's (lack of) commitment to skepticism (a moment in the pursuit of certainty) in contrast to psychoanalysis' praise of hysterical doubt.

The Žižekian *Cogito* and/as the Montaignian Subject of *Aphanisis*

The first thing to say about Žižek's reading of the Cartesian moment is that it is no standard Cartesianism: "The point, of course, is not to return to the *cogito* in the guise in which this notion has dominated modern thought (the self-transparent thinking subject), but to bring to light its forgotten obverse, the excessive, unacknowledged kernel of the *cogito*, which is far from the pacifying image of the transparent Self" (*TS*, 24). Descartes's error lies in his "ontologization of the *cogito*"[5]: the *cogito* is not a *res cogitans*; rather, "this *cogito* is the *cogito* 'in becoming.'"[6] Žižek laments the neglect of the *cogito* and its deleterious effects on thinking as such. Without the *cogito*, without the chance to "start with a clean slate," "to erase the entirety of reality" (*TS*, 34), the subject would be reducible to the socially given, enclosed in its organic community. Without the *cogito*, there is no possibility of critique. The virtues of the *cogito* thus lie not in its claims to self-sufficiency and self-transparency but in its performance of hyperbolic doubt, the ways in which it withdraws the self from the world, disclosing the "abyss of subjectivity," a void, or what Hegel dubs the "night of the world":

> One of Hegel's names for this abyss of subjectivity that he takes from the mystic tradition is the "night of the world," the withdrawal of the Self from the world of entities into the void that "is" the core of the Self, and it is crucial to notice how in this gesture of self-withdrawal (in clinical terms: the disintegration of all "world," of all universe of meaning), extreme closure and extreme openness, extreme passivity and extreme activity, overlap.[7]

As a locus of negativity, the *cogito* becomes indispensable for modern philosophy and psychoanalysis, a precondition for thinking the subject *otherwise*.

And yet as Ernesto Laclau observes, "this is a *most* peculiar way of being a Cartesian."[8] The Žižekian *cogito* couldn't be more at odds with the traumatophobic protocols Descartes himself outlined in *The Passions of the Soul*. Assessing philosophy's epistemic norms, Descartes pathologizes an excess of wonder; too much wonder paralyzes the subject of philosophy ("the entire body remain immobile like a statue"[9]), resulting in debilitating astonishment, a dreadful malady of the soul: "Astonishment is an excess of wonder which can never be anything but bad."[10] A healthy *cogito* must be measured and must avoid the unsettling effects of astonishment by successfully translating the new into the familiar, into a body of knowledge, and thus delivering on the mind's epistemic investment.

If the Cartesian *cogito* of *The Passions of the Soul* seeks a trauma-free approach to certainty, the Žižekian *cogito* dwells in negativity, insisting on its trauma-inducing radical separation from the world. While both introduce a gap between the subject and the symbolic ego, the former takes the form of a foundational substance, the latter a disturbing void. Modern philosophy will aggressively pursue the traumatophobic path laid out by Descartes, producing ever-more "masters and knowers of nature."[11] Psychoanalysis, however, will proceed differently, derailing the all-too-confident march of philosophy. This detour is in small part sparked by Freud's "narcissistic wound" to philosophy's humanistic subject, exposing and insisting on the ego's radical demotion: "*the ego is not the master in its own house.*"[12] The discovery of the Freudian unconscious subverts a philosophy of consciousness and disrupts the identification of the subject with ego. The full ramifications of the psychoanalytic split subject take up much of Lacan's energy. The early Lacan flatly rejects the unity of being and thinking, rewriting Descartes's "I think therefore I am" as "I am thinking where I am not, therefore I am where I am not thinking."[13] The unconscious fractures the Cartesian *cogito*, revealing that being and thinking fail to overlap. As Bruce Fink notes, "the unconscious has no being—it is where I *am* not—but it does plenty of thinking. I find my being where this unconscious thought does not occur, that is, in the ego as false being."[14]

Unlike its Cartesian counterpart, what we might call the Žižekian *cogito* is not embarrassed by the presence of the unconscious. On the contrary, it avows the unconscious. If the *cogito* as an engine of negativity records the void of the subject (it is not to be identified with the symbolic ego), the unconscious strips the traditional Cartesian *cogito* of its ideological claim to self-transparency. In both instances, what we get is a de-substantialized subject. Žižek often credits, and clearly is inspired by, the late Lacan's own return to the *cogito*, to the unsovereign *cogito* dominated by signifiers and led back to its "signifying dependence."[15] Lacan's "minimal cogito," as Ed Pluth points out, is "a subject without qualities."[16] Like Lacan, Žižek declines to identify the *cogito* with "the self-transparency of pure thought"; instead, he repeats Lacan's counterintuitive claim that the "*cogito* IS the subject of the unconscious—the gap/cut in the order of Being in which the real of *jouissance* breaks in."[17]

Žižek recasts Descartes's modernity, associating the birth of the *cogito* with "psychotic withdrawal" (*AR*, 183) and, as we have already seen, "the night of the world." Still, this is a Descartes that is not recognizable to most philosophers (Laclau's point). But rather than dwell on the peculiarity of Žižek's (over)reading, I want to pursue a missed opportunity to expand on the ways Lacan's investment in the subject leads him to juxtapose Descartes with his predecessor Montaigne, along with the ancient skeptics. Lacan's turn to Montaigne in his seminar of 1964, *The Four Fundamental Concepts of Psychoanalysis*, should not come as a surprise. In "Presentation on Psychical Causality" (1946), Lacan had already aligned Montaigne with Freud in their mutual troubling of the unity of the subject. We learned from Montaigne, Lacan tells us, that the subject is not "exempt from contradiction ... and learned even better when Freud designated it as the very locus of *Verneinung* [negation]."[18] Though we discover more Freud than Montaigne, the latter's reflections on the subject offer an inventive alternative to the Cartesian narrative of modern philosophy (that is, the path of the *cogito* that Lacan/Žižek are trying the read against the grain). And let us not forget that Descartes's inauguration of the *cogito* is a response to the challenges of Montaignian skepticism, which left the state of philosophy in a kind of epistemic paralysis. In *The Four Fundamental Concepts of Psychoanalysis*, Lacan returns to Montaigne and the question of skepticism to better isolate Montaigne's singular contribution to psychoanalytic thought:

> Scepticism does not mean the successive doubting, item by item, of all opinions or of all the pathways that accede to knowledge. It is holding the subjective position that one can know nothing. There is something here that deserves to be illustrated by the range, the substance, of those who have been its historical embodiments. I would show you that Montaigne is truly the one who has centred himself, not around scepticism but around the living moment of the *aphanisis* of the subject. And it is in this that he is fruitful, that he is an eternal guide, who goes beyond whatever may be represented of the moment to be defined as a historical turning-point.[19]

What makes Montaigne psychoanalysis' "eternal guide" is surprisingly not his modern brand of skepticism but rather his "*aphanisis* of the subject." We know from Lacan that *aphanisis* is constitutive of the subject and its endless source of alienation: "when the subject appears somewhere as meaning, he is manifested elsewhere as 'fading,' as disappearance."[20] Whenever the subject deploys language and substitutes meaning for being, *aphanisis* happens. Catherine Belsey situates Lacan's deployment of *aphanisis*, elucidating its psychoanalytic pertinence and meaning:

> Aphanisis (disappearance) was a term first used by Ernest Jones, who argued that the subject's ultimate fear was that desire would disappear. Lacan appropriates the term to discuss the disappearance, or sometimes the "fading," of the speaking subject itself, as it loses its purchase on meaning. I can disappear from what I am saying, and in the process make apparent *the provisional character of subjectivity*.[21]

Enlisting Montaigne in the cause of psychoanalysis, Lacan celebrates the essayist for having avoided both the paths of the skeptics and that of the (substantial) *cogito*. The skeptics' "heroic" adherence to the "subjective position that *one can know nothing*"²² and Descartes's discovery of certainty in the self-evidence of the doubting *cogito* ended up confirming and reaffirming the stable grounds of subjectivity. For Lacan, Descartes erred in his arrogance and hubris, in his investment in the humanist powers of consciousness, believing that they could yield certainty, that is, ground a permanent and constant "I," "a thing that thinks"²³ (*res cogitans*). "When Descartes introduces the concept of a certainty that holds entirely in the *I think* of cogitation . . . one might say that his mistake is to believe that this is knowledge. To say that he knows something of this certainty. Not to make of the *I think* a mere point of fading,"²⁴ writes Lacan.

But what exactly constitutes Montaigne's *aphanisis* of the subject is never spelled out. We are only told that Montaigne points us in a radically different direction. What we get is a subject dislodged from its humanist horizon, a subject that is paradoxically constituted by its own *aphanisis*. On the relevance of Montaigne for Lacan, Belsey speculates that "Lacan finds in Montaigne's apparent inconsequentiality, the seeming free association characteristic of the essays, a contrast with the rigorously thetic, law-abiding self-discipline of an Enlightenment philosophy confident that nothing in principle exceeds its totalising grasp."²⁵ Against modern philosophy's traumatophobic ethos, Montaigne is seemingly a breath of fresh air. Montaigne's traumatophilic musings resonate quite well with Lacanian psychoanalysis. The latter does not aim at immunizing the ego from external social hardship; it is not really concerned with curing individuals of their psychic disturbances. Rather, the point of Lacanian psychoanalysis is not to accommodate but to weaken fantasy's hold on individuals by compelling them to confront "the most radical dimension of human existence" (*HRL*, 3). And this traumatophilia in Montaigne—and, as we shall see, in Žižek—is deeply connected to a hermeneutics of skepticism, an incessant, hysterical questioning of authority, which, in turn, is indissociable in Montaigne from the essay form.

Lacan's brief gloss of Montaigne, however, implicitly decouples Montaigne's *Essays* from the question of skepticism, ignoring the ways *essaying* for Montaigne is intrinsically a form of skepticism, neglecting to appreciate the ways the *aphanisis* of the subject comes about precisely in the negativity of Montaigne's skeptical essaying. Indeed, it is a skepticism that touches the Real, that obliquely discloses the limits of meaning and creates the necessary conditions for *aphanisis*.

Lacan is surely correct to distance Montaigne from those who identify as skeptics, and in this respect, Lacan is arguably far more sensitive to the unsettling logic of the *Essays* than Pierre Charron, one of Montaigne's early disciples, who rewrote Montaigne's motto—"What do I know?"— preferring the more measured, and philosophically acquiescent, skeptical claim "I don't know [*Je ne sçay*]," which he engraved on the title-page of his revised *De la sagesse* (1604). There is great violence in translating "What do I know?" into "I don't know." "What do I know?" illustrates and enacts, through its interrogative form, the dialogic push and pull of forming and unsettling meaning. It sustains the becoming of the essay. Essaying generates meaning, necessarily abstracting from the particular, while, at the same time, signaling the limits of hermeneutic mastery, displaying its failures and imperfections. Attesting to the singularity of its object, its irreducibility to concepts, essaying—the embodiment of "What do I know?"—foregrounds that interpretation is "non-all."

I thus agree with Lacan that, unlike the ancient and early modern skeptics, Montaigne *persists* in his self-undoing, short-circuiting the skeptic's motto, "one can know nothing," transforming it into the double-voiced question, "What do I know?," which, at once, questions the fact of my knowing and probes the "what" of my knowing. But whereas Lacan would interpret Montaigne's gesture as a break with (the school of) skepticism, I see it as a reinvention of a more corrosive and traumatophilic skepticism. This skepticism is by no means foreign to Lacanian psychoanalysis; as Žižek notes, "the most outstanding feature of [Lacan's] teaching is permanent self-questioning" (*HRL*, 5). Hysteria is the figure of the *Montaignian* skeptic—of the subject: "the hysterical subject is the subject whose very existence involves radical doubt and questioning, his entire being is sustained by the uncertainty as to what he is for the Other; insofar as the subject exists only as an answer to the enigma of the Other's desire, the hysterical subject is the subject par excellence."[26] "Only hysteria produces new knowledge" (*IV*, 4), Žižek adds further, repeating Lacan. The challenge here is to apprehend *aphanisis* in light of Montaigne's *skeptical/hysterical* engagement with philosophical humanism and to be attentive to the knowledge produced by the essay: the most hysterical of genres.

Crippling Reason, or the Inhuman Core of Montaigne

As a mode of inquiry, the Montaignian essay slyly frustrates and eschews hermeneutic authority via its irresistible propensity to turn "a given into a question."[27] The essay disempowers the signifying subject and cripples reason, producing hysterical excess rather than measured results; it frustrates the desire for resolution and finality, preferring interrogations over answers. The essay's reluctance to yield meaning fosters an ethos of endless pursuit: "I put forward formless and unresolved notions, as do those who publish doubtful questions to debate in the schools, not to establish the truth but to seek it" (229). Lacking the properness of a philosopher, the essayist pursues—or rather staggers after—his subject wherever it pulls him: "I cannot keep my subject still. It goes along befuddled and staggering, with a natural drunkenness" (610). If such an essayist were to be considered a philosopher, he would an odd one, an "unpremeditated and accidental philosopher" (311), as Montaigne writes of himself.

In "Of Cripples," Montaigne hytericizes modern philosophy by questioning its attachment to "man" and "reason." Early in the essay, Montaigne stages a typical hermeneutical scene, where an insatiable desire to decipher governs his contemporaries' interpretive predilections. "They pass over the facts, but they assiduously examine their consequences. They ordinarily begin thus: 'How does this happen?' What they should say is: 'But does it happen?'" (785). Montaigne declines his would-be interpellation, to join the ranks of these overconfident metaphysicians. What their causal reasoning generates are not truths but something that resembles phantasmatic projections.

In assuming the question of "How does this happen?" the hermeneuts offer competing speculative accounts of the causes. You are implicitly being asked to choose between speculation A or speculation B. We appear to have here what Lacan refers to as the "*vel* of exclusion" (*vel* means *or* in Latin). Colette Soler gives a succinct account of its possibilities:

> It is a *vel* in which you have two elements, x and y for example. In the exclusive *vel*, if you have x, you can't have y. When x is true, y must be false ... for the *vel* to be satisfied. And when x is false, y must be true ... for the *vel* to be satisfied. However, both x and y cannot be false ..., for in that case the *vel* is not satisfied (it is false). Likewise, x and y cannot both be true ..., because then the *vel* is false. The *vel* accepts either one or the other as true or false, but not both at the same time.[28]

Each hermeneut is locked in an interpretive struggle, trying to answer the *how* question, to best his interlocutor. But by substituting "How does this happen?" for "But does it happen?", Montaigne cunningly recasts this *vel* as analogous to another *vel*,[29] the "*vel* of alienation," marking it as a forced choice, where you, in fact, have little say in the matter. You are as free, Lacan tells us, as an individual getting mugged, confronted with the "choice," "*Your money or your life*, or freedom or death."[30] This is a false choice. In either case, you lose something: either your life or "a life deprived of something."[31] The ideological framework of the choice gives the illusion that you have a voice in the matter. You become an agent in/of your own mystification. One speculation may be more obscurantist than the other, but either way you can only choose to mystify, since questioning the ontological status of the object ("But does it happen?") is not an option; it is *a priori* lost, sacrificed by the very framing of the inquiry, "How does this happen?"

Whereas an individual getting mugged is likely cognizant of the cruelty of the paradoxical "choice" being presented (in either case there is a loss), would-be hermeneuts are less likely to see the forced nature of the decision. They might be too eager to join the interpretive community and indulge in endless abstract, speculative debates: Is it cause A or cause B? In the latter forced choice, they experience themselves as free because, as Žižek would put it, they do not possess the very language to articulate our unfreedom (*WDR*, 2). A hermeneutic dogmatism naturalizes and reifies the facts so as to transform them into mere ornaments, the necessary background for the uninterrupted proliferation of speculations over *the being that happened*.

After François Laruelle, we might refer to such hermeneuts as "junkies of Being,"[32] as *causes*-junkies. Montaigne humorously calls these "comical prattlers" (785), "plaisants causeurs," punning on the double meaning of "causer"—"to talk about something/to someone" and "to cause something." Montaigne's "But does it happen?"—itself a manifestation of his motto "What do I know?", the sublime question that fuels the hysteric—jams the imposition of the other's forced choice. Montaigne hystericizes the master, the *causeur*, questioning his hermeneutic dominance in favor of a hermeneutics of skepticism. He implicitly says and asks: "Your causal reasoning makes no sense to me." "And why are you saying I'm interested in causes?" "Am I really like you?" "Why do you assume that?" "Do you really know that?" and so on. This questioning of hermeneutic authority, coupled by the essayist's refusal to be a fellow-*causeur*, sets the scene for Montaigne's *aphanisis*—his/the reader's exposure to the *real* Montaigne.

Taking stock of his self-image, Montaigne begins with a relatively uncontroversial observation: "we become habituated to anything strange by use and time" (787). But he quickly adds: "the more I frequent myself and know myself, the more my deformity *astonishes me, and the less I understand myself*" (787, emphasis added). Montaigne's own case, then, contradicts this general principle that identifies understanding with familiarity, knowledge with self-mastery. Astonishment here is no mere psychological unpleasantness, a mental hiccup in the pursuit of self-knowledge. As Žižek would say, we must elevate "astonishment" to the dignity of a fundamental philosophical attitude toward reality. Astonishment, in its immanence, discloses a barred Montaigne, a Montaigne haunted by a constitutive alterity—be it language, the unconscious, or the trace of others (the endless ancient and contemporary authors he dialogues with in the *Essays*). In this astonished state, the idea of auto-affection—of affect falling under the jurisdiction of the sovereign ego—vanishes. Essaying creates this moment of *aphanisis*; it *gives* its author an uncanny, precarious, and monstrous presence: "I have seen no more evident monstrosity and miracle in the world than myself" (787). Struck into astonishment, in this instance of *aphanisis*, Montaigne finds himself undetermined, at the very least momentarily, "floating in the unanchored void of an anonymous, faceless form of subjectivity."[33] Becoming monstrous entails self-destitution; it is tantamount to encountering yourself as a real neighbor—not the imaginary neighbor as the reader's mirror-image; not the symbolic neighbor who shares his wisdom à la Seneca with contemporary and future readers (a "French Seneca" as many of his early readers felt him to be[34]), but the uncanny neighbor, as Žižek insists, who incarnates "the unfathomable abyss of radical Otherness, of one about whom I finally know nothing" (*HRL*, 43). The bewildering experience of astonishment happens when fantasy fails to shield the individual from the "raw Real" (*HRL*, 57). Montaigne's astonishment is the ontological mood set by the traumatic realization of himself as neighbor, the experience of "the gap between what [he is] as a determinate being and the unfathomable X" (*HRL*, 44).

Astonishment, then, signals the unraveling of Montaigne's humanist project of self-study. Astonishment is after all what Descartes will warn us about in *The Passions of the Soul*: as an unhealthy excess of wonder, astonishment freezes the subject of knowledge. In "Of Cripples," however, Montaigne does not lament his "unsuccessful" translation, failing to recoup, as it were, on his cognitive investment. Rather, in his hysterical/skeptical essaying, Montaigne openly defies (self)reification and perpetually eludes spatial determination; he yearns for and thrives on astonishment—on this most unruly of cognitive passions—on the endless, multiple, and joyful pursuit of its objects (the self included). Unlike Descartes, who will seek to immunize himself against a pathologized, destabilizing experience of astonishment, Montaigne affirms the affectability and vulnerability of his self. The Montaignian essay does not ignore or neutralize the self's internal Otherness, but insists on its multiplicity and inconsistency, disclosing reason in its utter lameness, in stark contrast to modern philosophy's fantasy of sovereignty and auto-affection. Like the lame, reason limps; it is crippled. The essay astonishes the modern philosopher's gaze, disabling his powers of reason, and jamming his will to domesticate.

To be sure, Montaigne did not champion astonishment from the start. In his address "To the Reader," Montaigne outlines what he considers his modest project of self-portraiture: "I want to be seen here in my simple, natural, ordinary fashion, without straining or artifice; for it is myself that I portray . . . I am myself the matter of my book" (2). The essay form is the chosen medium for the accomplishment of Montaigne's self-study. The essayist's desire to grasp his self-image, however, proves much more difficult than expected. Many of his essays bear witness to the incoherence, fluidity, and elusiveness of the Montaignian "I." A few examples:

> Myself now and myself a while ago are indeed two. (736)
>
> Every minute I seem to be slipping away from myself. (61)
>
> We are all patchwork, and so shapeless and diverse in composition that each bit, each moment, plays its own game. And there is as much difference between us and ourselves as between us and others. (244)

> I cannot keep my subject still. It goes along befuddled and staggering, with a natural drunkenness. I take it in this condition, just as it is at the moment I give my attention to it. I do not portray being: I portray passing. (610–11).

Needless to say, Montaigne's self-portraiture is predicated on the success of his project of self-mastery—they are one and the same. Dissatisfaction, from the inability to pin down his subjectivity, prolongs the writing of the *Essays*. Ironically, writing was initially intended to discipline Montaigne's mind, serving a moral function, functioning as what Michel Foucault dubs a "technique of the self."[35] Montaigne first conceives of writing as a taming instrument. In his essay "Of Idleness," the author narrates how he came to writing.[36] In the beginning, Montaigne was looking forward to his retirement from active life, relishing the opportunity to cogitate in tranquility. But he discovers that within himself, to his dismay, resides an unruly imagination; he describes his mind as a "runaway horse," giving birth to "chimeras and fantastic monsters" (21). Because Montaigne's withdrawal from the public world did not translate into the anticipated self-care, he turns to writing to domesticate his imagination and to shame his mind of its monstrous production: "I have begun to put them in writing, hoping in time to make my mind ashamed of itself" (21). Writing is thus introduced as a psycho-immunological practice, a therapy for the mind, a prosthetic relief for Montaigne's self, hoping to shield him from the unsettling impurities of his imagination.

Montaigne's essayistic writing turns out to be what I've described elsewhere as an "autoimmune supplement"[37] of sorts; essaying immunizes *and* infects, transmuting the original model of the self that writing sought to safeguard. This is a shock to the early modern philosopher, a crisis-inducing event for the humanist subject, whose imaginary and symbolic self-image is in the balance. Becoming monstrous is indeed untranslatable in humanist terms. Why? It compels you to face the "inhuman core" of your humanity. Žižek turns productively, again and again, to this psychoanalytic insight. The humanist, in his fundamental desire for perfection (from the Latin *perfectio*, meaning completion)—fantasizes about purification, the evacuation of all excesses from the subject, disavowing, in turn, that "there is an inhuman core in all of us, or, that we are 'not-all human'" (*LC*, 17). Montaigne the essayist sets himself apart from the humanist circle; he does not belong to this community of (nostalgic) humanists; he is not one of them. We could formulate the difference between Montaigne and his humanist counterparts in terms of Žižek's ontologization of Lacan's formulae of sexuation.

Rather than referring to anatomical differences, the terms "masculine" and "feminine" describe instead two modalities or orientations, two ways a subject's enjoyment (*jouissance*) is organized or structured. For Lacan, the masculine logic of exception posits a subject who has unlimited enjoyment, who stands outside the law of castration that governs social symbolic existence; it is the sovereign exception that proves the universal rule of castration. The feminine logic, by contrast, sees no exception to the law of castration; it rejects the illusion of an uncastrated Man (and with it the possibility of absolute enjoyment), but at the same time takes castration to be non-all, never complete, or whole.[38] Whereas humanism arguably subscribes to a masculine logic to the extent that it posits the human as exceptional, sovereign, unitary, self-constituted, and outside animality or mere corporeality, Montaigne can be seen as embracing the feminine logic of the non-all, which gives the lie to the phantasm of humanism, to its ideological pretention of wholeness by ceaselessly pointing to its incompleteness and inconsistency. Unlike the humanist sage, Montaigne avers the "wound of subjectivity" and declines his interpellation as an undivided, sovereign subject, boldly avowing this non-all when he perceives himself as monstrous, that is, an unknowable and unrecognizable self. In this respect, the non-all mirrors the wayward logic of the essay.

Montaigne's status as a signifying subject is in perpetual crisis, reaching its apogee in "Of Cripples." In the alchemic process of becoming monstrous, we can also observe a shift from desire to drive: the endless circling around Montaigne as the sublime/monstrous object. Žižek succinctly captures the impact of this shift: "let us imagine an individual trying to perform some simple manual task—say, grab an object which repeatedly eludes him: the moment he changes his attitude, starting to find pleasure in just repeating the failed task, squeezing the object which, again and again, eludes him, he shifts from desire to drive" (*PV*, 7). We thus have two Montaignes: Montaigne the humanist, who sits down to write down his ideas, is the subject of desire, while Montaigne the essayist, who is constituted in the act of self-writing, riveted to signifiers, is the subject of the drive. The former predictably dreams of self-care as self-mastery (of successfully coinciding with himself: the project of self-portraiture), the latter embraces his incompleteness and imperfections, deriving an unexpected *jouissance* from the impossibility of his task.

As the subject of the drive, Montaigne's imperfections are not simply to be tolerated, that is, to be overcome or redeemed, as would be stipulated by Descartes: "There is no man so imperfect that we cannot have a quite perfect friendship when we think ourselves loved by him, and have a truly noble and generous soul."[39] No, in Montaigne's hands, imperfection and incompletion undergo a transvaluation of values. To paraphrase Žižek, only a lacking, vulnerable being like Montaigne is capable of friendship: the ultimate mystery of friendship is therefore that incompleteness is in a way higher than completion.[40] For his readers/would-be friends, imperfection would thus not be an obstacle to befriending Montaigne—in all of his neighborly figurations—but its very condition.

Notes

1. The will to "exorcize" "the Cartesian specter" is not unique to postmodern thinkers. Žižek adds to the list: "Deep Ecologist," "cognitive scientist," "Heideggerian proponent of the thought of Being," "critical (post-) Marxist," "feminist," and "Habermasian theorist of communication" (*TS*, 1). And we could add to the list Object-Oriented Ontologists and New Materialists, to name a couple recent objectors to the Cartesian legacy.

2. Slavoj Žižek, "Introduction: Cogito as a Shibboleth," in *Cogito and the Unconscious*, ed. Slavoj Žižek (Durham: Duke University Press, 1998), 7.

3. Michel de Montaigne, *The Complete Essays of Montaigne*, trans. Donald Frame (Stanford: Stanford University Press, 1957), 469. Henceforth all references to this edition will be stated parenthetically in the text.

4. Take for example, Jean-François Lyotard's enthusiastic endorsement of the Montaignian essay. Identifying it with postmodernism, to the extent that it eschews systematic thought and the hermeneutic comfort of "grand narratives," "the essay (Montaigne) is postmodern," as he succinctly put it (Jean-François Lyotard, "Answering the Question: What Is Postmodernism?" trans. Régis Durand, in *The Postmodern Condition: A Report on Knowledge*, trans. Geoffrey Bennington and Brian Massumi [Minneapolis: University of Minnesota Press, 1984], 81).

5. Žižek makes a similar argument when it comes to Plato: "The assertion of the gap between the spatio-temporal order of reality in its eternal movement of generation and corruption, and the 'eternal' order of Ideas—the notion that empirical reality can 'participate' in an eternal Idea, that an eternal Idea can shine through it, appear in it. Where Plato got it wrong is in his ontologization of Ideas . . ., as if Ideas form another, even more substantial and stable order of 'true' reality. What Plato was not ready (or, rather, able) to accept was the thoroughly virtual, 'immaterial' (or, rather, 'insubstantial') status of Ideas: like sense-events in Deleuze's ontology, Ideas have no causality of their own; they are virtual entities generated by spatio-temporal material processes" (*LN*, 36).

6. Žižek, "Language, Violence and Non-Violence," *International Journal of Žižek Studies* 2, no. 3 (2008): 9.

7. Žižek, "Afterword: Objects, Objects Everywhere," in *Slavoj Žižek and Dialectical Materialism*, ed. Agon Hamza and Frank Ruda [New York: Palgrave Macmillan, 2016], 190–1).

8. Ernesto Laclau, "Identity and Hegemony: The Role of Universality in the Constitution of Political Logics," in *Contingency, Hegemony, Universality: Contemporary Dialogues on the Left*, ed. Judith Butler, Ernesto Laclau and Slavoj Žižek (New York: Verso, 2000), 73.

9. René Descartes, *The Passions of the Soul*, trans. Stephen Voss (Indianapolis: Hackett, 1989). 58.

10. Descartes, *The Passions of the Soul*, 58.

11 René Descartes, *Discourse on Method and Meditations on First Philosophy*, trans. Donald A. Cress (Indianapolis: Hackett, 1998), 35.
12 Sigmund Freud, "A Difficulty in the Path of Psycho-Analysis," in *The Standard Edition of the Complete Psychological Works of Sigmund Freud*, ed. James Strachey et al., vol. 17 (London: Hogwarth, 195), 141.
13 Jacques Lacan, "The Instance of the Letter in the Unconscious, or Reason since Freud," in *Écrits: The First Complete Edition in English*, trans. Bruce Fink (New York: Norton, 2006), 430. Lacan initially frames psychoanalysis' relation to Cartesianism in strictly antagonistic terms: "It should be noted that this experience [of psychoanalysis] sets us at odds with any philosophy directly stemming from the *cogito*" (Lacan, "The Mirror Stage as Formative of the Function of the I as Revealed in Psychoanalytic Experience," in *Écrits: The First Complete Edition in English*, trans. Bruce Fink, 75).
14 Bruce Fink, *Lacan to the Letter: Reading Écrits Closely* (Minneapolis: University of Minnesota Press, 2004), 102–3.
15 Žižek draws on François Balmès, *Ce que Lacan dit de l'être* (Paris: Presses Universitaires de France 1999).
16 Ed Pluth, "Psychoanalysis, Science, and Worldviews," *Crisis & Critique* 5, no. 1 (2018): 335, 336.
17 Žižek, "Language, Violence and Non-Violence," 9.
18 Jacques Lacan, "Presentation on Psychical Causality," in *Écrits: The First Complete Edition in English*, ed. Jacques-Alain Miller, trans. Bruce Fink (New York: Norton, 2006), 146.
19 Jacques Lacan, *The Four Fundamental Concepts of Psychoanalysis, The Seminar of Jacques Lacan, Book XI*, ed. Jacques-Alain Miller, trans. Alan Sheridan (New York: Norton, 1998), 223–4.
20 Lacan, *The Four Fundamental Concepts of Psychoanalysis*, 218.
21 Catherine Belsey, *Shakespeare in Theory and Practice* (Oxford: Oxford University Press, 2008), 26, emphasis added.
22 Lacan, *The Four Fundamental Concepts of Psychoanalysis*, 223.
23 "But what then am I? A thing that thinks. What is that? A thing that doubts, understands, affirms, denies, is willing, is unwilling, and also imagines and has sensory perceptions" (René Descartes, *Meditations on First Philosophy*, trans. John Cottingham [Cambridge: Cambridge University Press, 1986], 19).
24 Lacan, *The Four Fundamental Concepts of Psychoanalysis*, 224.
25 Belsey, *Shakespeare in Theory and Practice*, 26–7.
26 Slavoj Žižek, "Lacan's Four Discourses: A Political Reading," in *Desire of the Analysts: Psychoanalysis and Cultural Criticism*, ed. Greg Forter and Paul Allen Miller (Albany: SUNY Press, 2008), 191.
27 Michel Foucault, "Polemics, Politics, and Problematizations," in *The Foucault Reader*, ed. Paul Rabinow (New York: Pantheon Books, 1984), 389.
28 Colette Soler, "The Subject and the Other (II)," in *Reading Seminar XI: Lacan's Four Fundamental Concepts of Psychoanalysis*, ed. Richard Feldstein,

Bruce Fink, and Maire Jaanus (Albany: State University of New York, 1995), 46.

29 Lacan also discusses the *"vel* of union," where unlike the exclusive vel, the *vel* is true even when both x and y are true (Lacan, *The Four Fundamental Concepts of Psychoanalysis,* 210; see also Soler, "The Subject and the Other (II)," 46).

30 Lacan, *The Four Fundamental Concepts of Psychoanalysis,* 212.

31 Lacan, *The Four Fundamental Concepts of Psychoanalysis,* 212.

32 François Laruelle, *Intellectuals and Power: The Insurrection of the Victim,* trans. Anthony Paul Smith (Cambridge: Polity, 2015), 9.

33 Adrian Johnston, *Badiou, Žižek, and Political Transformations* (Evanston: Northwestern University Press, 2009), 153.

34 François Garasse, qtd. in Olivier Millet, *La Première réception des Essais de Montaigne (1580–1640)* (Paris: Champion, 1995), 199. Similarly, Estienne Pasquier described Montaigne as "another Seneca in our language" (Millet, *La Première réception,* 146).

35 Michel Foucault, *Technologies of the Self: a Seminar with Michel Foucault,* ed. Luther H. Martin, Huck Gutman, Patrick H. Hutton (Amherst: University of Massachusetts Press, 1988).

36 "Of Idleness" is only one entry into the *Essays.* Montaigne multiplies their beginnings. In "Of Friendship," for example, Montaigne frames the *Essays* as a work of mourning. As a kind of substitute or compensation for the loss of his friend Etienne de La Boétie, Montaigne's writing seeks a reader capable of answering the call of friendship; he is writing to a reader, to a friend *à venir*—to a friend that could fill the vacated space of intimacy once occupied by La Boétie. Yet in the process of writing, Montaigne comes to realize that self-writing does not produce comfortable knowers but contributes further to the inventions of monsters. Montaigne's account of friendship is nothing less than astonishing, bearing the marks of his hysterical interrogative "What do I know?" Unlike Aristotle and Cicero, for example, who had magistrally argued for the voluntary aspect of friendship, Montaigne short-circuits their grammar by placing *chance* at the center of their friendship, thus foregrounding what was beyond his mastery and understanding. Montaigne did not orchestrate his first encounter with La Boétie, nor can he provide an explanation for *why* he was drawn to him (he does not, for instance, list the virtues of La Boétie). And when rhetorically pressured to provide an explanation for his love ("If you press me to tell why I loved him" [139]), Montaigne ends up answering with the following tautology: "Because it was he, because it was I [*Par ce que c'estoit luy; par ce que c'estoit moy*]" (188). This is a most bizarre answer. It functions as an explanation without actually explaining anything. Montaigne's reader—his would-be friend—is left astonished. Was this an example of perfect friendship or a lesson in the impossibility of mourning? Rather than choosing between the two (another instance of a forced choice), I prefer the Žižekian answer of the "Yes, Please!" Only a refusal of choice can sustain and prolonging the sublimity of Montaigne's essay.

37 Zahi Zalloua, *Theory's Autoimmunity: Skepticism, Literature, and Philosophy* (Evanston: Northwestern University Press, 2018), 51.

38 Jacques Lacan, *On Feminine Sexuality, The Limits of Love and Knowledge, 1972-1973: Encore, The Seminar of Jacques Lacan, Book XX*, trans. Bruce Fink (New York: Norton, 1998), 79.

39 Descartes, *The Passions of the Soul*, 64.

40 Slavoj Žižek, "The Real of Sexual Difference," in *Interrogating the Real*, ed. Rex Butler and Scott Stephens (New York: Continuum, 2005), 308.

8

Žižek and the Bartleby Paradox

I Would Prefer Not To?

Cindy Zeiher

"*You are decided, then, not to comply with my request—a request made according to common usage and common sense?*"

He briefly gave me to understand that on that point my judgement was sound. Yes: his decision was irreversible.[1]

We can imagine the varieties of such a gesture in today's public space: not only the obvious "There are great chances of a new career here! Join us!"—"I would prefer not to"; but also, "Discover the depths of your true self, find inner peace!"—"I would prefer not to"; Or "Are you aware how our environment is endangered? Do something for the ecology!"—"I would prefer not to"; or "What about all the racial and sexual injustices that we witness all around us? Isn't it time to do more?"—"I would prefer not to." (PV, 382)

It is not surprising that many different thinkers take up the writing of Herman Melville, because it is timeless in portraying humanity's arbitrary and precarious position in the world.[2] Melville is almost Pascalian in his presentation of the subject: his characters act as if, at any given moment, they have agency to choose, only to then realize that they have already, unconsciously made their choice long before. Melville's characters are often conspicuously ambivalent regarding the question of meaning until eventually realizing that they have already decided in favor of preserving subjective *jouissance* vis-à-vis meaning. The effect of this realization is always striking for Melville's characters: for example, *Mardi* considers the sheer joy of creating meaning while *Moby-Dick* considers the consequences of attributing too much meaning; *Pierre* is a character who suffers the frustrations of trying to find an attribution to all meaning, while *The Confidence Man* considers the humor of accepting the meaninglessness of everything. The narrative of *Bartleby* embodies giving meaning to chaos, a perfect project for the hysteric, a position of course occupied by Bartleby's employer. Arguably it is also a modernist project *par excellence* in its insistence on the plea for rationality as a way of regulating the tension between categorical distinction and representation of social conformity.

Žižek takes up Melville's character Bartleby as a force able to reckon with contemporary capitalist structures—it is the fantasy of capitalist ideology that Bartleby riffs against. Moreover, Žižek associates a strange political trust associated with the figure of Bartleby, whose refusal of oppressive capitalist structures manifests in the unrelieved monotony of office rules and space. His colleagues are either stupid, demanding, insightlessly ambitious, or simply biding their time, appropriately endowed by Melville with ludicrous names: Nippers, Turkey, and Ginger-Nut. However, Bartleby's employer respectfully uses his proper name, in line with his higher expectations of Bartleby's work as a scrivener, notwithstanding that this is mere hack work demanding little respect except for the requirement of accuracy. No wonder Bartleby prefers not to speak or engage with anyone. Initially, however, he continues to undertake his work seriously:

> At first Bartleby did an extraordinary quantity of writing. As if long famishing for something to copy, he seemed to gorge himself on my documents. There was no pause for digestion. He ran a day and night line, copying by sunlight and by candlelight. I should have been quite delighted with his application, had he been cheerfully industrious. But he wrote on silently, palely, mechanically.[3]

As Žižek notes, Bartleby is gradually being reduced to an automaton, the inevitable state of subjectivity rendered by workplace capitalism. Here the only choice available is a ready-made false choice, either to live and participate in capitalism or prefer not to, suffering and dying alone with hardly anyone caring that you preferred not to. This is what Bartleby opts for and it is no polite refusal, especially in the face of his employer's strange and opaque lingering care.[4] Žižek interprets the nothingness which Bartleby ultimately inhabits as a violent political act: "Sometimes doing nothing is the most violent thing to do" (V, 217). The deadlock of the false choice facing Bartleby is one which is, as Žižek implies, both new and yet familiar. Furthermore, claims Žižek, Bartleby's mantra must be taken seriously and at face value; that is, Bartleby refuses the existential conflict of choice:

> it says, "I would prefer not to" *not* "I don't prefer (or care) to" so we are back at Kant's distinction between negative and infinite judgement. In his refusal of the Master's order, Bartleby does not negate the predicate; rather, he affirms a non-predicate: he does not say that he *doesn't want to do it*; he says that *he prefers (wants) not to do it*. This is how we pass from the politics of resistance and protestation which parasitizes upon what it negates, to a politics which opens up a new space outside the hegemonic position and its negation. (*PV*, 381–2)

The political impasses we are faced with, for example adopting the position of enlightened, ethical consumer, do not erase but merely mask the oppressive forces and structures in which such a position is embedded. Sometimes it is better to simply do nothing, to opt out—of culture wars, protest, consumption, and remain passive in the face of capitalist structures which seek only their self-perpetuation. In this way Bartleby is, for Žižek, the ultimate hero, sacrificing himself by doing nothing in order to opt into resistance. In *The Parallax View*, Žižek explains what he means by opting out of ideological subjectivities:

> Better to do nothing than to engage in localized acts whose ultimate function is to make the system run more smoothly (acts like providing space for the multitude of new subjectivities, and so on). The threat today is not passivity but pseudo-activity, the urge to "be active," to "participate," to mask the Nothingness of what goes on. (*PV*, 334)

For Žižek Bartleby's existence incorporates the logic of his own contradiction: in *preferring not to*, he violently avoids any identification with anyone else and certainly does not forge one of his own. Perhaps such an uptake of nothingness is a privilege afforded to certain (male) individuals, perhaps not.... Regardless, it appears that Žižek reads Bartleby's opting out as opting into the Real, the space where he no longer needs to appear to be doing anything, where even his resistance is one of unconscious desire just simply doing its thing. This *thing* for Žižek is spatially oriented, the recognition of a void which is always-already there: "a politics which opens up a new space outside the hegemonic position *and* its negation" (*PV*, 381–82). Behind this reading of Bartleby and his location there is a certain assumption about the Real, that the subject, in this case Bartleby, is a signifier of the Real because he hovers within it, somehow devoid of the standards, rules, and regulations which structure the Symbolic. Of the Real, Lacan says,

> This real, the real at issue in what is called my thought, is always an odd or an end, a core. It is certainly a core around which thought embellishes, but the mark as such of this real is that it doesn't tie on to anything. This at least is how I conceive of the real.[5]

This mark of the Real is taken up by Luis Izcovich in a number of ways, for example,

> In *Television*, Lacan uses the expression, "grimaces of the real." What does this expression refer to and what does it explain? Lacan evokes it in relation to a question he takes from Kant—"what should I do?"—a question we often meet with in analysis [. . .]. The analyst does not respond to "what should I do?" but nor does he abstain from responding. More precisely, he does not respond as a master who knows what must be done. For the analyst is alert to the fact that the question of what to do appears systematically each time there is a failure of desire in the subject.[6]

Is such a systematic intervention the perfect application to the scrivener in *Bartleby*? Although the Real appears to set the standard for rules, that is, rules which stick to the subject, Lacan reminds us that rules are "senseless" and one can certainly "thumb one's nose in response."[7] Thinking along the same lines, Žižek suggests that rules are not always transparent; there are those which are obvious (don't kill your neighbor, don't sleep with your neighbor's wife, etc.) and there are those rules one can choose to break if such rules are contained within a certain mitigating logic (kill your neighbor if he threatens to kill you first, sleep with your neighbor's wife if you are in love with her). As Žižek states, "the existing order explicitly allows, although prohibits at the level of implicit unwritten prohibitions" (*FA*, 147). Although such meta-prohibition characterizes commands, society can be swayed so that the law is reconfigured to suit ideological preferences, especially when these align with some social supplement, such as a more progressive society, a more liberal outlook, and so on. In this odd way, the subject and indeed collectives of subjects undertake social and political causes under what is an essentially false guise: they are assuming agency when all the time this agency is no more than adherence to ideological commands creating a false sense of choice. This is where for Žižek the figure of Bartleby is important. Bartleby knows he has minimal agency and does not fight for even a semblance of this signifier; instead, he seems to simply command nothing at all.[8] Yet perhaps not exactly nothing, which is precisely the Bartleby paradox.

This paradox is one which interpellates both the falsity of choice and the silence which ensues. Of the falsity of choice we can say that embracing a system of values implies choices have already been made in that objects (and subjects) chosen or rejected reinforce such values. As Baudrillard suggests:

Choices are not made at random, but are socially controlled and reflect the cultural model within which they are made. It is not just any old goods which are produced and consumed; they must have some meaning with regards to a systems of values [. . .] The fundamental, unconscious, automatic choice of the consumer is to accept the style of a particular society (it is therefore no longer a choice (!) and the theory of the autonomy and sovereignty of the consumer is refuted).[9]

This is what underlies the Bartleby paradox: Bartleby is able to exclude the social command without compromising his subjectivity (because he has no investment in the subjective project), but this resistance to false choice can manifest only as silence. Bartleby truly confronts the masquerade of choice through repetition of his mantra and his self-incarceration instead of working and engaging in normal collegial relationships. By finally refusing even to eat he fully interpellates himself into the logic of false choice whose conclusion the subject cannot survive. In this way, Bartleby surrenders to his so-called symptom in a very specific way. In order to be a part of humanity through engaging with the social bond, everyone needs to include their symptoms, for example by getting along with those we don't much like, tolerating gatherings we don't want to be a part of, or laughing at jokes that are not especially funny. Rather than being exchangeable forms, these symptoms of needing to belong are part of the drive. But for Bartleby, drive manifests in the complete absence of activity; his drive is to resist not his symptom but its effect. This is a distortion of the Master's discourse in that Bartleby's position illustrates the impossibility of making a relation under such the Master's discourse itself; the rest of us are driven by our symptoms to fantasize and act out what that relation might be. Bartley simply opts out. Here Žižek's sequential reading of Bartleby rings true, in so far as it purports volunteerism as a direction that reinvention might take. However, this fails to accommodate division as a fundamental feature of subjectivity, for, like the rest of us, Bartleby despite trying, cannot just abandon the big Other.

We have all encountered times when our questions toward another are met with silence. Sometimes we accept this but at other times we feel the need to question why silence is occurring. We might then either just respect it or on the contrary, command an explanation from the silent subject. Although silence can beget speech, sometimes the more intense the command to speak, the more silence ensues. We are then faced with performing a final maneuver, that of imagining why there is silence. Bartleby gives us no clues as to why he *would prefer not to*. He is effectively speaking his silence. His employer, colleagues, all of us can only imagine why. Is he unhappy, bored, lonely, abandoned by his lover? Is he in therapy, homeless, on the run from authorities? Does he have a family? Bartleby offers a clarifying nothing in return, not even reassurance that he is in fact really absolutely fine! In offering nothing he transgresses everything, leaving us only with our imagination. Although Žižek might at this juncture encourage us to think of Bartleby as a signifier in the Real (i.e., Bartleby is an embodied enigma bearing a proper name), we must also think of him as a figure of the Imaginary who merely touches on the Real, in so far as he speaks clearly his desire (*parlé* as self-authorization) and not merely for the sake of speaking. Lacan draws attention to this inversion of the signifier when he says

> [d]istinguishing the dimension of the signifier only takes on importance when it is posited that what you hear, in the auditory sense of the term, bears no relation whatsoever to what it signifies . . . the signifier is the effect of the signified.[10]

In our imagination Bartleby might be anything—a closet psychopath, pervert, spy, alien, and so on. . . . In hovering around the Real such speculations can transgress any Law. Bartleby is, after all, just another subject and as such a divided subject. His lack is all too apparent, kept at bay only by the grammar of speech. This is what keeps Bartleby subservient to the Law, strongly invested in upholding it by being careful with his words to ensure that the meaning of what he says is absolutely clear—and yet the effect of his words is anything but. He threatens the ideological order precisely through being in this way of service to the Law. He is the ultimate fantasy figure whose "freedom of choice has been forced upon him" as Baudrillard puts it.[11]

Yet if Bartleby is truly resigned, why does he keep on speaking his mantra? Certainly, in doing so, he is imposing his conviction on his employer. However, we do know that he was not always so melancholic and catatonic but was once productive and driven. So we can speculate that the change in him is not because he is sick or dying. We might imagine that perhaps he has suffered some sort of loss, even something so profound that it is unspeakable. In the end we have no idea of what it is exactly he is preferring to refuse. He gives no clue as to his desire other than through the repetition of his mantra. He does not resist his apparent misery or focus on some future desirable status, whatever this might signify—having a promotion, a lover, a new car, or a holiday abroad. He simply gives himself over to the logic of his own misery, his mantra being the dominant symptom which determines his status of being in the world, a symptom which defines his lack and the reality of his subjective chaos. He disregards all competing tensions, offering nothing until the moment when his employer suggests that, given he is refusing to work, perhaps he ought to quit his job,

"I would prefer *not* to quit you," he replied, gently emphasizing *not*.[12]

This is perhaps the most poignant yet dignified statement Bartleby has yet offered. Yes, he would prefer not to quit and his employer not quit him. For his part, his employer grants the request by never again insisting that Bartleby leave, perhaps recognizing that what Bartleby is really asking is for his employer to accept this subtle variation on his mantra in a final protest against modernism's politico-cultural project: to take his words seriously and at face value. Of course, the hilarious irony here is that it is Bartleby's employer who is forced to leave the workplace in order to comply with Bartleby's *preferring not to*!

Although Melville is considered a romantic writer he manages to engage a certain preemptive and proto-modernist sensibility, especially the plea on behalf of individualism in the face of overwhelming structure, in which the subject vanishes because the will to episteme or knowledge (i.e. trust in knowledge alone as providing historical and social support to notions of justice and freedom) is foregrounded. The modernist subject is tasked to go along with this will, to accept that humanity, being ultimately controlled by structure, will always have to undertake boring repetitive work for the betterment of society and be perpetually disappointed by frustrated desire and longing. Any possible alternative social arrangements would require that human subjectivity be inspired to think outside the square, beyond traditional humanism or any semblance of the sacred: the modernist plea. The issue here is that trust in knowledge alone completely misses the uptake of subjective lack as implicitly a condition of the will toward knowledge. It is at this juncture we can say that while two *Bartlebys* emerge: Melville's modernist Bartleby and Žižek's political Bartleby, only one is a figure of conviction while the other represents a fantasy of what can't be realized.

In his repeated utterance, *I would prefer not to* Bartleby does more than employ grammar in order to say nothing: what he is doing is keeping at bay what we and arguably his frustrated colleagues, all command him to give up, namely his privacy to pursue a true question of freedom—whether to live or die.[13] We have little idea what Bartleby would prefer not to do but he is at least willing to utter words which, although monotonous, are sufficient for us to engage with him as a person rather than as an automaton of unthinking production.[14] When inevitably he dies alone it leaves only his mantra as a trace of his existence which at the same time provides a resounding echo of his subjectivity. How is this? We could say that is it because his mantra thrusts him into subjectivity yet also situates him as a subject refusing the conundrum of divided subjectivity (he refuses to be anything for anyone else). He is an enigmatic citizen who exhibits both barbarian, symbolic resistance and civilized, rational acceptance. Whether he is either an enlightened idiot or chronic melancholic, both are somewhat displaced modernist positions as subjects of knowledge yielding differing insights. There is nothing extra-linguistic, nothing special, about Bartleby's mantra. It reveals neither particulars nor generalities, contains little aspiration, and almost no command to another. What it does perfectly is to hystericize the subject by inhabiting two worlds: the workplace (the political Bartleby) and his own inner absurdist world (the modernist Bartleby).[15]

The German word *Grenzgänger* refers to the crossing of borders, commuting from one border to another and back again. Here, inhabiting one space does not preclude simultaneously inhabiting another even if this is only symbolic or representing a desire. Such a liminal space seems typically modernist whereas to be in a space which demands one to think beyond immediate concerns and worries requires traversing the symbolic imagination which is not necessarily coherent or rooted in surrounding structures. Perhaps we could even think of modernism as an epoch of such proximate immediacy. Žižek's reading of Bartleby certainly riffs on this and privileges the political subject by understanding Bartleby simply as a politicized figure whose narrative is a dialectic within the liminal space of border crossing: this Bartleby appears to give no thought to his surrounds and yet at the same time has no desire to leave and be elsewhere, he nevertheless explicitly traverses borders. Žižek's curiosity about Bartleby is marked by a silent question mark behind the mantra, *I would prefer not to*. While this gives Bartleby a speculative political character, it is one which arguably differs from Žižek's interpretation—that is, there is nothing concrete to Bartleby's politics whatsoever—suffused with the instability of time, space, and resistance to capitalist production and consumption. In this way, Žižek's Bartleby uses language to express his disdain for the structure in which he is interpellated but at the same time there nothing absolute about this antipathy. Žižek's omission of the question mark in his reading of Bartleby fails to allow for the division crucial to all subjectivity, instead of navigating the enigma of Bartleby along a trajectory of de-subjectified melancholy. By deliberately inserting the question mark to Bartleby's utterance, we could say that Žižek might understand him as an iconoclast who, rather than pursuing elsewhere some ideological discourse or Other, turns up at his place of employment every day precisely in order to break its rules. *I would prefer not to?* allows for some other traversal to be contemplated, which although is exactly what Žižek posits in his *Parallax*, attests to Bartleby's mark. For Žižek, the demands of the capitalist structure mute and confine Bartleby's subjectivity. Hence Bartleby's refusal is for Žižek a specifically passive refusal. However, it is also a refusal which is arguably contained within the paradox of an active silence marking his border crossing.[16]

Taking up Melville's conviction that Bartleby's mantra ends with a full stop, we might liken this silence as an *opting in* of a modernist subjectivity which truly surrenders to the absurdity—another nod to existentialism—of our insignificance. The repetition of this mantra asserts not that Bartleby is more interesting than anyone else, but rather that we are all equally uninteresting, even or especially if we *prefer not to* be. Being the only tool left for Bartleby, language is taken up by him in a subjective experiment to determine whether we could survive (let alone thrive) with *only* language at our disposal. In this way apparently freed from capitalist forms and structures, are we as subjects able to adopt any alternatives? If we are to take Žižek to his logical conclusion regarding his reading of Bartleby then it would seem that Bartleby's absurd, modernist experiment fully interpellates him in the workplace without him in the end even being a worker. At this point the office is transformed, its symbolism being turned upside down when Bartleby adopts it as his empty home. Here we can think of Bartleby as an illegal border-crosser (*Grenzgänger-schmuggler*), importing himself precisely in order to violate the customs and traditions of not only work but also life. He doesn't live *to* work but rather lives *at* work, therefore stealing the collective space work affords for only himself.[17]

That Bartleby initially turns up to work every day to do nothing and eventually never leaves underlies Žižek's contention that Bartleby is acting in accordance with overconformity to the law,[18] so much so that subjectivity vanishes leaving only the law to repeat his mantra. In this, contends Žižek, lies Bartleby's "politics of subtraction" (*PV*, 382) where differentiation between Bartleby the subject and the subjectivity which constitutes Bartley (his workplace, employer, etc.) either conform or converge to leave a marginal differentiation between the subject and the causes of subjectivity. Herein lies a very distinctive and particularizing feature of Bartleby, namely that he seeks no recognition of personal needs from anyone, which is sadly recognized and respected by his employer,

> This building too, which of weekdays hums with industry and life, at nightfall echoes with sheer vacancy, and all through Sunday is forlorn. And here Bartleby makes his home, sole spectator of a solitude which he has seen all populous—a sort of innocent and transformed Marius brooding among the ruins of Cathage!
>
> For the first time in my life a feeling of overpowering stinging melancholy seized me. Before, I had never experienced aught but a not unpleasing sadness. The bond of a common humanity now drew me irresistibly to gloom. A fraternal melancholy! For both Bartleby and I were sons of Adam.[19]

In this gloomy *Grenzgänger* (commute) of life lurks a certain dark humor, as when Bartleby qualifies his mantra: "At present I would prefer not to be a little reasonable."[20] The only way into the traumatized region of Bartleby's mind is his mantra which together with this sudden repudiation of reason is what we and Bartleby's colleagues have to wrestle with: no ordering, no deconstruction, no horrific moment, no hope of any explanation. Nevertheless, from this subjective exile Bartleby does convey something. Perhaps not only Žižek's political lesson of Bartleby, for he makes no attempt to overcome his isolation and alienation, to explain what led to his condition or to retrieve his lost identity. The only thing he retains and can truly count on is language. His reluctant, minimalist, grammatical consistency which marks his very existence is at once disturbing and hilarious. The ambivalence of his mantra is a statement of stoic conviction, rather than an invocation to the Law. Is this resistance not the modernist plea for the will to knowledge? Moreover, is this also not the very nature of the Bartleby paradox? Here the hysteric is anxious in refusing the body as part of hysteria. This is a refusal to make one's self the object to the master signifier (in Bartleby's case, the ego-ideal of capitalism) and also to make one's self a slave to the master signifier (again, for Bartleby, the ideal-ego of the existentialist). Thus the only identification is with the "act" or in the case of Bartleby, lack of action: *lack-tion*. Such *lack-tion* can be explicit to Žižek's modernist negativity to a leftist political project. However, Melville's conviction, an overlooked intervention by Žižek, is that Bartleby is nihilistic. It is important to distinguish what kind of nihilism is at stake here: Bartleby wagers on a reductive and not emancipatory nihilism.

Although an utterance of conviction, Bartleby's mantra conveys chaos rather than meaning to his employer,

"Prefer not to," echoed I, rising in high excitement, and crossing the room with stride. "What do you mean? Are you moon-struck? I want you to help me compare this sheet here—take it," and I thrust it towards him.
"I would prefer not to," he said.
I looked at him steadfastly. His face was leanly composed; his grey eye dimly calm. Not a wrinkle of agitation rippled him. Had there been the least uneasiness, anger, impatience or impertinence in his manner; in other words, had there been anything ordinarily human about him, doubtless I should have violently dismissed him from the premises.[21]

What is it that his employer is missing and perhaps Žižek is short-circuiting regarding the enigma of Bartleby? The most obvious reading of Bartleby, wherein the subject is deliberating distancing from the social, leads to Žižek's viewpoint that Bartleby is a political figure of "determinate negation" (*PV*, 382), moving from something to nothing and then to something-nothing else (the Hegelian maneuver), willing to undergo the void of nothingness in the abyss of desire, so opaque that it is thoroughly hystericizing. But let's not forget that Bartleby was able to avoid being dismissed because he appeared to or pretended not to care one way or the other. This impasse provides a supplement to the Law which in turn enables an ontological difference for the subject, one which literally "gives body" to negation and thereby allows for Žižek's political interpretation of Bartleby to emerge.[22]

A different interpretation of Bartleby's mantra of withdrawal does not separate material reality (fulfilling duties, chatting with colleagues, etc.) because by virtue of the arguably preexistent subjective void he is already intrinsically part of a material reality which has no ideological agenda. Bartleby's withdrawal not only signifies an ontological gap (as Žižek points out) but in addition creates another moment which is apolitical. He does not so much create an alternative order as Žižek suggests, but rather gives a repetitive voice both to the order which is already there and to the absurd, alienated materiality we find ourselves in. Bartleby becomes a frustrating object to be studied by his employer and colleagues, a "vagrant who refuses to budge!"[23] Are we not today often faced with such situations and subjects? Do we not dedicate time and energy to solving the problems of those who represent social decay and misery, by, for example, implementing this social investment program or that political idea in the hope that material reality can appear neatly stitched up and the vagrants of the world a bit better hidden? Do we not then, time and time again, have to face the failure of this suturing, when the structure of our beloved moralism fails and we vainly seek another way in the politics of collectivism or individualism? This is the situation Bartleby represents, not so much a revolutionary moment as a moment of revelation: that political pragmatism works only in the presence of understanding and agreement rather than an individual's moment. In this way, it is questionable as to whether Bartleby's *intervention* is constitutive of politics. His conviction is clear: he prefers to instead, do nothing. Here we could say that not only is this position de-subjectivizing but it is also de-politicizing. What is at stake here is the failure of symbolic pragmatism to galvanize the subject: Bartleby's mantra which he insists upon is ultimately a modernist paradox, not a political one. Interpreting this paradox as stoic refusal, all sorts of ethical and moral conundrums arise as the limits of politics begin to punctuate subjectivity. Here we can view *Bartleby* as a novella of modernist literature which centers on the apolitical existentialism of Bartleby, the divided subject.

Bartleby's nihilistic position can be thought of as a configuration of both modernist and contemporary contours of work in that he simply discards it in favor of nothing else. Although his workplace becomes eventually his place of residence, Bartleby doesn't live there because of comfort, warmth, and connection, rather he would simply prefer not to leave. There is little to explain this behavior, not even his past employment at the Dead Letter Office (notwithstanding that this might account for his melancholy) is adequate enough a motive in ascribing reason to Bartleby *preferring not to*. Only through the imaginaries of his colleagues and employer does the character of Bartleby emerge, moreover only via his mantra can these imaginaries be expressed. Given this modernist platform yet in the absence of any perceived truths, absolute or relative, the enigma of Bartleby certainly leaves everyone, not only his employer, perplexed. Žižek gives us another Bartleby to contend with (although it is not necessarily the one he purports in *Parallax*), one who is open to the question of desire via the absent and silent question mark. In the end however, Bartleby can be seen as the understated antihero of modernism. We admire his inner-strength, notwithstanding his ambivalence toward life. We are struck by his orderly sense of nothingness and the stoic nature of his utterances, although we have little idea of the neuroses which are driving him. In these ways Bartleby, or rather the divided Bartleby, possess integrity, a strange clarity, and even stranger freedom; he is a truly apolitical creation of enduring power and relevance. In this way we should prefer to think of Bartleby as a modernist figure of the apolitical.

Notes

1. Herman Melville, *Bartleby, the Scrivener: A Story of Wall-Street* (London: Melville House Hybrid Books, 1853; reprinted, 1999), 20.
2. Thank you to Nick Derrick, Todd McGowan, and Russell Sbriglia for their close engagement with earlier drafts of this text.
3. Melville, *Bartleby*, 18.
4. Here Russell Sbriglia offers the insight that it is the telling of the tale of Bartleby which is most cathartic for his employer (*A Gainful Loss: Melville avec Lacan*, unpublished manuscript).
5. Jacques Lacan, *Seminar XXIII: Sinthome* (London: Polity, 2016 [1975–76]), 104.
6. Luis Izcovich, *The Marks of a Psychoanalysis* (London: Karnac, 2017), 187.
7. Jacques Lacan, *Seminar XX: Encore* (London: Norton and Norton, 1998 [1972–73]), 29.
8. To elaborate, Bartleby appears to exhibit no investment in the signifier at all—whether it is to prolong the *jouissance* resultant from it or be released from its anguish.
9. Jean Baudrillard, *The Consumer Society: Myths and Structures* (New York: Sage, 1970), 70.
10. Jacques Lacan, *Seminar XIX: . . . Ou pire* (London: Polity 2018 [1972]), 131.
11. Baudrillard, *The Consumer Society*, 72.
12. Melville, *Bartleby*, 46.
13. We could say that *Bartleby* the novella sits nicely alongside *Moby-Dick* and *Pierre* as truly proto-existentialist works anticipating Nietzsche, Sartre, Camus, de Beauvoir, among others—a noteworthy point by Russell Sbriglia (*A Gainful Loss: Melville avec Lacan*, unpublished manuscript).
14. Here one is provoked to ask whether anyone can truly be thought of as an automaton.
15. It makes sense here that the real subject in Bartleby is the employer/narrator and not Bartleby who represents the opacity of the desire of the Other. Again, I owe this insight to Russell Sbriglia.
16. Ed Pluth and Cindy Zeiher, *On Silence: Holding the Voice Hostage* (London: Palgrave, 2019).

17 We can take this a bit further by suggesting that Bartleby takes over the psychotic structure of the workplace, where work is deemed not a problem one needs to attend to in life but rather a solution. Such signifiers so important to the social bond are struggled with only in the context of the pragmatics of work where knowledge and know-how envelop the subject. In this way, Bartleby is similar to Lacan's Joyce in that both share the same psychotic structure although for different reasons (although arguably both opt out). No compromise is made or position adopted by them because of their willing uptake of the symptom's *jouissance* which completely and fully serves their subjectivity (and drive), precisely what Lacan refers to as the pure symptom resultant from the psychotic structure.

18 It is interesting to note that Henry Krips reads Žižek's notion of overconformity as akin to ambivalence, when he says, "The concept of overconformity that I am suggesting here differs from Žižek's. That is, for Žižek, acts of overconformity are strictly legal actions that are not tolerated because they refuse to take advantage of the obscene underside of the law. Their "absurdity" arises, then, from refusing to engage the tolerated "common sense" illegal practices that make up the obscene underside of the law, even when the law threatens to make an ass of itself. By contrast, the "absurdity" of the acts of generalized overconformity that I have in mind here—their '*luniness*'—depends upon the undecidability of how to respond to them, which, in turn, has disruptive effects upon the audience who are unable to decide" (Henry Krips, "Politics of Overconformity: Bartleby Meets Žižek," *Communication and Critical/Cultural Studies* 9, no. 3 [2012]: 307–16).

19 Melville, *Bartleby*, 31.

20 Melville, *Bartleby*, 36.

21 Melville, *Bartleby*, 17–18.

22 In his reading of Žižek's Bartleby, Russelll Sbriglia (*A Gainful Loss: Melville avec Lacan*, unpublished manuscript) takes this further by suggesting that Bartleby literally embodies the unanswerable question, *Che Vuoi?* In his repetition, Bartleby so hystericizes his colleagues and his employer that we as readers cannot resist asking of Bartleby, "what do you want?!" Here Sbriglia rightly turns the unanswerable question of *Che Vuoi?* on its head—what does Bartleby want which is of such interest to us?

23 Melville, *Bartleby*, 51.

9

Hitchcock's Modernist Hauntology

Laurence Simmons

> Modernism is a tradition of those who have no tradition.
> GABRIEL JOSIPOVICI, *Whatever Happened to Modernism?*
>
> Cinema is the art of letting the ghosts return.
> JACQUES DERRIDA, *Ghost Dance.*

"The House Was a Character": The Gothic Modern

> [I]n a sense the picture is the story of a house. The house was one of the three characters of the picture.
> ALFRED HITCHCOCK.[1]

In the opening pages of *Everything You Always Wanted to Know About Lacan (But Were Afraid to Ask Hitchcock)* Slavoj Žižek, following a typology of Fredric Jameson, identifies the "Selznick period" of Hitchcock films that illustrate a modernism characteristic of an emergent auteurism and are formally identified by the presence of long, anamorphically distorted tracking shots which are thematically framed around the perspective of a traumatized female heroine. Žižek observes that what these films stage again and again in a shamelessly direct way is the different figure of "feminine masochism," of a woman enjoying her own ruin, finding a tortured satisfaction in her subjection and humiliation. Tania Modleski, in *The Women Who Knew Too Much: Hitchcock and Feminist Theory*, laments that Žižek neglects to discuss *Rebecca*, "*the* Selznick film par excellence," and suggests it is because he prefers to think about "women and men rather than women in relation to one another"?[2] So how are we to redeem this lack? This chapter begins by addressing the interanimation between modernism and the various motifs, tropes, and images of the Gothic in Hitchcock's *Rebecca* (1940) and by extension Hollywood narrative film in general. It proposes that it is the film's antiquated space of Gothic imagery and architecture that deflects attention from its exploration of the structure of the modernist moment. Through an analysis of the film's descriptive features of modernism—style, irony, subjectivity, attention to formal properties of a specific "film language," a refusal to stay put within specific generic categories, metaphysical, and aesthetic auto-resonances, self-reflexivity—it will be argued that what makes Hitchcock's film seem old-fashioned, and often ridiculous, is what makes it "modern" and alive.[3]

In the Foreword to the second edition of *Everything You Always Wanted to Know* Žižek, in a typically counterintuitive manner, insists that in order to discern the social relevance of Hitchcock's films we should "isolate the intensity of their formal patterns" (*EY*, viii). This, of course, is also a typical modernist move whereby formalism provided both the critical manual to the modernist text and was also the principle means by which it validated an "aesthetic of modernity." In the introduction to *Everything You Always Wanted to Know* Žižek proceeds to argue that any modernist work of art "is by definition 'incomprehensible': it functions as shock, as the irruption of a trauma which undermines the complacency of our daily routine and resists being integrated into the symbolic universe of the prevailing ideology." What Žižek describes as "the pleasure of the modernist interpretation consists in the effect of recognition which 'gentrifies' the disquieting uncanniness of its object" (*EY*, 1; 2).

Hitchcock's *Rebecca* therefore is available for this "gentrification," for reading as an instance of modernist self-reflexion, especially as it folds into its narrative trajectory generic citations of an earlier Gothic tradition. In engaging with such self-reflexivity, *Rebecca* traces a certain modernist impasse signalled, on the one hand, by anonymity of its protagonist (who from this point on I will refer to as "Fontaine")[4] and, on the other, in a romanticized addiction to an aesthetics of ruins (Manderley, the stately home at the film's center). One name for such an aesthetic is the Gothic. In considering questions of the Gothic in relation to *Rebecca*, as well as the background of English literature with which Hitchcock would have been familiar, we also need to acknowledge the direct influence of German expressionist filmmaking on Hitchcock who in his early career worked as a director in Germany, as well as being influenced later by the construction of mainstream cinematic narrative shooting and editing in Hollywood derived from the presence of film writers, directors, cinematographers who had left Germany for America in the 1930s, including Fritz Lang and F. W. Murnau.[5]

On the face of it, modernism would seem to be at odds with the Gothic. However, the burgeoning field of "Gothic modernism," in which the aesthetics of the Gothic *and* modernism are seen to cohere, and which uncovers the complex uses to which modernist texts put spectrality, confirms their connection. For Jerrold Hogle, "the Gothic is endemic to the modern" and he asks "how much the Gothic, despite its apparent countering of the modern, is deeply bound up with the contradictions basic to modern existence, even the 'post'-modernity of more recent decades."[6] Daniel Darvay uncovers a genealogy of modernism that traces its starting point to the emergence of the Gothic in the late eighteenth century.[7] For John Paul Riquelme, it is the "tendency to blur the distinction between opposites in both Gothic texts and modernist ones" which enables them, "especially when they converge, to expose problems in the hierarchical thinking at the heart of modern Western culture."[8]

It is Manderley, "a textbook Gothic mansion,"[9] which provides *Rebecca*'s strongest link to the "modernist Gothic." In his recreation of the quintessential Gothic location, Hitchcock highlights the fantasmatic quality of Manderley.[10] The film opens with a sense of uncanny ghostliness reminding its viewers that the relation to the past is never behind us. The film's first tracking shot up the drive through the fog in search of Manderley meets with the obligatory impasse at the stately gateway, then winds around an overgrown road to reveal the ruins of a concatenation of turrets, chimneys, and high gable roofs that produce a vivid skyline. This quality of the "fantasmatic" is again emphasized upon "Fontaine's" first arrival by car in a rainstorm "by having a windshield wiper clearing the heroine's field of vision. The new bride's first view of Manderley is explicitly framed, as though this were her own private film screen."[11] Later the "Gothic" height and vastness of Manderley's "Great Hall" with its Gothic mouldings, vast mullioned window-wall and high wainscottings overwhelms "Fontaine." Manderley's rambling and labyrinthine plan continually disorients her so she loses her bearings. "I feel so uncomfortable," she confesses to her husband Maxim.

Rebecca's bedroom, accessed through tall white doors, and then through a wall-to-wall transparent curtain, lies at the hidden heart of the house in the west wing of Manderley. The room is an *actant*, a surrogate for the absent Rebecca herself. Its décor at once amplifies and reflects the excessive emotional range of Rebecca's character. As such, space here evokes an unsettling spectrum of feelings: it is both promiscuous excess, evoked by the sensuality and tactility of her clothing and silk lingerie, and self-contained, inviolable, tomb- or crypt-like, evoked by the spatial and psychological thresholds to be crossed before entering. It is in this respect that, along with Kim Wheatley, we might propose that "Rebecca herself stands for the Gothic, which of course never dies."[12] As Mrs. Danvers proudly informs "Fontaine," and us, "Everything is kept just as Mrs de Winter liked it. Nothing has been altered since that last night. It's not used now. It's the most beautiful room in the house." "You've always wanted to see this room, haven't you Madam?" Mrs. Danvers avers when she catches "Fontaine" trespassing.

Manderley has another companion Gothic location in the boathouse, the site of Rebecca's sexual trysts, her death, and a site also haunted by her ghost. With its Gothic interior—cobwebs, piles of rope and tackle, stone walls, high door frames, a vast fireplace, and empty birdcage—together with Maxim's ghostly confessional rehearsal of Rebecca's death it, too, becomes a spectral space. Manderley thus conceptualizes the two poles of the continuum across which modernism's invocation of spectrality moves. On the one hand, the extravagant architecture represents an expression of excess that connotes a troubling space beyond the signifier. On the other, within the hidden spaces there is the recourse to turn on what might be called primal scenes in an extended sense—entering these rooms presents a voyeuristic intrusion into a space which has been the scene of a desiring and/or a murderous action in the past.[13] These past moments are speculated upon, imagined, remembered; they are not represented by the film directly but are present in its traces, which are encrypted or embalmed in a sealed, preserved location. They exist as complex displacements of an indirect, symbolic meditation about something else. It is thus not only the Gothic resemblance and atmosphere of the house that makes it uncanny, but also the spectral persistence of the past within its rooms. The sense of constant visitation from somewhere else makes it impossible for "Fontaine" to settle into a domestic and stable relationship with her new home, because everything about it forestalls "homeliness" while emphasizing an uncanny sense of being ill at ease. "Shadows loom all over her face. Constantly she presses herself against the walls and furniture as if she were looking for shelter."[14]

Spectrality: Modernism's Hauntology

> MRS DANVERS (to "Fontaine"): Do you think the dead come back and watch the living?

The figure of haunting which Manderley foregrounds, and we have raised, is acknowledged in the Gothic influences and precursors of Hitchcock's film. What is of interest here, then, is an effect of the already spectral nature of film itself. The haunting effect of *Rebecca* is inscribed at various levels in Hitchcock's film, whether the question is one of diegesis, the intermixing of genres (popular Romance and Gothic), or the determination to direct audience reception all of which mark the film as an exemplary modernist—and Gothic—text. It is a feature of the film's "formalism" that the Gothic in *Rebecca*, even though the film is not simply definable as Gothic, is itself haunted, doubled and redoubled, divided in two, and traced by several manifestations: the contrast of lighting and shadow; the emotive camera angles; and a character returning from the past to disturb the film's present. It is this figural and projected alterity which disrupts and therefore speaks to the condition of cinema itself. If *Rebecca* is concerned with the inescapable confrontation with a haunting past, or the possibility at least of glimpsing the indelible trace of such spectrality, as it takes on a momentarily visible form in various aspects of the film, it is also a film interested in the disturbance within the film industry of the very condition of its own production. Hollywood, the place of its production, is the site of its own fears and projections, the film's modernist self-awareness. For it is the gestures of a British past that haunt Hitchcock's American film (with British actors and a British "location" but one that is filmed in California).[15]

While the spectral does not belong exclusively, or primarily, to the realm of visual phenomena, cinema would provide a succinct focus for the metaphysical oppositions between presence and absence. To adapt a phrase of Jacques Derrida, "There is no essence or substance of film: film is not. It does not exist."[16] This notness is nonetheless not nothing. The condition of the visible, of visibility, is itself not visible. Invisibility is folded into the condition of visibility from the beginning. There is no visibility that is not also invisible, no visibility that is not in some way always spectral. In an interview with the film magazine *Cahiers du cinéma* Derrida claims: "At the cinema one believes without believing, but this believing without believing is founded upon a belief . . . It allows us to see new spectres appear that are protected within memory (and in their turn to then project them onto the screen), these phantoms haunt the films *already* viewed."[17] He makes a distinction between cinema that engages directly with the theme of spectrality, what Derrida names "the spectrality effect" (Hollywood horror, vampires, ghosts, even Hitchcock), and the spectral structure of the cinematic image as such. And, for him, the vision and the perception of detail in film are directly related to psychoanalytic procedures; it is film's uncanny (*unheimlich* to use the Freudian term) quality that links cinema and psychoanalysis. As Derrida elaborates a logic of this spectrality, he coins a neologism, what he refers to as *hantologie* [hauntology]—a neologism whose difference from the term it displaces (*ontologie*) can be heard in a slight shift from "o" to "a"—a shift that surfaces in other of Derrida's texts.[18] To watch film is to be in the presence of specters, the already-dead or the soon-to-be-dead, and it is also to be watched by them as they look back at us and see that we, too, shall die. The spectrality of cinema transforms the spectator of the film into a specter who can no longer maintain the distance between subject and object, seer and seen, the living and the dead. The film spectator becomes caught up in the becoming specters of the characters on screen. We the audience can no longer retain a distance and collapse into the spectral relations.

Thus film is always the scene in which haunting takes place, regardless of narrative concern, thereby revealing in the processes of apparition of the image the fact that the subject is structured by the fantasmatic. The possibility of film is an act of the unfolding and staging of a spectral relation. Both in terms of genre and production *Rebecca* deals with these structures of inheritance. The Gothic that serves to frame its narrative is also challenged by this "hauntology." With *Rebecca* the structure of haunting is signaled from the beginning with the incorporeal voiceover that commences to tell the "true" narrative of events. The film opens with a displacement that is also the sign of an unsuturable gap—the disruption between sound and vision—the hope that the invisible source of sound will offer access to or stand-in for narrative veracity. In a scenario that will echo that of her predecessor Rebecca, we hear the voice but never see the second Mrs de Winter, she too has become an absent figure.

> Last night I dreamt I went to Manderley again. It seemed to me I stood by the iron gate leading to the drive, and for a while I could not enter for the way was barred to me. Then, like all dreamers, I was possessed of a sudden with supernatural powers and passed like a spirit through the barrier before me. The drive wound away in front of me, twisting and turning as it had always done. But as I advanced I was aware that a change had come upon it. Nature had come into her own again and little by little had encroached upon the drive with long, tenacious fingers. On and on wound the poor thread that had once been our drive, and finally there was Manderley. Manderley—secretive and silent. Time could not mar the perfect symmetry of those walls. Moonlight can play odd tricks upon the fancy, and suddenly it seemed to me that light came from the windows. And then a cloud came upon the moon and hovered an instant like a dark hand before a face. The illusion went with it. I looked upon a desolate shell with no whisper of the past about its staring walls. We can never go back to Manderley again, that much is certain.

If *Rebecca* is a haunted text or, at least, if it manifests so many aspects of haunting, the uncanny, and the spectral, this is because there is no longer a sense of simple origin, for what is reflected is always split in itself, the entire film becomes the flashback of its anonymous narrative opening. Ultimately how we read *Rebecca* remains (deliberately) undecidable. It remakes as apparent its uncanny and haunted condition through its ghostly play of various cinematic modes of production, and its spectral dalliance with differing codes and rhetorical associations, so as to unsettle the viewer. Rhona Berenstein has noted the "ambiguous use of pronouns" in the opening monologue which imply subjective slippage between "Fontaine" and Rebecca.[19] "[L]ike all dreamers, I was possessed of a sudden supernatural power and passed like a spirit through the barrier before me": is this "Fontaine" or Rebecca speaking and, if it is "Fontaine," in speaking of herself as "spirit" or absent figure is she not associated with Rebecca, the absent body that haunts the film's narrative? "We can never go back to Manderley again, that much is certain": does that "we" denote "Fontaine" and Maxim, Rebecca and Maxim, or "Fontaine" and Rebecca? This is a film of broken couples and unsatisfactory relations: "Fontaine" and Mrs. Van Hopper; Maxim and Rebecca; Maxim and "Fontaine"; Rebecca and Jack Flavell; Rebecca and Mrs. Danvers.

"She'll Never Come Back No More": Modernism and *Das Ding*

MAXIM (to "Fontaine"): The thing has happened. The thing I have dreaded day after day night after night.

Žižek has been characterized by several commentators as the philosopher of the Real, and a collection of Žižek's shorter published articles is titled *Interrogating the Real* (2005). Indeed, Sarah Kay argues that the central topic over which Žižek obsesses, the Lacanian register of the Real, compels him to adopt characteristic (and frequently criticized) nonsystematic, fragmentary procedures. For his interventions may be understood as a series of "failed" or "missed" encounters with the forever-elusive Real as he attempts to engage with this interminably insistent-yet-inaccessible theoretical "object."[20] As Žižek makes clear: "At the level of the gaze, the Real is not so much the invisible Beyond, eluding our gazes which can perceive only delusive appearances, but, rather, the very stain or spot which disturbs and blurs our 'direct' perception of reality" (*PF*, 214). Another name for the Real is *das Ding* (the Thing) one of the central themes of Lacan's Seminar 7, *The Ethics of Psychoanalysis*.

> The Real is thus *simultaneously* the Thing to which direct access is not possible and the obstacle that prevents this direct access; the thing that eludes our grasp and the distorting screen that makes us miss the Thing. More precisely, the Real is ultimately the very shift of perspective from the first standpoint to the second. . . . [W]hat prevents us from accessing the Thing directly is the Thing itself. (*PD*, 77)

Das Ding, for Žižek, is not simply the intruder that destroys social harmony, the foreign body within the social texture (Rebecca), but is also that which guarantees the fantasmatic consistency of the social edifice (Manderley).

In this sense it remains a marker of the cusp between modernism and the postmodern:

> Within modernism, the Thing assumes either the form of "remnants of the past," of the inertia of prejudices to be cast away, or the form of the repressed life power to be unchained . . . we enter postmodernism when our relationship to the Thing becomes *antagonistic*: we abjure and disown the Thing, yet it exerts an irresistible attraction on us. . . . Postmodernism thus accomplishes a kind of shift of perspective in relation to modernism: what in modernism appeared as the subversive margin—symptoms in which the repressed truth of the "false" totality emerges—is now displaced into the very heart, as the hard core of the Real that different attempts of symbolization endeavour in vain to integrate and "to gentrify." (*E*, 123)

The Body Without a Name: Modernism's "Symptomal Reading"

Modernism, insists Žižek, engages in a "symptomal reading" the aim of which "is to ferret out the texture of discursive (symbolic) practices whose imaginary effect is the substantial totality" (*E*, 123). The namelessness of the film's central character, which as we have already noted poses a difficulty for critics of the film, who tend to substitute the name of the film actress Joan Fontaine, means she operates as a symptom, a stand-in, a visual, physical substitute for her absent predecessor. However, her namelessness also suggests an element of narrative freedom and Hitchcock's producer, Selznick, considered the strength of the story to lie in its unusually explicit encouragement of reader identification. In this way, she functions as a "stand-in" but a stand-in for "every woman."[21] The problem of "Fontaine's" "naming" relates to the radical nature of the specter, of how we "name" and identify the ghost. As Julian Wolfreys comments: "Names, conventionally applied, fix the limits of an identity. Yet this 'strange name'—*spectre*—names nothing as such, and nothing which can be named as such, while also naming something which is neither something nor nothing; it names nothing which is neither nothing nor not nothing."[22] "Fontaine's" non-naming is thus an attempt to get beyond the signifier, to the core of something beyond symbolic representation, the Real.

Rebecca is a name without a body, while the female protagonist ("Fontaine"), who is the spectator's chief point of narrative identification for the first three-quarters of the film, is never named in her own right. She is a body without, or in search of, a name. It is not by chance that the name "haunts" in another form in *Rebecca*, as signature initials, the continual reappearance of Rebecca's monogram throughout Manderley. As an incessant indicator of the presence of Rebecca, it is there on the writing materials in the morning room, on the rug in the boathouse, on the pillows in Rebecca's bedroom, on the napkins at the dining table. The producer of the film David O. Selznick even wanted the smoke over the burning Manderley to form an "R" in the sky thus providing another telling level of symbolism to the final fire. Hitchcock, thankfully, found the suggestion a little too precious and reverted to a shot of one of Rebecca's monogrammed pillows engulfed by flames.[23]

"A Large Tray of Cigarette Stubs": Modernism's Perplexed Gaze

Rebecca is for, and about, the watchful.
PATRICIA WHITE[24]

Žižek can be credited with a revival of interest in specifically Lacanian psychoanalytical film criticism, but his approach also represents a decisive shift from the traditional psychoanalytical film focus of Laura Mulvey's analysis of the gaze of mastery (1975)[25] and Jean-Pierre Oudart's notion of suture and cinematic identification (1977–78),[26] to concentrate on questions of fantasy and spectator enjoyment. Thus, concepts of the gaze and identification in Žižek's film commentary are linked to issues of desire and the fantasmatic support of reality as a defense against the Real. In her essay "Visual Pleasure and Narrative Cinema" Laura Mulvey identifies two types of pleasurable looking—scopophilia and narcissism both of which take the female form as their object. But in *Rebecca*, both viewing modes are severely problematized. The women in *Rebecca* defy the objectification of a desiring male gaze either through physical absence (Rebecca) or physical plainness ("Fontaine"). In this way, the extent to which these women "lack" (material presence or physicality) is their loophole. (Male) viewing pleasure in *Rebecca* is qualified because of this lack, not indicated upon it. As Tania Modleski has suggested: "For those under the sway of Mulvey's analysis of narrative cinema, *Rebecca* may be seen as a spoof of the system, an elaborate sort of castration joke, with its flaunting of absence and lack."[27] The pleasure of (male) looking and desiring is underpinned by the anxiety of castration and "lack," but within this film text "Fontaine" defines herself as lacking: "Every day I realise the things she had and that I lack." The important point being, this lack is predicated upon her comparison with a woman, Rebecca, and not the construct of "woman" as man's "other." In a crucial scene of the film the Mulveyian gaze is replaced by what Žižek describes as "the perplexed gaze":

> an expression characterised as one of "looking without seeing": the gaze is directed outside the frame, addressing us, the viewers, but we are treated "as if invisible or at least indifferent, occupying no important presence in the subjects vacant or bemused look" . . . the perplexed gaze . . . thus unsettles the viewer as well, making his or her gaze uncertain, simultaneously dislocated . . . and fixed into the unpleasantly exposed position of a voyeur. (*D*, 148)

This gaze exemplifies perfectly Lacan's thesis according to which the gaze I encounter "is not a seen gaze, but a gaze imagined by me in the field of the Other" (*EY*, 214). In *Rebecca* this gaze from "the field of the Other" is best exemplified in the scene in boathouse following the discovery of Rebecca's boat and body when Maxim "reconstructs" the fateful night and the event of Rebecca's death for "Fontaine."[28] He starts his account:

> "*She was lying on the divan a large tray of cigarette stubs beside her.*"

"Fontaine" looks to her right and we follow her gaze to an full ashtray in the middle of the divan which also seems to bear the imprint of a (reclining) body. There is a single magazine thrown on the divan as well as a tea setting on the tray table in front. We have not seen the 'spectral' ashtray, the tea setting nor the trace of the human form in the divan before this moment nor will we see them after.[29]

> "*Suddenly she got up and started to walk towards me.*"

The camera now pans upward and then towards where Maxim is standing.

Maxim recounts Rebecca's words: "*When I have a child neither you nor anyone else could ever prove it wasn't yours. You'd like to have an heir, wouldn't you Max, for your precious Manderley . . . when you die, Manderley will be his.*"

As he utters these words the camera moves slowly past a clock on the wall, two vases full of dead flowers in front of a painting of a boat being tossed on rough waves.[30]

> "*She was face to face with me, one hand in her pocket, the other holding a cigarette.*"

The camera comes close, now fixes Maxim in the left of the frame and stops panning.

"I must have struck her. She stood staring at me. She almost looked triumphant. Then she started towards me again, smiling. Suddenly she stumbled and fell."

Maxim opens the door and the camera pans down to the rope and metal tackle including a large reflective anchor visible on the floor.

"When I looked down . . . ages afterwards it seemed . . . she was lying on the floor."

Maxim walks to the centre of the room followed by the camera. He then turns and looks back at the rope, anchor and tackle.

"She'd struck her head on a heavy piece of ship's tackle."

As Neil Badmington clarifies, "The camera remains in the present, from which Rebecca is absent. But not *simply* absent . . . The ghostly composition of the sequence—the way in which the camera moves and frames what lies before it in the present—intensifies the spectrality effect that riddles the entire film."[31] What we have here with the full ashtray, the imprint of a body on the divan, and the ship's tackle is a form of *anamorphosis*, where anamorphosis designates an object whose very material reality is distorted in such a way that a gaze is inscribed into its objective features. Lacan's example is Hans Holbein's *The Ambassadors* where a face (skull) that looks grotesquely distorted and protracted acquires consistency; a blurred contour, a stain, becomes a clear entity if we look at it from a certain biased standpoint. Anamorphosis undermines the distinction between objective reality and its distorted subjective perception; in it, the subjective distortion is reflected (in part by the reflecting anchor in this case) back into the perceived object itself, and, in this precise sense, the gaze itself acquires a supposedly objective existence. We are now a long way from Mulvey's gendered gaze.

Žižek ascribes to Hitchcock, a prolonged meditation upon the gaze as that which reveals the Real as a merciless, autonomic, and lethal position which is only in the end our own, as well as the mark of our desire, and a concern with ideological interpellation. In his comments on Hitchcock's *Psycho* (1960), which apply equally to *Rebecca*, "the viewer is forced to face the desire at work in his/her seemingly 'neutral' gaze," to question the ideology of a pure gaze which "pretends to float freely in an empty space, not charged by any desire" (*EY*, 223). How does this questioning occur? In the section called "A triumph of the gaze over the eye" Žižek notes the importance of the gaze, but also its fundamental emptiness as far as meaning or symbolic use is concerned. For Žižek, the transfixed gaze, "isolates a stain of the Real, a detail which 'sticks out' from the frame of symbolic reality—in short, a traumatic *surplus of the Real over the Symbolic*; yet the crucial feature of these scenes is that this detail has no substance in itself—it is, so to speak, 'substantiated,' caused, created, by the transfixed gaze itself" (*EY*, 235–36). It is this that brings about the split between reality and the Real.

Two Stories or One?: Modernism's Frame

In *The Indivisible Remainder* Žižek insists that "modernist dialectics provides another example of how the frame is always included in, is a part of, the framed content in modernism, a theory about the work is comprised in the work, the work is a kind of pre-emptive strike at possible theories about itself" (*IR*, 202). Elsewhere Žižek notes that "many Hitchcock films seem to rely on a between-two-frames dimension . . . what we are lured into taking as the full story is all of a sudden displaced, reframed, relocated into, or supplemented by, another story" (*MC*, 62). In *The Monstrosity of Christ* he cites a text by Jacques-Alain Miller which elaborates an idea by Ricardo Piglia that

> a story always has a double characteristic and always tells two stories at the same time, which provides the opportunity to distinguish the story which is on the first plane from the number 2 story which is encoded in the interstices of story number 1. . . . There is a modern form of the story which transforms this structure by omitting the surprise finale without closing the structure of the story, which leaves a trace of a narrative, and the tension between the two stories is never resolved. This is what one considers as being properly modern: the subtraction of the final anchoring point which allows the two stories to continue in an unresolved tension. (*MC*, 62–3)

Is this not precisely the structure and the final narrative twist of *Rebecca* when story number 2 (Maxim's "murder" of Rebecca) only appears when the narrative seems to have come to a conclusion. The twists of the plot which may seem superfluous in story number 1 (Maxim's attempted suicide on the cliff, his distraction and irascibility, and the visit of Flavell) become essential for story number 2. The second story, the enigma of Rebecca's death is never satisfactorily told. Nevertheless, while the two narrative registers are at the same time distinct (secrecy and reticence as opposed to confession; ingenue "Fontaine" and femme fatale Rebecca), they are also simultaneous (the opening after the flashforward starts with Maxim's clifftop "suicide" while revisiting the site of Rebecca's first "betrayal").[32] As Žižek observes, this redoubling of the hidden counter-narrative is a typical modernist subversion of the "standard self-enclosed linear narrative" (*MC*, 65).

The theme of self-reflexive double imitation abounds in *Rebecca*: Mrs. Danvers punishes "Fontaine" through the ploy of double imitation when she tricks her into wearing the outfit that copies the dress of one of his ancestors for Maxim's fancy dress ball. It is a dress that Rebecca has also worn in a previous ball and so "Fontaine" becomes "Rebecca" by imitating the ancestor that Rebecca has previously imitated, and Rebecca is brought back from the dead by default. It is a theme that will subsequently be repeated by Hitchcock in the scene of the imitation of Carlotta Valdes's portrait in *Vertigo*. In the home movie sequence, the film literally and self-reflexively contains a projected film within its own projection. In engaging with such self-reflexivity *Rebecca* traces a certain modernist impasse. As we have suggested, Hitchcock's film is haunted, doubled, redoubled, and traced by several Gothic manifestations and modes drawn from literature (from the original story by Daphne du Maurier to the work of Jane Eyre), German expressionism (we can think here of Hitchcock's early work in Germany), the silent screen, and Hollywood adaptations. The identity of the Gothic divides itself from and in itself, thereby haunting the very nature of the Gothic itself, through internal transgressions and returns, from the Gothic's "others." Hitchcock brings together two contrasting, yet overlapping, modes of filming and representation, British and Hollywood, as to explore the limit of each form, their inability to address each other. The two Rebeccas (Rebecca and "Fontaine") can be seen as spectral embodiments of two film traditions, and these are inscribed at the level of the film camera: moments of stillness and moments of excessive movement; the "perplexed gaze" and skewed, emotive camera angles; the importance of the set and a focus on facial responses and visible codes of emotional response; the importance of minor characters and the presence of "stars"; the doubling of the audience gaze.

"Not a Hitchcock Picture": The Vanishing Mediator

What are we to make of Hitchcock's apparent dismissal of *Rebecca*? He reported to François Truffaut: "Well, it's not a Hitchcock picture, it's a novelette, really," dismissing the story as "old-fashioned . . . feminine literature," "lacking in humour."[33] Tania Modleski has suggested that these comments display Hitchcock's concern to disassociate himself from a female-authored text and the female subjectivity the story entails, in particular its female transgressive authority.[34] Modleski locates a crucial juncture in Hitchcock's *oeuvre* in the narrative structure of *Rebecca*. She sees Hitchcock's own dismissal of the book as "novelletish" and his rejection of his film as "not a Hitchcock film," symptomatic of a denial of what in fact is an obsession in Hitchcock's films: the bisexuality of the human subject. As noted in the introduction to this essay, she has also suggested that Žižek's lack of extended commentary on *Rebecca* reflects his determination "to support Hitchcock's own characterization of the film as 'not a Hitchcock picture.'"[35] Rebecca's, and by implication "Fontaine's," sexuality is at most equivocal. While we can interpret the clues in the film indicating Rebecca's (Mrs. Danvers contends, "She despised all men. She was above all that") and "Fontaine's" ("I'm not the sort of person men marry") homosexuality we do not have to do so. We can decide subjectively. Modernism entails just this filling in of gaps, but at the same time the repressed content, and the absence around which Rebecca centres, can never be filled in. For it is in this way, Žižek argues, we experience "the void as such, which, of course, is ultimately none other than the void of subjectivity" (*FR*, 148).

So can we not turn around Modleski's comments and suggest they reflect the film's modernity? In the case of *Rebecca* what occurs repeatedly is the dissolution of fixed places (Manderley in ruins) and times (the film itself seems "out of time" and the diegesis is one long flashback), as well as fixed identities ("Fontaine" who initially appears childlike and thus inhabits the pre-symbolic to become confident and enter the Symbolic). We recognize that the gaze always comes from somewhere else, how someone (Rebecca) or something (her murder/suicide), a diffuse presence, is always watching from some other place or, somewhere other than the place from where one watches another watching. Another way to understand Hitchcock's dismissal of *Rebecca* is that it functions as a "vanishing mediator" between the Gothic and modernism, and between British and American cinema, just as the "vanished" Rebecca can be understood as a "vanishing mediator" between "Fontaine" and Maxim. The term "vanishing mediator" is borrowed by Žižek from Fredric Jameson (from his essay "The Vanishing Mediator; or, Max Weber as Storyteller").[36] Jameson's essay represents an attempt to historicize the overlooked or invisible moments in large-scale historical processes: the role of Protestantism within the rise of capitalism; the part played by opposition socialist parties in the fall of communism. The vanishing mediator thus mediates the transition between two seemingly opposite traditions and then "vanishes," as Protestantism, and religion in general, has done under capitalism. It is the conjecture of Lacan, notes Žižek, that the passage from the premodern to the modern individual does not occur directly but "there is something in between the two, a kind of 'vanishing mediator'" which "accounts for the repressed 'genesis of modernity'" (*IR*, 115). On several occasions, Žižek develops and expands the concept beyond the purely political to encompass "the vanishing mediator" as a kind of necessary gap or absence in any text which is constituted by what must be left out, an undecidability in the unfolding of a narrative that, as Rex Butler observes, "is only thinkable against the background of how events actually did turn out, an 'undecidability' that is not to be realized but that haunts and makes possible every reality."[37]

"No Whisper of the Past": Hitchcock as Postmodernist

FRANK CRAWLEY (to "Fontaine"): We none of us want to live in the past.

At the film's conclusion, as the camera prepares for its final penetration of Manderley and Rebecca's inner sanctum, it lingers "Gothic-like" at the window of the west wing, framing the figure of Mrs. Danvers in black silhouette amid the roaring flames of the fire she reportedly started. As the camera enters the burning house moving toward Danvers, a horrible sound draws her gaze upward. Then, in a sudden point-of-view shot, the roof falls in upon her and the world of the film in upon us. Danvers may not survive but the camera does and the film continues for a few more seconds as we track onto Rebecca's bed, the real site of the film's sexual enigma, and its "primal scene," as the monogrammed envelope of Rebecca's transparent négligée is engulfed in flames. As Žižek remarks of Hitchcock's endings, they are always ambiguous offering the possibility "that other possible outcomes are not simply cancelled but continue to haunt our 'true' reality as a spectre of what might have happened."[38]

For Žižek:

> A modernist work of art is by definition "incomprehensible"; it functions as a shock, as the irruption of a trauma which undermines the complacency of our daily routine and resists being integrated into the symbolic universe of the prevailing ideology; thereupon, after this first encounter, interpretation enters the stage and enables us to integrate this shock—it informs us, say, that this trauma registers and points towards the shocking depravity of our very "normal" everyday lives ... What postmodernism does, however, is the very opposite: its objects *par excellence* are products with a distinctive mass appeal ... the aim of the postmodernist treatment is to estrange its very initial homeliness. (*EY*, 1–2)

Nevertheless, in the passage from modernity to postmodernity he insists that "postmodernity is not a 'synthesis' of both extremes, traditional realism and modern subjectivism, it is not the unity of both one-sided positions; it is a self-relating repetition of the modernist break, its application to itself, it is modernity brought to conclusion" (*D*, 112). Postmodernity is thus understood by Žižek as a form of regression, "a way of betraying the modernist break" (*LN*, 255).[39]

We have made an argument, along with Žižek, for Hitchcock as a modernist artist and his film *Rebecca* as exemplary of that modernism. Following Žižek, we have also suggested that one can understand the difference between modernism and postmodernism by "analysing the effect of horror in Hitchcock's films" (*LA*, 143). "At first," Žižek argues, "it seems that Hitchcock simply respects the classical rule ... according to which one must place the terrifying object or event outside the scene." By not showing Rebecca directly "one fills out [her] absence with fantasy projections" (*LA*, 143; 144). But then there is something where there was nothing, in the scene in the boathouse where Maxim conjures up Rebecca's gaze, the object of fear becomes both "something" and the focus for the camera. It is as if by reflecting on and calling up the past "one realizes that one is confronting the source of an inexplicable terror" (*LA*, 144). This terror is intensified by the fact that what was once in the past is now brought into horrible and menacing proximity.

Hitchcock's modernism itself might thus be grasped as a profound movement of disarticulation. To the extent that mainstream Hollywood puts to work and subsumes modernist aesthetic experimentation into reiterable techniques for the purposes of the apparent unity of representation, we might argue that which is modernist about *Rebecca* is already spectral in as much as it returns disruptively from all attempts at representation on the part of the film itself. The film foregrounds its disjointing, mixing, and disarticulation of genres (Gothic, Modern, Popular Romance) all of which in turn destabilize the stability of representation on which those very genres rely. If this is the case, then *Rebecca* occupies a distinctly eccentric, and yet central place, in Hitchcock's *oeuvre*; it disturbs the historical continuity of cinema and our relation to it, as a form of displacement in and from itself. The figure of the absent character Rebecca is conceived of as a kind of impossible mediator between tradition and modernity. There is both fascination and ironic difference as modern viewers of a seemingly "old-fashioned" film are replicated in the relation of Hitchcock the filmmaker to European and North American cinema. *Rebecca* thus replicates a tension between tradition and modernity and, as Žižek has noted of *Psycho*, "epitomizes the incapacity of American ideology to locate the experience of the present, actual society into a context of historical tradition" (*EY*, 232). Are we then not forced to ask, along with Žižek: "Yet is Hitchcock for all that, a 'postmodernist' *avant la lettre*?" (*EY*, 2).

Notes

1 François Truffaut, with Helen G. Scott, *Hitchcock*, revised ed. (New York: Simon & Schuster, 1985), 131.
2 Tania Modleski, *The Women Who Knew Too Much: Hitchcock and Feminist Theory*, 2nd ed. (New York: Routledge, 2005), 133.
3 For Hitchcock and modernism in general, see David Trotter, "Hitchcock's Modernism," *Modernist Cultures* 5, no. 1 (2010): 106–26.

4 The second Mrs. de Winter remains nameless and is referred to by most critics as "I" or "Fontaine." She is unnamed in Daphne du Maurier's original novel. When questioned about the lack of name du Maurier disingenuously stated "she could not think of one," *The Rebecca Notebook and Other Memories* (Garden City: Doubleday, 1980), 3.

5 Hitchcock's early influences were German: he worked briefly on one German film and directed two of his own. The influence was both stylistic and associated with the work of two key directors but also tied to a specific German production model and its associated aesthetics. François Truffaut called him "the most German of all directors on the other side of the Atlantic": *Correspondence, 1945–1984*, ed. Gilles Jacob and Claude de Givray, trans. Gilbert Adair (New York: Farrar, Straus and Giroux, 1990), 179. While working on a British-German co-production *The Blackguard* (*Die Prinzessin und der Geiger*) in 1924 at the Ufa studios in Neubabelsberg he observed Fritz Lang and F. W. Murnau at work. The experience was pivotal and his biographer Donald Spoto quotes Hitchcock: "My Models Were Forever after the German Filmmakers of 1924 and 1925," in *The Dark Side of Genius: The Life of Alfred Hitchcock* (New York: Ballantine, 1984), 74.

6 Jerrold E. Hogle (ed.), *The Cambridge Companion to the Modern Gothic* (Cambridge: Cambridge University Press, 2014), 7; 6.

7 See his *Haunting Modernity and the Gothic Presence in British Modernist Literature* (New York: Palgrave Macmillan, 2016). See also Andrew Smith and Jeff Wallace (eds.), *Gothic Modernisms* (Houndmills: Palgrave, 2001). Avril Horner and Sue Zlosnik provide a full account of du Maurier's relationship to the Gothic genre and the influence of the Bronte sisters. They suggest that her novels offer "interesting examples of how Gothic writing is inflected by both personal and broader cultural values and anxieties." See Avril Horner and Sue Zlosnik, *Daphne du Maurier: Writing, Identity and the Gothic Imagination* (London: Macmillan, 1988), 2.

8 John Paul Riquelme, "Modernist Gothic," in *The Cambridge Companion to the Modern Gothic*, ed. Jerrold E. Hogle (Cambridge: Cambridge University Press, 2014), 28.

9 Kim Wheatley, "Gender Politics and the Gothic in Alfred Hitchcock's *Rebecca*," *Gothic Studies* 4, no. 2 (2002): 134.

10 Indeed, despite Hitchcock's extensive location scouting no actual houses fitted his prerequisites and given that war in Europe had commenced and the script required a house both intact and in ruins a decision was made to recreate Manderley as a series of combined sets, miniatures and mattes. See Steven Jacobs, *The Wrong House: The Architecture of Alfred Hitchcock* (Rotterdam: 010, 2007), 178–9.

11 Jacobs, *The Wrong House*, 167.

12 Wheatley, "Gender Politics," 134.

13 For "primal scenes" in Rebecca, see John Fletcher, "Primal Scenes and the Female Gothic: *Rebecca* and *Gaslight*," *Screen* 36 (1995): 341–70.

14 Jacobs, *The Wrong House*, 192. Jacobs earlier describes the labyrinthine structure of Manderley as a form of "architectural elephantiasis" calling it "an exaggerated example of the most spectacular Victorian country houses," 81. Tania Modleski observes of "Fontaine's" relationship to the house: "she is continually dwarfed by the huge halls in which she wanders, and even the doorknobs are placed shoulder-level so that the viewer receives a subliminal impression of her as a child peeking in on or intruding into an adult world that provokes both curiosity and dread," *The Women Who Knew Too Much*, 47.

15 For Hitchcock's relationship with Hollywood and his first American producer, see Leonard J. Leff, *Hitchcock and Selznick: The Rich and Strange Collaboration of Alfred Hitchcock and David O. Selznick in Hollywood* (London: Weidenfeld and Nicholson, 1988). The whole of chapter 3 of Leff is devoted to *Rebecca*. For Hitchcock's own account, see "In the Hall of Mogul Kings," in *Hitchcock on Hitchcock: Selected Writings and Interviews*, ed. Sidney Gottlieb (Berkeley: University of California Press, 1995), 227–30. Also Thomas Schatz, *The Genius of the System: Hollywood Filmmaking in the Studio Era* (London: Faber and Faber, 1995). Chapters 15 and 20 deal with Hitchcock's relationship with Selznick.

16 Jacques Derrida, *The Instant of My Death/Demeure*, trans. Elizabeth Rottenberg (Stanford: Stanford University Press, 2000), 28: "There is no essence or substance of literature: literature is not. It does not exist."

17 Jacques Derrida, "Le cinéma et ses fantômes," *Cahiers du cinéma* 556 (2001): 75–85 [77–8] (my translation).

18 Derrida introduces the term "Hauntology," in *Specters of Marx: The State of the Debt, the Work of Mourning, and the New International*, trans. Peggy Kamuf (New York: Routledge, 1994), 10.

19 Rhona J. Bernstein, "'I'm Not the Sort of Person Men Marry': Monsters, Queers, and Hitchcock's *Rebecca*," in *Out in Culture: Gay, Lesbian and Queer Essays on Popular Culture*, ed. Cory C. Creekmur and Alexander Doty (Durham: Duke University Press, 1995), 239–61 [244].

20 Sarah Kay, *Žižek: A Critical Introduction* (Cambridge: Polity Press, 2003), 48.

21 Selznick quoted in Modleski, *The Women Who Knew Too Much*, 43.

22 Julian Wolfreys, *Victorian Hauntings: Spectrality, Gothic, the Uncanny and Literature* (Basingstoke: Palgrave Macmillan, 2002), xi.

23 Tom Cohen in his account of Hitchcock's unclaimed signifiers suggests the letter R also stands for "repetition," *Hitchcock's Cryptonomies 1* (Minneapolis: University of Minnesota Press, 2007), 7.

24 *Rebecca* (London and New York: British Film Institute, 2021), 41.

25 Laura Mulvey, "Visual Pleasure and Narrative Cinema," *Screen* 16, no. 3 (1975): 6–18. Reprinted in her *Visual and Other Pleasures* (Bloomington: Indiana University Press, 1989).

26 Oudart, Jean-Pierre, "Cinema and Suture," *Screen* 18, no. 4 (1977–78): 35–47.

27 Modleski, *The Women Who Knew Too Much*, 53. The film contains a telling comic ironic deflation of "visual pleasure": the line-up of the gazing eyes of the staff upon "Fontaine's" arrival at Manderley; Maxim declares to "Fontaine"

that his sister Beatrice "can't wait to look you over"; during the home movie scene "Fontaine" complains that "It is very difficult with people looking me up and down as if I were a prize cow."

28 I have been prompted to think about this scene by Neil Badmington's insightful close reading of it in his *Hitchcock's Magic* (Cardiff: University of Wales Press, 2011), 75–7.
29 Tania Modleski writes that the effect "dynamizes Rebecca's absence," *The Women Who Knew Too Much*, 50.
30 With viewers' hindsight we can read these "signs" as time ticking for the cancer-ridden Rebecca, dead flowers that counter the large vases of fresh flowers displayed throughout Manderley and, of course, Rebecca's boat scuttled on a storm-tossed sea.
31 Neil Badmington, *Hitchcock's Magic*, 77–8; 79. As Badmington also notes, Hitchcock will repeat a similar mechanics of murder eight years later in *Rope* when Rupert Cadell imagines the scenario of David Kentley's death, 81–3.
32 Note how this "double story" is also the structure and narrative twist of both *Vertigo* and *Psycho*.
33 Truffaut, *Hitchcock*, 127.
34 Modleski, *The Women Who Knew Too Much*, 43. For Patricia White Hitchcock's disavowal is to be read "in terms of his contentious yet productive relationship" with Selznick, *Rebecca*, 17.
35 Modleski, *The Women Who Knew Too Much*, 134.
36 Fredric Jameson, "The Vanishing Mediator; or, Max Weber as Storyteller," in *The Ideologies of Theory, Essays 1971–1986. Volume 2: The Syntax of History* (Routledge: London, 1988), 3–34.
37 Rex Butler, *Slavoj Žižek: Live Theory* (London: Continuum, 2005), 22.
38 "Is There a Proper Way to Remake a Hitchcock Film?" in *Hitchcock: Past and Future*, ed. Richard Allen and Sam Ishii-Gonzales (London: Routledge, 2004), 257–74 [267]. Patricia White offers two alternatives for the monogram to be engulfed in flames: "R is for Revenge," and "R is for Revenant," *Rebecca*, 75.
39 Žižek rejects the idea of modernism and postmodernism as consecutive stages of historical development: "'postmodernism' is rather the name for a regression, for a refusal to follow the consequences of the modernist break" (*LN*, 255).

10

Žižek's Redemptive Reading of Richard Wagner's Ambivalent Modernity

Erik M. Vogt

Theodor W. Adorno's publications[1] on the work of Richard Wagner constitute, according to Slavoj Žižek, a crucial shift in the history of Wagner interpretations. They develop a Marxist approach that endeavors to account for Wagner's music dramas as sites of societal antagonisms by means of micrological analyses of the complex structures of Wagnerian music (*WWWS*, viii). Moreover, Adorno's deciphering of Wagnerian art "as a monument to betrayed revolution, paradoxically combining the conservative rejection of capitalist modernity with formal elements of the very commodity fetishism he was fighting," reduces Wagner's anti-Semitism not to a "personal idiosyncrasy"; rather, Adorno's interpretation recognizes it "as a feature inscribed into the very artistic texture of his works" (*WWWS*, viii). Žižek recalls in that context that Adorno's later texts elaborate on the provocative thesis that Wagner's art is not fully determined by its layers of anti-Semitism and reactionary nationalism, but that one should consider it in terms of its innovative and progressive musical characteristics. Adorno's early texts on Wagner conduct an ideology critique that firmly inscribes Wagnerian artistic theory and practice into the (bourgeois-capitalist) landscape of fascism. However, the issue of ideology critique recedes in his later texts on Wagner; instead, they concentrate on the modern historicity of Wagnerian music, and they articulate the imperative to engage in experimental practices of interpretation and performance. Adorno's readings of Wagner work out the ambivalent modernity of Wagnerian art in terms of both its progressive and regressive aspects. It is this Adornian legacy of criticizing and rehabilitating Wagner to which Žižek intends to remain faithful in his own interpretations of Wagner that elaborate further on Wagner's ambivalent modernity.

Adorno's account of Wagnerian art is part of a larger project to conceptualize National Socialism that wards off any attempt at relativizing National Socialism as a mere historical accident and uncovers its origins in the fundamental process determining bourgeois-capitalist society. Adorno reads Wagner's overt anti-Semitism before the background of his ambivalent attitude toward bourgeois-capitalist society: an ambivalent attitude that combines masochistic appeals to pity on the part of the oppressors with sadistic tendencies to ridicule victims through cruel and violent humor. This ambivalent attitude becomes evident in figures such as Mime, Alberich, and Beckmesser that represent barely concealed anti-Semitic portraits of Jews. Wagner's anti-Semitism is articulated primarily via the quasi-natural categories of immediacy and Volk; it anticipates the constitutive elements of National Socialist anti-Semitism.[2] Death and annihilation (of the Jews) are operative in Wagner's fantasy of redemption; they are also present in the Wagnerian confounding of sexual pleasure and death that takes place in the name of some ascetic ideal: "Pleasure and death become one: Brünnhilde abandons herself at the end of Act III to her beloved Siegfried for a 'laughing death,' at the moment when she means to awaken and return to life, and Isolde, too, experiences her corporeal death as the 'highest bliss.'"[3] These regressive moments affect the technical structure of the Wagnerian music drama in many of its aspects: in its motivic and harmonic construction; in its instrumentation and amplification of the orchestral forces; in its development of new instruments and in its sonority; in its manipulation of time and its coercive integration of music, text, dramatic action, and stage into the new totality of the music drama[4] whose organizational form is that of phantasmagoria—a type of aesthetic semblance that exhibits the commodity character of the music drama and reduces the artwork to a mere object of consumption by concealing its production process.[5] Wagner's hyper-rational music drama reproduces the existing societal division of labor. At the same time, it generates an ecstatic phantasmagoria that is, however, overtaken by the fate of disintegration. It conjures away the negativity of both art and society by recognizing the antagonism of bourgeois-capitalist society and art; on the other hand, it substitutes society for the music drama and mythologically sacrifices individual autonomy to the collectivist forces of the societal status quo.

However, Wagner's use of myth and mythology contains an ideological-critical potential in that it renders the truth about the social fate of the individual and about the dominance of myth and law. Wagner's demonstration of the mythical character of the law in bourgeois-capitalist society suggests that "with this regression to myth, bourgeois society salutes itself by name in Wagner."[6] That is to say: "If in the *Ring* mythic violence and legal contract are confounded, this not only confirms an intuition about the origins of legality, it also articulates the experience of the lawlessness of a society dominated in the name of law by contact and property."[7] According to Adorno, Wagnerian art possesses relevance because it brings the delusional context of bourgeois-capitalist society to the surface; it lets emerge something new, once one realizes that certain layers of his work have historically receded. For instance, nationalism as one essential layer has been "cleared away . . . to see another emerge from underneath."[8] This is made possible by the fact that Wagnerian artworks are "not complete in themselves. They create a magnetic field of all possible intentions and forces, of inner tendencies and countervailing ones, of successful and necessarily unsuccessful ones. Objectively, new layers are constantly detaching themselves, emerging from within; others grow irrelevant and die off."[9] Any historicist approach to Wagnerian art must therefore be rejected. One can identify the new in Wagner only by means of a focus on the historicity of Wagner's work. This focus on historicity brings to the fore Wagner's modern musical nominalism and his art of transition; it also highlights the epic character of Wagner's art and its "temporal core" that can be adequately rendered only by interpretations and performances of Wagner's works that "force what is false, flawed, antinomical out into the open."[10] Consequently, one must bestow legitimacy on Wagnerian music as a prototype of modernity. This undertaking can be successful if one recognizes Wagner's musical techniques as devices that have generated fundamental structural transformations in music by means of which music has emancipated itself.

From Wagnerian Art's Proto-Fascism . . .

Žižek's fidelity to Adorno's reading of Wagner occurs in terms of a radicalized critique of historicist approaches to the issue of anti-Semitism in Wagner. It proceeds via the decontextualization of Wagner's music dramas so that one can decipher them as different failed structural configurations and variations containing the new in form of still unexplored potentialities. The emphasis on the Wagnerian music dramas as past failed attempts is supposed to question the historical totality named "Wagner": furthermore, it is supposed to show that the relevance of Wagnerian art is decided retroactively by its inscription into the symbolic network and that its relevance emerges from the impasses characterizing the different music dramas (*OSD*, 103). Žižek's basic hypothesis is that Wagner's sexualized politics provides the matrix for anti-Semitic proto-fascism. This anti-Semitic proto-fascism becomes discernible precisely in the way in which Wagner's work stages the relation of law and (erotic) transgression. But Wagner's sexualized politics provides the matrix for the concomitant perverse Christianity in *Parsifal*. This basic hypothesis enlists Adorno's ideological-critical analysis of the *Liebestod* in *Tristan and*

Isolde. Žižek's appropriation of Adorno's ideological-critical reading is, however, framed by the inscription of Wagnerian music into the tradition of romanticism. This tradition of (musical) romanticism is characterized by an inversion of the pre-romantic relationship between music and language in that music is not subordinated under language anymore; consequently, music now renders *jouissance* in such a manner that it can no longer be integrated into the symbolic universe. This shift in the relationship between music and language implies furthermore that music pretends to be (and gets elevated to) the *organon* of truth. Since it is at the same time nothing but the immediate expression of emotions and affects, its status as lie becomes apparent (*WAG*, 179)—a lie that also defines Wagner's music dramas and their phantasmatic satisfaction of the desire for the (allegedly) lost object. For this reason, Žižek's interpretations of Wagner do not ascribe to music the status of truth; rather, they suggest to "reverse the standard notion of the primacy of music in opera" (*WAG*, 180). Music assumes in Wagner the status of a "screen obfuscating the true message, which resides within the action on stage" (*WAG*, 180). One cannot therefore identify the truth-content of Wagnerian art in its music, but in its dramatic stage action and in the libretti. Dramatic stage action and the libretti subvert the passionate romanticist immersion into the musical texture often enforced by Wagner. In contrast to Adorno, Žižek locates Wagner's modernity not in the music of Wagner's music dramas, but in their dramatic stage actions and libretti. The modernist, subversive moments often manifest themselves in the long, epic narratives permeating Wagner's late music dramas; they interrupt the musical flow, and one should grasp them as symptoms of the failure of the very idea of *Gesamtkunstwerk* in that their artificiality belies the Wagnerian project of an organic art.[11]

The "fundamental matrix" of the Wagnerian music drama consists in "man's redemption through woman's willing self-sacrifice" (*TWIH*, 187). This Wagnerian fantasy concerning the sexual relationship contains the key for the political meaning of his work.[12] Wagner's phantasmatic rendition of woman's redemptive self-sacrifice constitutes a certain "pathology" (already identified by Adorno) to which both man and woman are subjected: While "the man to be delivered is no longer an innocent hero, but a suffering sinner, ... the woman, his redeemer, acquires the unmistakable features of hysteria, so that we obtain a kind of redoubled, mirrored fantasy" (*TWIH*, 188). The Wagnerian fundamental matrix of the suffering man condemned "to wander in the domain 'between the two deaths'" and woman's self-sacrifice appears at its purest already in *The Flying Dutchman*; one can also find it in *Parsifal*, Wagner's last work. Žižek suggests interpreting *Tristan and Isolde* as "the zero-level work ... and then to read the later works ... as the variations on this theme, as posts on the path of the disintegration of Tristan's unique synthesis that culminates in the much-celebrated *Liebestod* ... as its final resolution" (*OSD*, 105). This conceptualization of the *Liebestod* implies the recognition that the proverbial Wagnerian hero is a sinner who, due to having committed an unspeakable crime in the past, is condemned to lead an "undead" existence (*OSD*, 106). It also implies the necessity to work out the affinity between this "undead" existence and the Freudian death drive in that both represent the "uncanny excess of life" (*OSD*, 107). Accordingly, one can venture the claim that Wagner's music dramas revolve around this uncanny excess that "inscribes itself into the human body in the guise of a wound that renders the subject undead . . . ; when this wound is healed, the hero can die in peace" (*OSD*, 107). This linkage between undead existence and redemptive death illuminates the gesture shared by Tristan and Isolde: their embrace of "their disappearance into the abyss of nothingness as the climactic fulfillment of their love" (*OSD*, 113).

The *Liebestod* also exhibits the central feature of courtly love: it constitutes a transgression that suspends all socio-symbolic relations and culminates in ecstatic self-annihilation. *Tristan* is, however, not apprehended in an adequate manner through the transgressive *Liebestod*. This account fails to grasp the ways in which *Tristan*'s text and dramatic action undermine the fantasy of the *Liebestod*. Referencing Jean-Pierre Ponelle's Bayreuth production from 1983, Žižek illustrates his contention that the music of the finale of *Tristan* has the status of a lie. That is to say: In "music, it is as if the two lovers die together, whereas in reality, they die one after the other, each immersed in his or her own solipsistic dream" (*OSD*, 123). Repeated interruptions and allegedly external obstacles in *Tristan* mark the inherent impossibility of ecstatic immersion into the *Liebestod*. They also reveal Isolde's death as Tristan's own phantasmatic supplement—a supplement that indicates that the figure of Isolde is a male symptom, a male misogynistic fantasy serving as shield against female desire. Wagner's *Liebestod* constitutes an ideology of transgression falsely promising full satisfaction. One can interpret Wagner's adherence to transgression as recoil from hysteria and its consequences for the sake of clinging to the fantasy of the redemptive power of an unfettered sexual relationship (*OSD*, 134).

Wagner's fantasy of the possibility of the sexual relationship provides the framework for an account of his conception of politics, since his fantasy of woman as "the ground that bears man" (*OSD*, 138) entails the subordination of woman under the male order: "For that reason, the elevation of and subordination to the essential woman goes hand in hand with the exploitation of and domination over actual flesh-and-blood women" (*OSD*, 139). The finale of *Tristan* is a deceptive finale. The ecstatic self-annihilation of the two lovers based upon the false dichotomy between societal constraints and true love does not represent the truth of *Tristan*. In addition, Ponelle's production clearly shows that Isolde's love song addresses itself to a phantasmatic "third gaze" as the true object of this fantasy (*OSD*, 221). This phantasmatic scene is supported by a relation to the big Other, and the presence of the big Other explains why Wagner's *Tristan* is not yet "properly modern" (*OSD*, 221). The reference in Isolde's *Liebestod* to the big Other "in the guise of an ideal witness supposed to register what is going on" ultimately suggests that, for Wagner's *Tristan*, "the big Other still exists" (*OSD*, 221).

Wagner's sexualized politics can also account for the way in which *Parsifal*'s rendition of the relationship between society and community pretends to restore community against the alienated structures of society. The restoration of community is based upon a ritual with features indicating once more the (Wagnerian) "defense against the real of feminine desire" (*OSD*, 160). Žižek reiterates here Michel Poizat's account of *Parsifal* in terms of a narrative about the "closed incestuous community, immobilized by the *jouissance* of the privileged object-thing (Grail), which is derailed when Amfortas, its leader, succumbs to feminine seduction" (*OSD*, 160). Accordingly, the role of the figure of Parsifal consists in reconstituting this closed community by healing Amfortas's wound caused by Kundry. Kundry represents an artificial montage of "the devastating seductress and the angelic redemptrix" and renders possible "an imaginary solution that allowed Wagner to bring *Parsifal* to conclusion" (*OSD*, 163). This imaginary solution consists in Parsifal's identification with Amfortas's wound at the very moment in which he receives Kundry's kiss and then rejects her to heal Amfortas's wound. Parsifal's adherence to the Wagnerian fantasy of having the "wound healed only by the spear that smote it" explains why Parsifal misrecognizes Kundry's subject-position after the kiss. It also makes evident why his rejection of Kundry, a desiring woman in love with him, is but another iteration of the Wagnerian reduction of woman to a mere symptom of man. Wagner's imaginary solution is indicative of his inability to confront "the 'feminine' nature of Parsifal's identification with Amfortas at the moment of Kundry's kiss" (*TWIH*, 205); furthermore, Parsifal's succumbs to perversion, that is, to self-objectivation that involves a self-instrumentalization on behalf of the *jouissance* of the big Other. What is more, *Parsifal*'s circling around the *jouissance* of the big Other, that is, the obsession with the Grail containing Christ's blood, points to the origins of Wagner's anti-Semitism. These origins find expression in the rejection of the Jewish idea of the formal, empty law and in a type of perverse Christianity that is condensed into the Wagnerian syntagm that reads as follows: "the redemption of the redeemer!"[13] That is to say: "Christ does not have to die to redeem us. As such, Parsifal bears witness to a deep perturbation in the 'normal' relationship of life and death: the denial of the will to life, yet simultaneously the fantasy of a life beyond death" (*TWIH*, 208).

The political implications of Parsifal's perverse Christianity point to the fact that Parsifal's succession of Amfortas signifies the "the replacement of the traditional patriarchal authority by the totalitarian object-instrument of the Other's *jouissance*, the safekeeper of God's enjoyment (epitomized by the Grail)" (*TWIH*, 208). The reconstituted totalitarian Grail community is an anti-Semitic community. Parsifal's rejection of Kundry relies on the phantasmatic logic of the eternal feminine. Furthermore, it contains an anti-Semitic logic in that it represents Kundry as an external, corrupting, and destructive force standing in opposition to the totalized, organic unity of the Grail community and its enjoyment. That is, Kundry appears as a figure that wants to "steal" the enjoyment of the community; she wants to "steal" the very "Thing" that has allegedly been given to the Grail community for good; this "Thing" is presented as something that remains forever out of reach for Kundry *and* as something that is threatened by her. The construction of this external opposition between the Grail community and Kundry produces the fantasy that the Grail community is—or could be—devoid of antagonisms in that any possible or factual corruption can only occur from the outside. It is therefore only fitting that Parsifal, the "pure fool," constitutes nothing but the obverse of Kundry. His power of salvation and redemption also comes from outside the Grail community and serves as the exception that confirms the very fantasy supporting the male, anti-Semitic identity of the Grail community.

. . . To Its Implied Critical Theory of Fascism . . .

Do the fantasies of the *Liebestod*, of the lethal experience of transgression and of the self-enclosed male and anti-Semitic Grail community, represent Wagner's only approaches to the Real or is it possible to elaborate a different approach to the Real? One can find hints for a different Wagnerian approach to the Real in Žižek's critical engagement with Poizat's account of the true disturbance of the Grail community. In contrast to Poizat's reading, according to which the finale of Parsifal restores the equilibrium that was temporarily upset by Amfortas's desire for Kundry—a reading that falsely identifies Amfortas's wound as emblematic for symbolic castration and not for the "Real of an undead partial object" (*OSD*, 173)—Žižek locates the disturbance of the equilibrium in Titurel's fixation on the Grail, "the thing-*jouissance*" (*OSD*, 173). However, a profoundly different conception of the Real can be found in Wagner's tetralogy *The Ring of the Nibelung* and its presentation of the relationship between law and love.

Far from suggesting a simple unity or synthesis of law and love, Wagner's *Ring* examines this problematic relationship before the background of a crisis of public symbolic authority in the late nineteenth century. This crisis points to a split law that the *Ring* renders in the guise of the opposition between Wotan and Alberich, that is, the opposition between "contractual symbolic authority and the spectral, invisible master" (*OSD*, 136). Wagner's accomplishment consists in his recognition that the allegedly external opposition between Wotan and Alberich is in fact the opposition inherent to Wotan himself. In other words, the very gesture of establishing the rule of law contains within itself necessary violence. It is for this reason that the instituted law appears as wrong or crime. The narrative of the *Ring* that involves the violent establishment of the law proves to be a narrative about a violence that continues to haunt the legal order from within. The *Ring* presents (mythically) the violent and excessive funding gesture of the law within the world of contract and exchange instituted by Wotan; it also shows that Wotan's violent founding gesture is repeated by incidents such as Alberich's violent appropriation of the gold. Two conclusions follow from this state of affairs: On the one hand, Wagner recognizes that "the very balance of exchange is grounded on the disturbance of the primordial balance, on a traumatic loss that opens up the space of social exchange" (*OSD*, 136). On the other hand, Wagner still clings to the fantasy that one can restore the primordial balance, and this fact explains his—anti-Semitic—repudiation of bourgeois-capitalist society.

Although Wagner's ambivalence toward bourgeois-capitalist society constitutes the basis of his anti-Semitism, any full account of Wagnerian anti-Semitism must consider the fact that it is inscribed into modernity as the "the reign of exchange, . . . the dissolution of organic links and of modern industry and individuality" (*OSD*, 137). Since this aspect of modernity forms the crucial theme of the *Ring*, it is no longer possible to claim that Wagner's position is simply antimodern; rather, Wagner approaches modernity in a contradictory fashion—"he wants to enjoy its fruits while avoiding its disintegrative effects" (*OSD*, 137)— and this internal contradiction is externalized and projected onto the Jews. Consequently, one cannot derive Wagnerian anti-Semitism from an antimodern stance; rather, one should decipher it in terms of a (failed) synthesis of modernity and societal corporatism. The displaced reference of Wagnerian anti-Semitism to modernity can also explain why one should not mistake the *Ring* for a straightforward anti-Semitic treatise. One can demonstrate that Wagner construes the anti-Semitic figure of the "Jew" not as ultimate reference point but rather as "cipher of ideological and societal antagonisms (*WWWS*, xiv). This account of Wagnerian anti-Semitism in terms of an encoded cipher for the societal antagonisms that are presented *and* denied in his work entails the opportunity to read certain characters in Wagner's music dramas against the grain. That is to say, one can question their reductionist portraiture found both in the reactionary apologetic tradition typical of right-wing Wagner interpretations and in the denunciatory historicist tradition common among certain left-wing Wagner interpretations.[14] While the recognition of the split status of law and authority in Wagner sheds new light on Alberich as obscene figure of enjoyment, it can also account for Wagner's critical depiction of both Hagen as proto-fascist figure and of Siegfried as "inhuman monster" (*WWWS*, xv). More importantly, this reevaluation of the *Ring* can address the question of the origin and existence of evil in such a way that any anti-Semitic explanation is undermined by locating the origin of evil in Wotan himself (and no longer in Alberich). Thus, one can no longer account for the origin of evil in terms of an external opposition; one must recognize the external opposition as effect of an internal contradiction. This perspectival shift renders problematic the familiar anti-Semitic position, according to which the disturbance of corruption always occurs from outside via an alien body throwing out of joint the alleged equilibrium of the societal organism. The *Ring*'s depiction of the relationship between Wotan und Alberich—Alberich as the externalization of Wotan's immanent antagonism (*WWWS*, xviii)—renders tangible the immanent inconsistency of the law; that is, it depicts the law as a mere assemblage of rules; it demonstrates that the law is not-all since its own structuring principle eludes it. Incidentally, Žižek's resolution of the relationship between Wotan and Alberich in favor of Wotan betrays another affinity to Adorno in that Adorno interprets the *Ring* in a Hegelian manner as the narrative of Wotan's coming to self-consciousness.[15]

. . . And Pauline Redemption

How does the finale of the *Ring* relate to the other finales of *Tristan* and of *Parsifal*, that is, to the *Liebestod* and the reconstituted self-enclosed Grail community? Does it also exhibit phantasmatic features that would render it an imaginary and failed finale? Žižek follows the hypothesis submitted by Philip Kitcher and Richard Schacht,[16] according to which one should understand the tetralogy of the *Ring* in terms of a series of existential projects that, although different from each other, constitute failures. After expounding the failed finales of *Rheingold*, *Walküre*, and *Siegfried* (*WC*, 71–3), he engages with the finale of *Götterdämmerung* to determine whether this finale is part of the series of Wagner's failed attempts at redemption. Recall that *Meistersinger* expresses the impossibility of the sexual relationship in (resigned) marriage, while *Tristan* and *Parsifal* render it as *Liebestod* and as asexual compassion (*WAG*, 195). The finale of *Götterdämmerung* sticks out in that it brings about a genuine "solution to the deadlock, in the guise of Brünnhilde's act"; that is, her self-immolation must be identified as "a gesture of supreme freedom and autonomy" (*WAG*, 195–6).

But in what sense is Brünnhilde's self-immolation an act? Does it not represent a mere *suicidal passage à l'acte*? Is it not simply another variation on the fantasy of female sacrificial death that one encounters repeatedly in Wagner? Can one even claim that there is a difference between Brünnhilde' end and that of Isolde? According to Žižek, the constitutive difference between Isolde's death and Brünnhilde's self-immolation is the following one: while Isolde's death is nothing but the hallucinatory product of the dying Tristan, that is, a male fantasy, one should conceptualize Brünnhilde's self-immolation as an act by means of which Brünnhilde's love for Siegfried is neither a hallucination nor a disavowal but constitutes a veritable transformation. This transformed (act of) love both preserves and goes beyond her failed erotic love for Siegfried and discloses the possibility for Brünnhilde to become "all-knowing."[17] To be more precise, Brünnhilde gains the" highest knowledge" through Siegfried's betrayal: "The purest had to betray me, so that a woman becomes knowing!" (*WAG*, 209). One should approach his correlation between the acquisition of the "highest knowledge" and betrayal via the "motif of renunciation" that is "the most important leitmotif in the entire tetralogy" (*WAG*, 209); it also articulates the crucial linkage between love and power, albeit in a distorted fashion. Fully reconstructed, this linkage becomes legible as the following sentence: "Love's highest need is to renounce its own power" (*WAG*, 211). This sentence announces that a crucial shift regarding the status of love has occurred. One passes from erotic love in which the love relation is usually posited as direct goal to a different kind of love. This different kind of love subjects the fantasy of love as self-annihilation (in *Tristan*) and the psychotic rejection of love (in *Parsifal*) to a radical critique. What is more, it renders visible—before the background of "the failure of the intense sexual relationship"—a love "which says yes to all passing, but no less sublime, human achievements" (*WAG*, 212).

It is via Brünnhilde's act of love that the *Ring* enters the territory of "authentic" Christianity and its specific conception of the relationship between law and love. Žižek suggests that the finale of *Götterdämmerung* contains the contours of a Christian Wagner. The motif of redemption exhibits even an affinity with St. Paul's notion of love. Both Wagner and St. Paul conceive love as a necessary supplement. Žižek employs this affinity between Brünnhilde and St. Paul as an opportunity to put forth his speculative conclusion, according to which Brünnhilde's version of Pauline love might be stated in the following manner: "If I am the most natural innocent living being, but do not have love, I am nothing; if I am the greatest law-giver, but do not have love, I am nothing; if I am the greatest hero, but do not have love, I am nothing. Now abide natural innocence, law, and heroism; but greater than these three is love" (*WAG*, 220). Consequently, the *Ring* is a Pauline work since its central issue consists "in the failure of the rule of Law, and the shift that best encompasses the inner span of the *Ring* is the shift from Law to love" (*WAG*, 222). In other words, Wagner's *Ring* overcomes the ideology of erotic love as paradigm of love and accomplishes the shift from "*eros* to *agape*" (*WAG*, 222) and from perverse Christianity to authentic Christianity. Wagner's authentic Christianity is no longer caught in the vicious cycle of law and transgression. It reveals the split or antagonism of the law in the law (and in society) without recourse to an obscene, phantasmatic supplement. It no longer operates within the matrix of an external conflict between the law and a transcendent Other; rather, it operates within the matrix of an always-already existing minimal split of the universal law with itself, of an antagonism inscribed in this universal law itself. This results not in a universal law and its exception or transgression but in an antagonistic universal. It is this insight, according to which modern law and society are inherently antagonistic and "Other-less," that manifests the dimension of Pauline's political love. In Pauline's political love, the rule of law appears as "not-all": it displays the impossibility of the law to claim its self-immanence via the construction of an Outside, that is, via an exception. The relationship between the rule of law and the act of Pauline love—of Pauline love as enactment of an abyssal self-referential gesture enabling the "not-all" of the Symbolic Law—points to a new configuration of the relation between universal rule of law and exception. One can conceive of it as an endless process of self-enclosure and self-application of the logic of exception. This process renders visible the contours of Pauline's political love understood as an endless and constantly divisive struggle for a transformation of the law from within.

Brünnhilde's self-immolation, the genuine finale of the *Ring* redeeming the imaginary finales of *Rheingold*, *Walküre*, and *Siegfried*, contains even Christ-like traits "in the precise sense that Christ's death marks the birth of the Holy Spirit, the community of believers linked by *agape*" (WAG, 224). As agent of political love, Brünnhilde opens the space for the possibility of organizing an emancipatory and egalitarian collective. Žižek interprets the human crowd silently watching and surviving the catastrophe in terms of a community of believers no longer finding (or seeking) support or guarantee in God or a big Other. It is an abandoned human collective hearing the motif of redemption without a clearly established message. This means that the finale of *Götterdämmerung* does not guarantee "redemption-through-love: redemption is merely possible" (WAG, 225). Brünnhilde's act represents "the openness of a New Beginning, and it is up to humanity to live up to it, to decide its meaning, to make something of it" (WAG, 225). Incidentally, Žižek's Pauline reading of the finale of the *Ring* has also consequences for his account of *Parsifal*. While his early interpretation deciphers the Grail community as an anti-Semitic collective disavowing its own internal antagonism by externalizing it in form of the figure of Kundry, his rereading claims not only that the Grail community represents an authentic Christian community, but also that *Parsifal* "logically follows the Ring" (WWWS, xxvii). That is, *Parsifal* accomplishes the transition from the nameless and anonymous crowd surviving the final of the Ring to the self-organization of a new human political collective. In this respect, Žižek even suggests the possibility of interpreting *Parsifal* as a dramatic anticipation of Bertolt Brecht's learning plays (WS, 56–64).[18]

Finally, the finale of the *Ring* suggests once more that Wagner's art is grounded in modernity. The invocation of an abandoned human collective as finale of *Götterdämmerung* marks the moment in which Wagner's art decisively forgoes any attempt to provoke the answer of the big Other—of God or the eternal feminine—or to rely on the guarantee of the big Other; instead, it accepts the nonexistence of the big Other. Moreover, Wagner's aesthetics of contamination bears witness to the modernity of his art.[19] Irrespective of Wagner's own intentions of purity and purification, his music dramas repeatedly repudiate a "pure" reconciliation of content and form. Their excessive dimension imposes itself as stain of the repressed onto the musical form; this stain of the repressed disturbs Wagner's conjured harmonious finales that confound redemption with purification.

Notes

1. These publications include *In Search of Wagner*. With a new foreword by Slavoj Žižek; trans. Rodney Livingstone (London: Verso, 2009) and "Wagner's Relevance for Today," in Theodor W. Adorno, *Essays on Music*. Selected, with Introduction, Commentary and Notes by Richard Leppert; trans. Susan H. Gillespie (Berkeley: University of California Press, 2002), 584–602. In addition, there are other essays on Wagner in Adorno, *Gesammelte Schriften 13*, ed. Rolf Tiedemann (Frankfurt: Suhrkamp, 1997), 497–504, and in Adorno, *Gesammelte Schriften 18*, 204–9; 210–25.

2. Adorno, *In Search of Wagner*, 16. I paraphrase here some of the defining characteristics of Wagnerian anti-Semitism that Adorno identifies at the beginning of his text.

3. Adorno, *In Search of Wagner*, 4.

4. Adorno, *Gesammelte Schriften 13*, 497. Adorno does not strictly distinguish between the notions of music drama and total work of art. For a succinct account of this crucial distinction, see Udo Bermbach, *Der Wahn des Gesamtkunstwerks* (Weimar: Metzler Verlag, 2004), 210–15.

5. Adorno, *In Search of Wagner*, 74–5.

6. Adorno, *In Search of Wagner*, 108.

7. Adorno, *In Search of Wagner*, 108.

8. Adorno, "Wagner's Relevance for Today," 585.

9. Adorno, "Wagner's Relevance for Today," 587.

10. Adorno, "Wagner's Relevance for Today," 600.

11. Žižek shows that these epic narratives often follow the performative logic of declaratives (*WC*, 81).

12. For the relationship between sexuality and politics in Mozart, see Mladen Dolar's claim that "in Mozart's operas, all politics is sexual politics" (*OSD*, 43).

13. For a detailed account of the relationship between Judaism and (perverse) Christianity, see Erik M. Vogt, "Das Christentum als Religion des Atheismus. Žižek's materialistische Lektüre des Christentums," in *Wieder Religion?*, ed.

Marc de Kesel and Dominiek Hoens (Vienna: Turia + Kant, 2006), 199–219. See also Erik M. Vogt, *Slavoj Žižek und die Gegenwartsphilosophie* (Wien: Turia Kant, 2011), 21–39.

14   One example for the latter is Marc A. Weiner's book *Richard Wagner and the Anti-Semitic Imagination* (Lincoln: University of Nebraska Press, 1997).

15   For a discussion of the monistic versus dualistic resolution of the relationship between Wotan and Alberich, see Johanna Dombois and Richard Klein, *Richard Wagner und seine Medien* (Stuttgart: Klett-Cotta, 2012), 157–94.

16   Philip Kitcher and Richard Schacht, *Finding an Ending: Reflections on Wagner's Ring* (Oxford: Oxford University Press, 2004).

17   For a critical reading of Brünnhilde's self-immolation as act, see Dombois and Klein, *Richard Wagner und seine Medien*, 173.

18   Žižek's rereading of *Parsifal* is influenced by Alain Badiou's account of *Parsifal* and its focus on the question of political ceremony. See Alain Badiou, *Five Lessons on Wagner*, trans. Susan Spitzer. With an afterword by Slavoj Žižek (London–New York: Verso, 2010), 135–59. For a summarizing commentary on Badiou's reading of *Parsifal*, see Erik M. Vogt, *Ästhetisch-Politische Lektüren zum 'Fall Wagner'* (Vienna – Berlin: Turia + Kant, 2015), 224–50.

19   For an account of the Wagnerian aesthetics of contamination from the perspective of Jacques Rancière, see Erik M. Vogt, *Zwischen Sensologie und ästhetischem Dissens* (Vienna – Berlin: Turia + Kant, 2019), 119–72.

11

Žižek's Critique of the Authoritarian Personality

Geoff Boucher

The global resurgence of authoritarian populism has sparked renewed interest in the classical Frankfurt School work on the authoritarian personality, especially Adorno's contribution.[1] It has also drawn attention to recent research that measures the prevalence of right-wing authoritarian attitudes in society and relates these to political allegiances. According to veteran authoritarianism researcher Bob Altemeyer, who represents a post-classical continuation of Adorno's classical work, right-wing authoritarians represent a genuine threat to democracy.[2] Alarmingly, global surveys indicate that right-wing authoritarians represent a durable 10 percent–15 percent of the population of every country.[3] In the United States, this figure might be as high as 18 percent of adults, with an additional 23 percent of adults rating as having "moderate" sympathy for authoritarian attitudes.[4] The disturbing fact that 41 percent of Americans are potentially sympathetic to authoritarian politics indicates a significant potential constituency for a populist leader with some authoritarian policies. Indeed, that figure is highly suggestive in light of Donald Trump's electoral performance in 2016 and 2020. Readers will not be surprised to learn that the best predictor of a vote for Trump was a high score on the right-wing authoritarianism (RWA) scale.[5]

A persistent question raised by both classical (Adorno) and post-classical (Altemeyer) research, however, concerns the political influence of right-wing authoritarians. Authoritarian personalities represent a small minority of the total population, yet under conditions of social dislocation, they are capable of winning political power. Why? Intuitively speaking, it seems clear that the authoritarian personalities "convert" moderates into authoritarians. Not surprisingly, classical research focused on political anxiety as a gateway into acceptance of fascist propaganda.[6] But how is this supposed to work? Both classical and post-classical research present a static conception of the authoritarian personality as a durable syndrome that originates in childhood. The problem with this is that you cannot convert someone from a moderate into an authoritarian if this requires retrofitting a personality structure that begins with the relation to the parents. For this reason, Adorno developed an ingenious—but implausible—theory: the authoritarian personality is the hidden structure of the modern individual; fascist propaganda merely activates this latent disposition.[7] Somewhat more plausibly, Altemeyer points to processes of resocialization that happen in authoritarian enclaves.[8] But what makes a moderate susceptible to resocialization in the first place?

In this chapter, I present a Žižekian interpretation of the authoritarian personality that I think provides intellectually satisfying, sociologically plausible, and politically effective answers to these urgent questions. In the process, I explain how Žižek's Lacanian theorization of the authoritarian personality represents a modernist rethinking of Adorno's classical synthesis of Marx and Freud. By reframing the authoritarian personality, not as a "sado-masochistic character," but as a perverse form of subjective structuration, Žižek foregrounds a psychodynamic model of authoritarian subjectivity, one that is driven by anxiety. On this reading, perverse subjectivity is not a fixed "thing," or a static "character," but represents a subject-position adopted in response to heightened anxiety, one that depends on the defense mechanism of denial (or disavowal): "I am not a racist, but . . . " Within Lacanian theory, the mechanisms of repression, disavowal, and foreclosure are increasingly regressive responses to the anxiety caused by what Žižek calls "enjoyment," a transgressive and excessive desire "beyond the pleasure principle." When the subject is overwhelmed, rising anxiety triggers the resort to regressive defenses, shifting the subject-position of the individual and making them susceptible to entirely new ideological conceptions about social reality. But this depends in turn upon the breakdown of that socio-symbolic authority which is supposed to hold transgressions in check. The resort to regressive defense mechanisms is always accompanied by the subject's perception that "society is falling apart" because "authority is disintegrating" and "transgressions are everywhere." Perverse subjectivity, then, or the "authoritarian personality," revolves upon a shifting relationship between authority, transgression, and anxiety, within which the effort of the pervert (i.e., the authoritarian) is to commit a supreme transgression in order to *make*, to force, a potent authority into existence.

The Frankfurt School's Discovery of the Authoritarian Personality

According to the classical position of Adorno and cothinkers, the authoritarian personality is a "syndrome," consisting of covariant social attitudes, the presence of which predicts aversive prejudices. Authoritarian personalities exhibit:

- rigid conventionalism—a prescriptive adherence to existing social norms and institutional regulations;
- authoritarian submission—a submissive attitude of unquestioning obedience toward established authorities;
- authoritarian aggression—a punitive attitude toward designated out-groups and critics of conventions.[9]

Additionally, authoritarian personalities regard the world as a dangerous place and deal with this with stereotyping and superstition. They characteristically have destructive feelings and a fascination with sexual degeneracy. They also tend to be unimaginative and lack empathy. Adorno's explanation for this syndrome invoked an Oedipal scenario involving the disciplinarian father, cold mother, and a culture of stereotypes.[10] He hinted that the resulting sadomasochistic character was in actuality the underlying structure of the modern individual. Yet Adorno admitted that the genuine authoritarians in the Frankfurt School's survey represented less than 25 percent of the sample.[11] The dialectical gymnastics that he engaged in to make this tiny minority into a "virtually universal . . . personality structure" can be set aside as unconvincing.

It is crucial to notice the importance of economic collapse, political paralysis, and class struggle in the Frankfurt School's explanation of classical fascism. Adorno and cothinkers did not for a moment deny the Marxist interpretation of fascism as a counter-revolutionary mass movement that arises in a social crisis. Despite its "anticapitalist" rhetoric, fascism is a militarization of politics that aims at the restoration of order, which means, it is a pro-capitalist stabilization of the class basis of society. The Frankfurt School invoked Freud to explain how such a politics could possibly recruit masses from the middle strata (especially the white-collar employees), winning them away their enlightened self-interest—which is to support social transformation by mass egalitarian parties. Fascism's ultra-nationalist ideology mobilizes aversive prejudices to designate "enemies of society" who can be destroyed with impunity, and its propaganda has a noticeably irrational tenor, filled with logical contradictions and conspiracy theories. The irrationality of fascist ideology suggests an unconscious component that the psychoanalytic thinkers in the Frankfurt School traced to the structures of paternal authority in the modern, middle-class family.

[The authoritarian personality] follows the "classic" psychoanalytic pattern involving a sadomasochistic resolution of the Oedipus complex, [as] pointed out by Erich Fromm under the title of the "sadomasochistic" character. According to Max Horkheimer's theory . . . in order to achieve "internalization" of social control which never gives as much to the individual as it takes, the latter's attitude towards authority and its psychological agency, the superego, assumes an irrational aspect. The subject achieves his own social adjustment only by taking pleasure in obedience and subordination. This brings into play the sadomasochistic impulse structure both as a condition and as a result of social adjustment. In our form of society, sadistic as well as masochistic tendencies actually find gratification. The pattern for the translation of such gratifications into character traits is a specific resolution of the Oedipus complex which defines the formation of the syndrome here in question. Love for the mother, in its primary form, comes under a severe taboo. The resulting hatred against the father is transformed by reaction-formation into love. This transformation leads to a particular kind of superego. . . . In the psychodynamics of the "authoritarian character," part of the preceding aggressiveness is absorbed and turned into masochism, while another part is left over as sadism, which seeks an outlet in those with whom the subject does not identify himself: ultimately the outgroup.[12]

Among an important minority of the population, then, an unconsciously ambivalent relation to the disciplinarian father forms, which leads to a personality structure that at once resents and craves strong authority, and which clings to the rules that provide order, as a defense against the terrifying temptation of forbidden desire. Fascist propaganda, for instance, represents designated out-groups as engaged in transgressive enjoyment that urgently deserves the strictest punishment, but it also, paradoxically and irrationally, insists that the restoration of order can legitimately include the enactment of forbidden desires against the persons of these "enemies of society." Although not all authoritarians are fascists (because most authoritarian personalities under normal circumstances are conscious of the potential consequences of subversive actions), the authoritarian personality gravitates toward aversive prejudices and believes that violence is legitimate. According to Adorno and cothinkers, therefore, the authoritarian personality is a proto-fascist character structure, typically produced by the familial circumstances of a certain class milieu, one whose activation by right-wing agitators depends on two essential conditions: social crisis; and, fascist propaganda.

The contemporary RWA research of Bob Altemeyer and cothinkers represents a post-classical extension of the classical framework of the authoritarian personality.[13] Altemeyer's research is solidly grounded in empirical data, which shows that the authoritarian personality is an authentic discovery in social science.[14] However, Altemeyer is neutral about psychoanalytic explanations, grounding subjective structure in social learning, especially styles of socialization.[15] Adorno routinely speaks of "strict discipline, lack of cathexis and stereopathy," reflecting the strict father, cold mother, and defenses against "deviant" desires, respectively.[16] By contrast, Altemeyer's work describes a syndrome of authoritarian aggression, authoritarian submission, and rigid conventionalism and is agnostic about whether this is the result of Oedipal dynamics or some other process.[17] According to research following Altemeyer, authoritarian personalities represent between 10 percent and 15 percent of the population in the developed world.[18] Altemeyer documents the aversive prejudices, belief in the legitimacy of violence, hostility toward mass society, and democratic politics, that make authoritarian personalities a genuine threat to democracy.[19] Fortunately, authoritarian politics and religious fundamentalism compete for recruits within the same pool, and, until recently, religious fundamentalism has tended to isolationism rather than interventionism.[20] Furthermore, authoritarian parties tend to be fissile, because the tendency to militarize every disagreement into us/them polarization does not promote organizational longevity, as the history of fascist parties and authoritarian movements in the United States and Canada demonstrates.[21] Finally, disturbingly, authoritarian movements are often led by pathologically narcissistic and sociopathic variants of the authoritarian personality. Altemeyer has discovered that "double high" combinations of the "Social Dominance Orientation" with RWA represent the pathology of choice for would-be American Hitlers.[22]

The Authoritarian Personality as Perverse Subjectivity

Although Žižek is in general highly critical of the Frankfurt School, in his critique of the category of "totalitarianism," Žižek develops a concept of perverse subjectivity that is effectively coextensive with the concept of the authoritarian personality. However, Žižek's rethinking of the subjectivity behind authoritarianism represents a modernist rethinking of the authoritarian personality that is relational and dynamic, rather than essentialist and static, something that flows from his use of Lacan's reformulation of Freud. What Žižek shows is that the key to the authoritarian personality is not an individual's family background, but rather, the changing relationship between political anxiety, transgressive enjoyment, and social authority, and the way that this affects different subjects.

From the Žižekian perspective, the authoritarian personality involves a perverse structuration that may be described as a proto-totalitarian subjectivity. In light of the fact that Žižek rejects the term "totalitarian," that might seem a strange claim. What Žižek is refusing, however, in critiquing the term totalitarianism, is the ideological phobia toward radical politics that liberalism develops as a defense mechanism—the idea that *every* politics goes beyond negative liberty and parliamentary democracy necessarily leads to Auschwitz or Siberia. Žižek rejects the false dichotomy of liberalism or totalitarianism. His entire work is dedicated to developing an alternative to this dichotomy. Not for a moment, though, does Žižek deny that *some* forms of radical politics (for instance, Stalinism and Nazism) *do* result in the gulag or the camps. On the one hand, it is urgent that the left fully grasp the nature of right-wing authoritarian politics and the threat that it poses today. On the other hand, in opposing RWA, it is crucial that the Left does not fall into the trap of proposing left-wing authoritarianism. In reality, then, some of Žižek's most penetrating insights into perverse subjectivity happen in the context of an analysis of the same regimes that liberalism describes as totalitarian. Against the background of Altemeyer's finding on religious fundamentalism as the "other authoritarian personality," it is significant that the rest of Žižek's pointed insights into perverse subjectivity happen in the context of his analysis of Christian theology.

As Žižek describes it, in the political field, perverse subjectivity involves rigid conventionalism, authoritarian aggression, and unquestioning obedience toward leader figures—exactly the characteristics of the authoritarian personality. Discussing Lacan's article "Kant avec Sade," Žižek points out that the Sadeian executioner rigidly implements a (deviant) set of social norms, a supposed Highest Good, acting as a superegoic figure of the enforcement of conventions, and taking no pleasure whatsoever in this exercise of this "moral duty" (*TK*, 232–3). As in the Nazi criminal Adolph Eichmann's defense that he was a good Kantian, unquestioningly obeying the legitimate instructions of the Führer, the pervert's sadistic aggression is "justified" as the mere execution of a merited punishment (*TK*, 230–1). This submissive relation to authority is the necessary complement to unrestricted aggression against designated out-groups, because the pervert has in fact completely abdicated moral reasoning and become the passive instrument for the implementation of the Highest Good as defined by the supreme leader. "The Sadeian executioner," Žižek concludes, "works for the enjoyment of the Other, not for his own: he becomes a sole instrument of the Other's Will. And, in so-called 'totalitarianism,' this illegal agent-instrument of the law, the Sadeian executioner, appears as such, in the shape of the Party, agent-instrument of historical Will" (*TK*, 234).

Žižek's general theory of the authoritarian personality recognizes that the rigid enforcement of conventions does not necessarily mean conformity to mainstream social norms. This is because the regulations in question are those that govern the authoritarian pervert's irrational beliefs about social order and transgressive enjoyment. According to the pervert, social order is threatened by transgressive enjoyment that is enacted by marginalized groups, who are "undermining society." The pervert's response is to "make it stop," by performing a "supreme crime" designed to force into existence the social prohibitions required to utterly quash this transgressive enjoyment. In the sadistic form of perversion that generates RWA, this supreme crime involves enacting transgressive enjoyment upon the marginalized groups themselves. Žižek summarizes this with extraordinary economy as the thesis that perverse subjectivity involves becoming the "instrument for the enjoyment of the Other," in an effort to disavow the "non-existence of the Other." Žižek supports this interpretation with a key statement from Lacan, which indicates that perversion "is an inverted effect of the phantasy" that screens the nonexistence of the Other (*HRL*, 105 Lacan cited). In perversion, the subject positions themself as an object for the enjoyment of the Other, in a strategy designed to simultaneously avoid subjective division and guarantee the fullness of the Other (*HRL*, 105). He then goes on to maintain that "this passage throws a new light on political totalitarianism":

> When confronted with the task of liquidating the Jews of Europe, Heinrich Himmler, the chief of SS, adopted the heroic attitude of "Somebody has to do the dirty job, so let's do it!": it is easy to do a noble thing for one's country, up to sacrificing one's life for it—it is much more difficult to commit a crime for one's country. . . . My violation of spontaneous ethical instincts of pity and compassion is turned into the proof of my ethical grandeur: to do my duty, I am ready to assume the heavy burden of inflicting pain on others. (*HRL*, 105–6)

In the masochistic form of perversion constitutive of left-wing authoritarianism, the supreme crime involves the incitement of authority to enact this transgressive enjoyment upon the subject, who places themselves in the position of "traitor" and "saboteur." Žižek continues:

> A true Stalinist politician loves mankind, but nonetheless performs horrible purges and executions—his heart is breaking while he is doing it, but he cannot help it, it is his Duty towards the Progress of Humanity. This is the perverse attitude of adopting the position of the pure instrument of the big Other's Will: it is not my responsibility, it is not me who is effectively doing it, I am merely an instrument of the higher Historical Necessity. The obscene [enjoyment] of this situation is generated by the fact that I conceive of myself as exculpated for what I am doing: I am able to inflict pain on others with the full awareness that I am not responsible for it, that I merely fulfil the Other's Will. (*HRL*, 105)

Thus, in both cases, the pervert enjoys the very transgressive enjoyment that they claim to suppress, and they do so in the name of making themselves into the instrument of "vengeance," or "justice," against the supposed "transgressors."

The Logic of Fetishism

According to Žižek, then, the central characteristic of totalitarian subjectivity is perverse self-instrumentalization. This effort to become the instrument for the Other is something visible in fundamentalism, Hitlerism, and Stalinism. The pervert strives to become the instrument that guarantees the existence of the Other, while at the same time, and in contradiction with this aim, forcing an articulation of the Symbolic Law, as if the Other needed to be made to exist. Indeed, the defense mechanism of disavowal (also known as denial) is all about that performative contradiction, something whose formula has been expressed by Octave Mannoni: "I know all very well that . . . but nonetheless, I continue to assert that . . ."[23] In his work on totalitarianism, Žižek develops Mannoni's insights into a Lacanian political theory. This makes possible a typology of totalitarian subjectivity, which can be used to map these styles of the authoritarian personality onto fetishism, sadism, and masochism. The example of fundamentalism involves fetishism, but it illustrates the basic dynamic for all forms of totalitarian perversion:

> The perverse solution forms the very core of "actually existing Christianity": with modernity proper, we can no longer rely on the pre-established dogma to sustain our freedom, on the pre-established Law/Prohibition to sustain our transgression—this is one way of reading Lacan's thesis that the big Other no longer exists. Perversion is a double strategy to counteract this nonexistence: an (ultimately deeply conservative and nostalgic) attempt to install the Law artificially, in the desperate hope that it will then take this self-posited limitation "seriously," and, in a complementary way, a no less desperate attempt to codify the very transgression of the law. In the perverse reading of Christianity, God first threw humanity into Sin in order to create the opportunity for saving it through Christ's sacrifice. (*PD*, 53)

In fundamentalism, the Other is God. The fundamentalist maintains that humanity wallows in sinfulness, just as if divine law were mere imagination, the holy text a psychotic delusion and God did not exist. Nonetheless, the fundamentalist vigorously affirms that God exists and that humanity will be judged according to divine law, as set forth in the holy text. Accordingly, the fundamentalist expends extraordinary energy on a literal interpretation of scripture. This is a (fetishistic) strategy to *make* God exist, through the conversion, the transformation, of the believer into an instrument of divine will. Now, the God of fundamentalism demands from the believers that, in order for some to be saved, the believers must ruthlessly consign the entirety of humanity to the category of reprobate sinners destined for hellish punishments. Accordingly, the fundamentalist highlights the depravity and worthlessness of human beings, their ecstatic writhing in a cesspool of sin, and insists that everyone's protestations of innocence are evidence of their monstrous secret crimes. Although the fundamentalist maintains that they do everything possible to hasten the advent of the end times, which will bring to a stop the spectacle of humanity flagrantly violating the Ten Commandments, in reality, they dread the terrifying pronouncement of God's judgment on the sinfulness of the believer themselves. Against this background, the fundamentalist's ritualized observance of a literal interpretation of the holy text—their rigid conformity to divine decrees—actually acts as an avoidance mechanism. Each jot and tittle of the law is collected and curated as if it had the magical property that it anticipated the annihilating moment of God's judgment—that is, the fetishization of the holy text provides a guarantee for the existence of the Other.

Žižek also uses fundamentalism to illustrate the economy of sacrifice at work in perverse subjectivity, and its relation to authority. The pervert regards themselves as called upon to make a terrible sacrifice to the Other (*DSST*, 44–54). To placate the Other, sometimes the pervert sacrifices themselves, hoping that their suffering might provoke a manifestation of the Law. Alternatively, the pervert sacrifices the other, again hoping that the suffering of the victim will provoke a manifestation of the Law. In the context of totalitarianism, Žižek returns to the *Akedah*, the traumatic scene of the commandment by God to Abraham to sacrifice Isaac, common to Judaism, Christianity, and Islam, to clarify the idea of self-instrumentalization as involving a perverse sacrifice to the "dark god" (*DSST*, 44–5; 102–8). The pervert cannot accept that authority can be founded on a symbolic substitute for real sacrifice, because this removes the guarantee that the Other exists; instead, the pervert carries out the sacrifice as an alternative to the symbolic pact. A perverse Abraham, instead of letting the angel intervene to prevent the sacrifice of Isaac, would mercilessly go through with the deadly ritual slaughter, in order to make certain that God exists. A perverse Isaac would insist on, would provoke, the sacrificial ritual. This is equivalent to saying that the anxiety aroused in the pervert by the possibility of the nonexistence of the Other is absolutely intolerable, for self-instrumentalization and the logic of sacrifice (as well as the fetish) are defense mechanisms that are evoked by the proximity of the Real (i.e., anxiety). As Žižek analyses the modality of authority that belongs to fetishism:

> [F]etishism *strictu sensu* [is] the matrix of *totalitarian authority*: the point is no longer that the other ("ordinary people") would be deceptively manipulated, but that we are ourselves those who—although we "know very well" that we are people like others—at the same time consider ourselves to be "people of a special mould, made of special stuff"—as individuals who participate in the fetish . . . [the] direct embodiment of the Will of the [Other]. . . . The breach between cynicism and totalitarian[ism]

can be illustrated by different attitudes to the experience that "the Emperor has no clothes." ... The totalitarian too does not believe in the symbolic fiction, in his version of the Emperor's clothes; he knows very well that the Emperor is naked ... but *just because* the Emperor is naked we must hold together the more, work for the Good, out Cause is all the more necessary ... (*TK*, 251–2).

For the pervert, traditional authority has collapsed—it is a mere symbolic fiction that no longer conceals the fact that everybody is enjoying forbidden transgressions, starting with designated out-groups and extending to authority figures themselves. Indeed, the fundamentalist knows very well that the authority figures involved in the logic of sacrifice—for instance, the fundamentalist preacher who calls for the cleansing of society, or the reactionary president who manipulatively invokes millenarian expectations—are corrupt and mendacious. But for that very reason, it is necessary to vigorously execute the sacrificial victims. When this logic of sacrifice and authority shifts locus from mythology to history, in political perversions, it becomes extraordinarily destructive.

Totalitarian Perversions

In Hitler's Nazism, the Other is the Aryan Race and its manifest superiority. By contrast, in Stalinist communism, the Other is the Historical Necessity of communist society. In his work on totalitarianism, Žižek's discussion of both Nazism and communism exhibits their commonalities before making an argument about their differences (*DSST*, 61–87 and 88–140). Intriguingly, for Žižek, unlike Adorno, instead of RWA, it is *left-wing* authoritarianism that is paradigmatic—think of

> a Stalinist Communist who loves humankind, but none the less performs horrible purges and executions; his heart is breaking while he's doing it, but he can't help it, it's his Duty towards the Progress of Humanity ... What we encounter here is the properly perverse attitude of adopting the position of the pure instrument of the big Other's Will: "it's not my responsibility, it's not I who am actually doing it, I am merely an instrument of a higher Historical Necessity." The obscene [enjoyment] of this situation is generated by the fact that I conceive of myself as exculpated for what I am doing: "isn't it nice to be able to inflict pain on others in the full awareness that I'm not responsible for it, that I am merely an agent of the Other's Will?" (*DSST*, 119).

Nonetheless, the logic of sacrifice that governs these horrible acts is exemplified by Nazism rather than Communism:

Was not Nazism precisely a desperate attempt to restore ritual value to its proper place through the Holocaust, that gigantic sacrifice to the "obscure gods," as Lacan put it in *Seminar XI*? ... The sacrificial gesture does not simply aim at some profitable exchange with the Other to whom we sacrifice: its more basic aim is, rather, to ascertain that there is some Other out there who is able to reply (or not) to our sacrificial entreaties. (*DSST*, 44; 64)

Adopting the perverse subject-position of becoming an instrument for the enjoyment of the Other, and conducting a perverse sacrifice designed to make the Other exist, that is, to guarantee the existence of the big Other, are therefore the same thing, regarded from the perspectives of the executioner and the victim, respectively.

In Hitlerism, then, the Other is the racially pure national state, which demands from the Nazi the renunciation of moral responsibility, in the commission of terrible deeds that are designed to finally exterminate the alien intruders supposed to have polluted the master race. At the same time, the Nazi is fully aware that what is demanded is a supreme crime, that is, not simply a foundational act that happens to violate the norms of a historical community, but an abominable transgression that entirely voids the humanity of the perpetrator. The Nazi sacrifices the Jews in order to force the intrinsic superiority of the Master Race to become manifest; surely it is not accidental that the extermination program was significantly intensified *after* the Battle of Stalingrad, once the automatic supremacy of the Nazi war machine was seriously called into question.

In Stalinism, the Other is the necessary process by which history culminates in communist society, which demands from the communist the abdication of ethical standards and political restraints in the punishment of the traitors within the ranks, who have supposedly diverted the historical process toward counterrevolution. Here, a logic of perverse *self*-sacrifice is particularly evident. Žižek discusses Bukharin's show trial in detail, aiming to demonstrate how the aim of the proceedings was to recruit the accused into the role of self-accuser, in the name of exhibiting fidelity to Historical Necessity. What is fascinating about Bukharin is that he refuses to accept this perverse subject-position: Bukharin writes desperately to Stalin, pleading for some articulation of a limit to the guilt that Bukharin is called upon to admit to, that is, a statement that the accused did not, in the final analysis, fully participate in traitorous enjoyment (*DSST*, 102–10).

Against this background, Žižek proposes that the figures of abjection created by the totalitarian perversion—the "Muslim" of the concentration camps and the "Trotskyite" of the show trials—are somehow different because self-sacrifice includes the dimension of tragedy (*DSST*, 73–80). This argument makes up in ingenuity what it lacks in plausibility. Better, perhaps, to simply notice that whereas fascism involves the authoritarian restoration of (a fundamentally unjust) social order, the tragedy of communism is that it was a miscarried effort to create a just society, one that did not begin as a left-wing authoritarianism. Beyond this, Žižek's insight into the difference between the executioner's prey and the torturer's victim is that Hitlerism involves sadism (the sacrifice of a victim to make the Other exist, to "purify the race") while Stalinism involves masochism (the self-sacrifice that makes the Other exist, that "vindicates the cause"). Both sadist and masochist seek to transpose their own anxiety onto the sacrificial other (the victim, the torturer)—their motto should be, "somebody stop me!"—at the same time as their sacrifice provides a guarantee for the existence of the Other.

The connection between anxiety and authority now becomes visible. Social authority normally shields the subject from the anxiety that transgressive enjoyment might happen, through the mechanism of repression: the subject identifies with (the master signifier of) social authority while repressing the desire to transgress; this desire only reemerges in the form of neurotic symptoms, such as hysterical bursts of protest, obsessive (police) rituals, and, political phobias to do with potentially transgressive activities. The existence of the Other—the legitimacy and significance of nation, religion, or party—is guaranteed through unconscious beliefs. But under conditions of an augmentation of anxiety—for instance, a social crisis—a disintegration of traditional authority sets in, and the "void" of the question of the potential nonexistence of the Other emerges forcefully (*DSST*, 149). Authority seems to break down. Transgressions are everywhere. The cause is placed in question. It is at this point that perverse subjectivity presents itself as a possible solution: anxiety can be relieved through disavowal, rather than repression, and the fantasy supporting the existence of the Other can be salvaged—at the cost of a certain irrationality, even destructiveness. This, rather than an Oedipal character fixed from childhood onward, is the Žižekian response to the problem of the authoritarian personality and its political influence.

Lacan's Modernist Rethinking of Freud

As we have seen, Žižek discusses perverse subjectivity in the highly theoretical terms of the "non-existence of the Other." Perversion involves the effort to become the "instrument of the enjoyment of the Other," in order to "make the Other exist," that is, to force an enunciation of the Law. That might sound arcane, but it is actually straight to the point. Žižek's conceptual abstractions are justified by Lacan's development of a general theory of perverse subjectivity, within which Freud's conceptions of fetishism, sadism, and masochism are special cases. Lacan's general theory of psychoanalysis is a modernist rethinking of Freud, which shifts attention from "things" to "relations," and from special cases to structural forms.

For Freud, perversion involves the relative weakness of the father figure and the subject's belief in the existence of the "maternal phallus."[24] Belief in the "maternal phallus" implies that the subject both does, and does not, acknowledge the possibility of castration. Specifically, what the subject at once denies and affirms is that the "paternal castration threat" is truly effective. Accordingly, perverse sexuality revolves around simultaneously avoiding and provoking the fantasy scenario in which the maternal phallus is revealed while the paternal threat is articulated. The implication is that perverse sexuality involves high levels of anxiety combined with transgressive enjoyment. Fetishism is the effort to stage the entry of the characters into this scene without the performance of the entire act. Typically, an object proximate to the revelation of the maternal phallus (e.g., shoe, button, panty) is selected as the fetish object. The strategy of the fetishist therefore represents the perverse equivalent to neurotic phobias. By contrast, masochism is the attempt to endlessly postpone the delightful and terrifying moment of simultaneous revelation and castration. As with fetishism, the ritual of pleasure and degradation or suffering is substituted for the climactic moment. In this respect, masochism is the perverse equivalent to obsession. Finally, sadism is the effort to provoke some intervention that prevents the transgressive and anxiety-provoking culmination of this spectacle of eroticism and punishment. The game of the sadist is to develop exactions that are truly exorbitant—excessive and impossible—in order to force the partner to say "stop!" before things go too far. In this respect, sadism is the perverse equivalent to hysteria.

Lacan provides the general theory of psychoanalysis that englobes (and corrects) Freud's special theory of psychoanalysis, just as general relativity reduces special relativity to a highly restricted local instance, one with special boundary conditions and some idealizing abstractions. Lacan reformulates psychoanalysis in terms of the relation between the subject and the Symbolic Order, something represented to the subject through social authority and conceptualized psychoanalytically in terms of the position adopted toward the Other. The Symbolic Order (of linguistically mediated intersubjective agreements, especially kinship arrangements and moral norms, as stated through prohibitions) is instituted in the subjective economy through the advent of the Symbolic Law, which is the rule that desire must pass through permitted signification in order for the subject to request satisfaction from the other. The result of the Symbolic Law is the constitution of the Other, normally through repression, that is, the unconscious as something "structured like a language," consisting of symbolizations of prohibited desire linked to transgressive forms of enjoyment.

In Lacanian theory, perversion does not describe deviant partial objects and erogenous zones, but rather is defined structurally, by the subject's relation to the Other, something determined by the connection between the fundamental law and transgressive enjoyment. Lacan reframes Freud's "paternal threat of castration" as a special case of the statement of prohibitions that is enunciated through the Symbolic Law. He recasts Freud's "maternal phallus" as the prohibited symbol of transgressive enjoyment. Finally, Lacan rethinks Freud's "denial" (of castration) as the disavowal of the Symbolic Law, that is, the performative contradiction between the affirmation of transgressive enjoyment and the acknowledgment of a fundamental prohibition. From the Lacanian perspective, as we have seen, the formula for perverse enactment is: "I know very well that . . . but nonetheless I continue to insist that . . . ."

Conclusion

In the political field, perverse subjectivity is all-too-familiar: "I am not a racist, but nonetheless . . . ." The pervert knows all very well that the master race does not exist, but all the same, insists on transgressions that imply it does exist. Unlike Adorno, for whom perversion involves pregenital sexual pleasure, for Žižek, perversion can define enjoyment in any way whatsoever—from the Jewish conspiracy against Western civilization to Trotskyite sabotage of the Bolshevik Revolution. Sometimes, the enjoyment in question is lurid. Take, for instance, QAnon, where the global conspiracy of "bureaucrats, technocrats and plutocrats" is only completed by the dark fantasy that these elites are involved in Satanism, pedophilia, and cannibalism. But it is important not to fixate on the "substance" of enjoyment, for it could be literally anything. In Žižek's many discussions of xenophobia and the "problem of the neighbors," he points out that enjoyment is really whatever it is that the neighbors are supposed to be getting up to, from strange foods, to alien music, to running a crackhouse from a suburban bungalow or performing clitoridectomies on the kitchen table. It is not *what* the neighbors are doing that is crucial, but the supposition that this is transgressive and that authority should prevent it (but has failed to do so). This leads to the anxiety that transgressions are so ubiquitous and the transgressors so rampant, that the next victim of the roto-rooter rectum probe (or whatever) may be the subject themselves. It goes without saying that the only patriotic thing to do under these circumstances is to perform savage tortures on the neighbors, inflicting their own monstrous enjoyment on them, or to smash one's way into their houses of worship and murder a few dozen of them, in order to show—what? That there are resolute men and women ready and willing to support a potent authority figure who doesn't give a damn about human rights and legal niceties, and who is ready to put a complete stop to all of these goings on . . . *this* is what perversion is, in Žižek's theory. It should be familiar from recent political history. It is high time that we mapped out its moving parts, so as to throw sand in its gears.

Notes

1. See, for instance, Peter Gordon, "The Authoritarian Personality Revisited," in *Authoritarianism: Three Inquiries in Critical Theory*, ed. Wendy Brown, Peter Gordon, and Max Pensky (London: University of Chicago Press, 2018), 45–84. See also Jeremiah Morelock, "Introduction: The Frankfurt School and Authoritarian Populism—A Historical Outline," in *Critical Theory and Authoritarian Populism*, ed. Jeremiah Morelock (London: University of Westminster Press, 2018), xiii–xxxvii. And: Panayota Gounari, "Authoritarianism, Discourse and Social Media: Trump as the 'American Agitator,'" in *Critical Theory and Authoritarian Populism*, ed. Jeremiah Morelock (London: University of Westminster Press, 2018), 207–27.
2. Bob Altemeyer, *Enemies of Freedom: Understanding Right-Wing Authoritarianism* (Mississauga: Jossey-Bass, 1988).
3. Karen Stenner, *The Authoritarian Dynamic* (Cambridge: Cambridge University Press, 2005).
4. Matthew MacWilliams, *On Fascism: 12 Lessons from American History* (New York: St Martin's Press, 2020).
5. Matthew MacWilliams, "The One Weird Trait that Predicts Whether You're a Trump Supporter," *Politico Magazine*, January 17, 2016.
6. Theodor Adorno, *The Psychological Technique of Martin Luther Thomas's Radio Addresses* (Stanford: Stanford University Press, 2000).
7. Adorno et al., *The Authoritarian Personality* (New York: Wiley, 2019), 7.
8. Bob Altemeyer, *The Authoritarian Specter* (Cambridge, MA: Harvard University Press, 1996).
9. Adorno, *Personality*, 228.
10. Adorno, *Personality*, 751.
11. Adorno, *Personality*, 6.
12. Adorno, *Personality*, 759.
13. Bob Altemeyer, *The Authoritarians* (free online ebook: theauthoritarians.org, 2006), available online: https://www.theauthoritarians.org/options-for-getting-the-book/.
14. Jos Meloen, "The Fortieth Anniversary of *The Authoritarian Personality*," *Politics & the Individual* 1, no. 1 (1991).
15. Altemeyer, *Enemies of Freedom*.
16. Adorno, *Personality*, 228, 751.
17. Bob Altemeyer, *Rightwing Authoritarianism* (Winnipeg: University of Manitoba Press, 1981), 170.
18. Karen Stenner and Jonathan Haidt, "Authoritarianism Is Not a Momentary Madness, but an Eternal Dynamic within Liberal Democracies," in *Can It Happen Here? Authoritarianism in America*, ed. Cass R. Sunstein (New York: Harper Collins, 2018), 175–95.

19 Altemeyer, *Enemies of Freedom*.
20 Bob Altemeyer, "The Other 'Authoritarian Personality,'" *Advances in Experimental Social Psychology* 30 (1998), 47–92.
21 MacWilliams, *On Fascism*.
22 Bob Altemeyer, "What Happens When Authoritarians Inherit the Earth? A Simulation," *Analyses of Social Issues and Public Policy* 3, no. 1 (2003); "Highly Dominating, Highly Authoritarian Personalities," *The Journal of Social Psychology* 144, no. 4 (2004), 161–9.
23 Octave Mannoni, "'I Know Very Well, But All the Same . . .'" in *Perversion and the Social Relation*, ed. Molly Anne Rothberg, Denis Foster, and Slavoj Žižek (Durham: Duke University Press, 2003), 68–92.
24 Otto Fenichel, *The Psychoanalytic Theory of the Neuroses* (New York: W. W. Norton, 1996).

12

What Is Worth Salvaging in Modernity

A Realist Perspective from Non-Philosophical Marxism to Žižek's Universalism

Katerina Kolozova

Refracting the Vectors of Modernity through the Lens of Non-Philosophy

I intend to propose a comparative reading of two perspectives on the notion of subjectivity and its centrality for the legacy of modernity that both purport the possibility to think of or in relation to the Real albeit by admitting its radical foreclosure, that of non-Marxism and Žižek's universalism as conceived in his works of the early 2000s. Non-Marxism is, let us explain briefly, an approach to Marxism inspired by the method provided by François Laruelle called non-philosophy or nonstandard philosophy that seeks to radicalize what it identifies as both the scientific and realist core of Marx's thought. It is realist, or rather "correlating with the real,"[1] without establishing "amphibology" between the Real and thought[2] by way of ridding Marxism of philosophy or rather the "principle of philosophical sufficiency."[3] In what follows I will provide an explication of what the *principle of philosophical sufficiency* (PPS) refers to as conceptualized by François Laruelle, whereas, at the moment, suffice it to say that it is comparable to Marx's extolling of the principle of praxis over that of philosophy as a critique of the philosophical "self-mirroring," a thesis that pervades *Critique of Hegel's Philosophy in General* (Marx, *Manuscripts*), *German Ideology* (1968), *Theses on Feuerbach* (1969). The self-mirroring thought (philosophy is) subsumes the Real itself reducing it to a postulate, to its transcendental aspect exclusively rather than reversing the hierarchy whereby thought submits to the Real albeit radically foreclosed for philosophy's totalizing ambition.[4] Instead of revisiting the dialectics between thought and the real, or reviving a Kantian dilemma, in his critique of Feuerbach's materialism and the critique of Hegel's philosophy under the aforementioned several titles, in particular in "Critique of Hegel's Philosophy in General," Marx proposes that a shift toward "objectivism" would proffer a proper foundation for a truly scientific discussion of human reality. It is probably an undisputable fact that subjectivity-centered thinking and anthropocentric ontology, epistemology, and morality have determined the civilizational legacy of modernity: it begins with Kant's practical philosophy and metaphysics of morals, if we must choose a single philosophical threshold in the Western history of ideas. Certainly, it coincides with the birth of republicanism as the model state promulgated by the French and the American Revolution and the completion of the enlightenment project.

Kant's own vision could however only develop into a "liberal" or individual-centered foundation of a rationally organized society, and a society that presumes it is moved by invisible yet rational forces immanent to it. The individual is one's own sovereign, metaphysical, political, and legal materialization of the *cogito*-modeled foundation of human subjectivity and its metaphysics (*CU*). The republican sovereign is the sum of such individuals called "the nation." In contradistinction, the enlightenment project also led to a form of reason that has called itself "objective" and "scientific." In fact, scientific breakthroughs *stricto sensu* that emerged as part of the enlightenment did bring forth a form of reason that sought to achieve "objectivity," grounded in a materialist episteme and empirical study, whereas ridding thought of metaphysics has been its goal from the onset. Philosophies close to these traditions espoused the ambition of transcending metaphysics but also much of what remains of philosophy itself once one had engaged in the task of overcoming metaphysical constraints of thought (culminating in Wittgenstein).

In spite of the ambitions of philosophy and the social sciences, the possibilities of objectivity and scientific exactitude have remained reserved for the natural and the exact sciences whereas what came to be the humanities, as well as the social sciences, has been struggling to rid itself from the subjective perspective ever since. With the emergence of poststructuralism, these constantly frustrated efforts ceased by way of transforming them into the realization that not only in the humanities (and the social sciences) and philosophy but also even in the sciences themselves one was unavoidably "subjective." I call this a transformation instead of a shift because, counterintuitively to its purported ambition, the affirmation of thought's ultimate impossibility to fully account of the Real is premised on the realization about the impossibility to achieve absolute objectivity. Considering the expectation of absoluteness and thus the criterion of the absolute are in place, in spite of the admitted impossibility, the reasoning of this type remains entrapped in philosophical metaphysics. To paraphrase François Laruelle, the equation real = fiction has been replaced by fiction = real, but the equation is still the same.[5] In other words, deconstruction, Deleuzian theory, and the entire continental tradition of the linguistic turn in philosophy have merely put the entire structure of the classical philosophical tradition upside down while remaining constricted by the laws of the very same culture.[6] To conclude, an account of what is "objective," to what extent or in what sense, has remained an impossibility for the poststructuralist episteme and it is so because an account of absolute metaphysical certainty of it is treated as impossible. In such an expectation that is absolute, the concession of impossibility is absolute too and the premise of absoluteness has, therefore, not been abandoned.

Nonetheless, there emerged discourses of both modernity and objectivity in the nineteenth century that pleaded for an objective point of view, such as positivism, logical empiricism, and Marxism. In the present chapter, I will focus on Marxism or rather Marx's original writings approached with the epistemic scaffold provided by Laruellian non-philosophy. Objectivity as an inherently materialist criterion of scientific relevance, according to Marx "Critique of Hegel's Philosophy in General" (in Marx, *Manuscripts*: s.p.),[7] neither seeks to emulate the exact sciences nor espouse positivism insofar as it is anthropocentric and thus retains a nonscientific episteme. Marx's vision is epistemologically positioned beyond what he called a Hegelian legacy of subjectivity-centered thought that entertains idealism even when cloaked as materialism.

> The chief defect of all hitherto existing materialism—that of Feuerbach included—is that the thing, reality, sensuousness, is conceived only in the form of the object or of contemplation, but not as a sensuous human activity, practice, not subjectively. Hence, in contradistinction to materialism, the active side was developed abstractly by idealism—which, of course, does not know real, sensuous activity as such.[8]

Marx's vision of modernity has never been that of (human) subjectivity structured thought, which, even when pretending to be objective, remains immanently idealist. Marx's project of dismantling Hegel's philosophical and political project as one ensuing from (and amounting) to the ideal of a universal egoist, to paraphrase Marx (1959)[9] ends up as a radical critique both of Hegel's notion of (political) state and concomitant conceptualization of secularism.

In Karl Marx's politico-philosophical project, subjectivity, political state, and secularism are not what a modern society should consist in but quite the opposite their transcendence by way of sublation when confronted with a materialist, objective science of the species-being of humanity. Secularism is, argues Marx in *The Jewish Question*, a name for a "political" state that has alienated itself from the society precisely by way of relegating everything pertaining to the individual to the so-called "civil society."

> The relation of the political state to civil society is just as spiritual as the relations of heaven to earth. The political state stands in the same opposition to civil society, and it prevails over the latter in the same way as religion prevails over the narrowness of the secular world—i.e., by likewise having always to acknowledge it, to restore it, and allow itself to be dominated by it. In his most immediate reality, in civil society, man is a secular being. Here, where he regards himself as a real individual, and is so regarded by others, he is a fictitious phenomenon. In the state, on the other hand, where man is regarded as a species-being, he is the imaginary member of an illusory sovereignty, is deprived of his real individual life and endowed with an unreal universality.[10]

The split between the purely "political state" and the "civil society" is immanently bourgeois maintaining an alienation of the citizen from the reality of the social relations taking place in the "civil society," but also an alienation of the "private person" from their role of "citizen."[11]

In *Less Than Nothing*, Slavoj Žižek argues that subjectivity-centered reason and secularism lie at the core of modernity: "[. . .] it is absolutely crucial for emancipatory politics to remain faithful to the universalist/secular project of modernity" (*LN*, 70), and a bit further in the same text, he proffers an addition to this definition by saying "premodern organic society that denies the infinite right of subjectivity as the fundamental feature of modernity" (*LN*, 206). He is most probably right when one looks at the liberal-democratic tradition based on the idea of the republican enlightenment-inspired idea of modernity. Yet, I argue, there are insufficiently explored niches of alternative possibilities for the modernist political, epistemic, and onto-metaphysical potential predicated on the aforementioned critique forwarded by Marx.

Let us explore how an abstraction such as "humanity" can be rendered real, proffering a materialist account of it, albeit while affirming the realness of its abstract nature, and in doing so avoiding the trap of idealism as well as anthropocentrism. In order to do so, one ought to embrace Marx's notion of objectivity and consider social relations as objects among objects, seen from a "third party's perspective," a concept

I will elaborate in the pages that follow. Humanity is an abstraction that is real, but that does not make it a self-standing idea. It is rather what I might call a "real abstraction" constituting the species-being of humanity. Such abstractions are called real by the Austrian Marxist epistemologist Alfred Sohn-Rethel (1978). Regardless of the fact that an abstract category such as "humanity," but also "labour," "value," is predicated on a material reality that is its embodiment and an ontological property, it is also real in and of itself insofar as an abstraction. By affirming its realness as an abstraction, one does not fall back into idealism, but quite to the contrary—its real abstractness is affirmed as well as its material effects. However, the real abstraction of "species-being" of humanity or *Gattungswesen*[12] is not an ersatz-entity, it is not an *ousia*—it is yet again a product of human (cognitive) labor that is inhabited by incalculable number of physical bodies, and should be addressed as such, as that reality shaping and instituting category it is.

By decentering scientific thought from humanity as its legislating principle, as its teleological sense, by transcending the anthropocentric limitations of a posture of thought structured in line with the empty form of subjectivity that nonetheless emerges from humanist semantics, Marx pushes us further in the direction of posthumanism than constructivist discourse ever did. On the other hand, such a procedure of decentering does not imply anti- or transhumanism, it remains radically humanist as Marx keeps arguing, and not only in his early works (consider *Grundrisse* (1973) and in *The Communist Manifesto* (1969). As object of study among other objects of study, humanity, seen in its very material foundations of social relations insofar as real abstractions, returns to nature as realization of human "existence":

> The human aspect of nature exists only for social man; for only then does nature exist for him as a bond with man—as his existence for the other and the other's existence for him—and as the life-element of human reality. Only then does nature exist as the foundation of his own human existence. Only here has what is to him his natural existence become his human existence, and nature become man for him.[13]

This realization is possible through a communist resolution of the fundamental contradiction of capitalism—humanity's estrangement from nature, materialized as social relations of a political-economic base but also of a metaphysics pertaining to said base, inextricably constituting one another. Building on the non-idealist or perhaps anti-idealist basis of modernity, we might explore a possibility for the left that builds on Marx's scientific project, which is, however, something quite different and more often than not at odds with the tradition of "scientific Marxism" in Leninist vein. Here, we are engaged in a reading of Marx's authorship, and, in this process, we are aided by the methodological instruments furnished by François Laruelle and Alfred Sohn-Rethel.

Marxian Objectivity of the Subject from the Perspective of Sohn-Rethel's Epistemology

Sohn-Rethel's epistemology[14] relies on one simple premise—a materialist methodology, science, and the science of the species-being of humanity more specifically, including political economy, must have a materialist account of the abstractions that constitute human lives. Social relations, economy being part of it insofar as human productivity, are abstractions that have a real or material effect on human realities, as well as on other forms of living and non-living physical reality. Economic reductivism is not part of the reasoning I propose building on Marx's and Sohn-Rethel's texts: economic analysis is always political-economic and it is intrinsic to a particular worldview, or simply—metaphysical position. Or put in Marx's own words (that do not include the word "metaphysical") it is described as follows:

> To the extent that we are considering it here, as a relation distinct from that of value and money, capital is capital in general, i.e. the incarnation of the qualities which distinguish value as capital from value as pure value or as money. Value, money, circulation etc., prices etc. are presupposed, as is labour etc. But we are still concerned neither with a particular form of capital, nor with an individual capital as distinct from other individual capitals etc. We are present at the process of its becoming. This dialectical process of its becoming is only the ideal expression of the real movement through which capital comes into being. The later relations are to be regarded as developments coming out of this germ.[15]

As argued earlier, let us underscore, a position on human alienation, a possible eschatology of its resolution through a return to nature, is a metaphysical stance. I have elaborated this argument in detail elsewhere,[16] whereas for the moment, suffice it to say—one's belief in human progress through technology, even the very belief in progress is not only ideology but also metaphysics, and, therefore, not even sciences can avoid metaphysics entirely. They should not be seeking to do so either as metaphysical quizzing is what moves sciences and overall human productivity—one can, however, rid this process of the problem called "principle of philosophical sufficiency."[17] To affirm that an abstraction, such as social relations or value is a reality in its own right, however, does not mean that there is no material or physical *determination of the last instance*.[18] The determination of the last instance should not be confused with essence or substance or "purpose or reason of being" of the forms of physical reality of objects of scientific enquiry.

I choose to refer to "forms of physical reality" due to the fact that Nature is a notion heavily indebted to philosophy and theology (as a form of philosophy), an argument brought forth by authors such as Donna Haraway (1990)[19] but also those associated with the "speculative turn,"[20] for example, in the work the non-philosopher Anthony Paul Smith's (2013).[21] I also tend to avoid the use of "material," even though I do not insist on discarding its use entirely, for the same reasons Marx avoided it and instead resorted to the terms "real" and "physical" (sometimes "sensuous" too): to circumvent the possibility of being mistakenly assumed to espouse the spontaneous use of "philosophical materialism," for example, that of the Young Hegelians and Feuerbach whom Marx criticized. The core of this critique is the argument that Feuerbach remains entrapped in a form of idealism because his materialism is subjected to the same legislating principles that found and govern philosophy (all philosophy, its apex being Hegel). A central legislating principle that institutes philosophy as a vicious circle of auto-referentiality, a view comparable to Laruelle's critique of "the principle of sufficient philosophy," is, argues Marx in Critique of Hegel's Philosophy in General as noted earlier, the centrality of the notion of Subjectivity, demonstrating that it is always-already human subjectivity, unavoidably so. Even if semantically emptied of human content, Subjectivity, and in particular in Hegel's phenomenology, can be but human due to the very structural conditioning of thought.

In other words, philosophy cannot escape the *form* of idealism, and that is why philosophical materialism, be it Feurbachian or Hegel-inspired Leninist materialism, is merely different semantics filling up the same structure, that of idealism. In order to overcome this problem, and move philosophy toward science of humanity's "species being" Marx argues an *Ausgang* (exit) from philosophy is required (*Theses*). Marx's own work, the execution of his project in *Capital* and *Grundrisse* is a demonstration of how one departs from philosophical "abstractions" that are in fact generalizations, "philosophically spontaneous" abstractions, cumulative imaginary projections combining science, philosophy, common sense, and mythology of the quotidian in a vague assemblage of a manifest image of realty), only to arrive at the concreteness that constitutes them. This permits an extraction of abstractions in the methodological, not ontological sense, extrapolations of formalized and formalizable notions from the examined material reality.[22] The prerequisite for such a posture of thought and an ensuing process of scientific operation that nonetheless departs from philosophy is to shift the position of the philosophical gaze, to carry out a non-Euclidian shift, and, thus, do away with a *subjectivity centered thought*.

As already noted, subjectivity as the legislating principle of philosophical enquiry is identified, in particular, in Marx's *Critique of Hegel's Philosophy in General* but elsewhere too, as the main culprit of philosophy's self-centeredness, auto-referentiality, and inability to produce accounts of the real. Let us remark, in passing, that it would not be an error to liken this barred Real with the Lacanian real, if that helps get the point across more easily, but also to Laruelle's always-already foreclosed real. In *Hegemony, Contingency, Universality* (2000), co-written with Judith Butler and Ernesto Laclau, Žižek demonstrates that it is possible to construe a political language around the Real albeit while affirming its radical foreclosure, or rather that any political language is necessarily conditioned by the Real (*CHU*, 223). In this sense, his argument is very similar to that of François Laruelle in *Introduction to Non-Marxism* (2013), a scientific language, including that of radicalized Marxism, is affected by the immanence of the Real,[23] while nonetheless affirming the Real's "indifference,"[24] non-reciprocity, by way of the method of "unilateralization."[25] In said exchange with Butler and Laclau, Žižek demonstrates not only that universalism is the path of true socialist emancipation but also that universalism is possible only by way of "interrogating the Real" (*ITR*), as a form of realism informed by the sensibilities of poststructuralism yet moving away from its particularistic and atomist utopia. Laruelle's notion of the generic, occurring more persistently in his later works, and Žižek's concept of the universal seem to be similar in the sense that they are both aided by attributing relevance to the real in creating a new episteme and a novel political language, one that transcends the boundaries of the poststructuralist paradigm.

This universal subject megalomanically expanded by Hegel to the universal principle defining all possible reality morphed into the Spirit that cuts across history and ultimately manifests itself realized or materialized through the negation of its materiality, is a mere projection of the human ideal, of enlightenment humanism taken to its infantile extremes bordering with the grotesque. Subjectivity-centered metaphysics, ideology, and civilizational foundation, that of what I term earlier as the liberal-democratic and bourgeois modernity, is an inherent contradiction within the wider legacy of enlightenment determined modernity. Scientific reason (in contradistinction to Reason insofar as Spirit), the pursuit of objective and positive knowledge, and, finally, materialist metaphysics (or an inevitable foundationalism) is the dialectical other of said contradiction. A Marxian stance would expect a sublation leading to a materialist worldview, social relations that are not at odds with nature treating it as mere resource but rather as an inalienable element of the *real abstraction* they are, determined by the direct "interests of the proletariat"[26] or the "free producers."[27] Subjectivity-centered thinking is replaced by what Marx proposes as properly materialist method, that of the "third party view,"[28] a resolution of the contradiction through sublation according to generically conceived and not only Hegelian dialectics.[29]

Marx's Posthumanism and Why We Should Call It Non-Humanism

The solution to the inevitably idealist constitution of any philosophy or simply of philosophy itself Marx proposes is a methodological one—even though it implies a metaphysical shift too—to assume a third party's position that sees human subjectivity and thus humanity as object among objects. This is, I argue, a posthumanist proposal par excellence. It enables a radical defense of the "species being" of humanity in ecological balance with nature and technology, one placed beyond anthropocentrism (always-already present in any form of subjectivity-centered philosophy).

> To be objective, natural and sensuous, and at the same time to have object, nature and sense outside oneself, or oneself to be object, nature and sense for a third party, is one and the same thing.[30]

Building on Marx's proposal to exit philosophy's self-circumscription but rejecting the idea of fully doing away with philosophy as untenable, François Laruelle proposes a science of philosophy and a science operating with the conceptual repository of philosophy that would transcend a single yet key axiomatic problem—that of the principle of philosophical sufficiency. As explained earlier, the principle of sufficient philosophy refers to and is grounded in the procedure of philosophical amphibology, as Laruelle terms it. He elaborates the problem of the amphibology of thought and the Real in the following way: philosophy's identity of the last instance[31], rather than generalization, consists in the presupposition that the Real and thought ought to establish an ontological unity, become one and the same thing, an ambition sciences proper never had. The Real is thus always a philosophical product, and whatever its decision on what constitutes the Real co-constitutes thought itself too. That implies that the admission of poststructuralism that the Real in itself is inaccessible and thus any discourse of the Real should be abandoned as futile, is simple the obverse of the old metaphysical expectation that thought should penetrate, control, and become one with the real. I would add that any philosophy, beginning with the Greek, is determined by the ambition to produce truth that would be more real than the Real itself, the Real itself rid of meaning being recast as senseless and therefore worthless of any examination. One can easily notice that such is the stance of poststructuralism too—being unable to account of the real, fiction is declared to be more real than the Real itself or simply the only Real available to us and therefore the only Real there is.[32]

All philosophy is indeed idealism—thought and the Real are equated in the form of philosophical truth, there is no other form of truth in philosophy, one that would be beyond the aspiration of such an equation, even when said equality is declared impossible, as in poststructuralism. The first and foremost category of philosophy, Being is the principle, "principle" in the temporal and axiological sense of the word, product of the amphibology at issue: thought and the Real constitute a single form of reality, transcendence (a truth) posturing as immanence, whereby the Real and the thought that relates and mediates it are unified into an Entity—*to ôn*, that is presumed to be the "true real," thus not merely real but Real endowed with truth. This dream of reality imbued with truth, with (human) Spirit, elevated or sublimated reality whereby the Real becomes more real than the Real itself because human knowledge and the Real have collapsed in a perfect unity, this unity is what Laruelle's identification in the last instance (not reduction) of all philosophy to the act of philosophical decision is all about. Therefore, to criticize "philosophical decisionism" in Laruellian terms is not to claim that philosophy or science should not postulate about the Real but rather not to decide what it is in and of itself and instead admit its radical foreclosure. Once this foreclosure is admitted, thought seeks to mediate it, explicate it, convey knowledge (and therefore control) of it without seeking to "merge" with it, and institute a union of thought and the real. To assume this posture of thought means, according to Laruelle, to assume a position vis-à-vis human cognitive activity and reality as exteriority that is by its constitution equal to that of scientific thought. In this way, one might remain with philosophy and continue operating with "philosophical material" while staying outside of it, miming the scientific posture and ambition of thought.

Therefore, the relation is unilateral—the Real remains indifferent to thought's ambition, whereas the latter continues to "clone" the Real as Laruelle would say. Thereby, a radical dyad of thought and the Real is constituted, never amounting to a unity of the two elements, to a reconciliation of a duality, to acquiescence of their tension but quite to the contrary affirming it. The dyad is radical because it always remains a dyad, it is not a duality or dualism that seeks to be overcome either through some synthesis of reconciliation (the vulgar dialectics) or a playful affirmation of a paradox (postmodernism). Also, it is not an ontology—it does not speak the truth of how things are with regard to what *is* and what *isn't* (real), it does not legislate the Real (already affirmed as foreclosed). It is a method. The "non"—in non-philosophy and non-Marxism does not stand for "anti-," but quite the opposite—radicalization of the conceptual core in the both by way of ridding the doctrines of their philosophical legacy structured in line with the "principle of philosophical sufficiency."

Doing away with anthropocentrism as the foundation of all philosophy leads us to the notion of the nonhuman (rather than posthuman), which in line with the episteme of non-philosophy would mean radical humanism rid of the philosophical concept of the human, placed beyond any form of anthropocentrism and human-centered thought. At the level of subjectivity, we can apply the same method and recognize the prelingual Real at the heart of the nonhuman on the one hand and the signifying automation the language is and its effect—the Subject, on the other hand. The Real of the human-in-human is indifferent to the processes of signification just as the Real of some exteriority is indifferent vis-à-vis the unilateral tendency of "thought" (Laruelle) to signify it, relay it, mediate it, create knowledge or "truth" of it. This originary alienation is never to be overcome by the nonhuman conceived as a radical dyad (of a foreclosed Real and the signifying automaton and its effect, the subject). It is a real abstraction that yields material effects, an abstraction that yields effects of the Real, an instance of transcendence, and a material reality of cognition that is real and allows for a materialist account in and of itself. Finally, this is a purely formal category, just as "labor" or "social relations" are and as such it cannot be reduced to some semantic contents—such gesture, in Marxist terms, would be an error of reification, and an analogy of capitalist commodity fetishization.

Thinking oppression from the "third party perspective," a method developed by Marx, abandoning human-centered thought, which remains such even when it is termed post-, trans- or even antihumanist, enables scientific practice of philosophical enquiry, aided by the method of Laruelle's nonstandard philosophy and Marxism. Anthropocentric philosophical reason and its capitalist rationalizations can be surpassed through the notion of the nonhuman, which does away with subjectivity-centered thought as proposed by both Marx and Laruelle. It is a posture of thought that enables a radical structural critique of an endless sequence of intersecting forms of inequality and subjugation of humanity by being situated beyond subjectivity-centered reasoning. The latter is a form of thought that inevitably engenders the dogma of identity politics even when trying to be antidogmatic (postmodernism/poststructuralism), obfuscating the possibilities of structural resistance and reimaging a world beyond capitalism.

Notes

1 François Laruelle, *Philosophie et Non-philosophie* (Liège: Pierre Mardaga, 1989), 93–5.
2 Laruelle, *Philosophie*, 12; 23; 27–9; 34–6.
3 Laruelle, *Philosophie*, 17.
4 Laruelle, *Philosophy*, 24–31.
5 Laruelle, *Philosophie*, 231.
6 Laruelle, *Philosophie*, 179–86.
7 The Soviet edition of this and other titles in English by Marx I am citing here were available to me only online and without pagination. In order to be more specific, I am referring to titles of chapters such as "Critique of Hegel's

Philosophy in General," which is part of the *Economic and Philosophical Manuscripts of 1844*.

8   Karl Marx, *Theses on Feuerbach*, trans. W. Lough (Moscow: Progress Publishers, 1969).
9   "The self-abstracted entity, fixed for itself, is man as abstract egoist—egoism raised in its pure abstraction to the level of thought" (Marx, *Manuscripts*: "Critique of Hegel's Philosophy in General").
10 Karl Marx, *Economic and Philosophical Manuscripts of 1844:* "The Jewish Question," trans. Gregor Benton retrieved from *Internet Marxist Archive*, s.p., available online: https://www.marxists.org/archive/marx/works/1844/jewish-question/ (accessed June 18, 2021).
11 Paulin Clochec, "Le libéralisme de Marx," *Actuel Marx* 2.56 (2014): 115.
12 Marx, *Manuscripts*.
13 Marx, *Manuscripts*: "Third Manuscript: Private Property and Communism."
14 Alfred Sohn-Rethel, *Intellectual and Manual Labor: Critique of Epistemology*, trans. Martin Sohn-Rethel (London: Macmillan, 1978).
15 Karl Marx, *Grundrisse: Outlines of the Critique of Political Economy*, trans. Martin Nicolaus (New York: Penguin Books, 1973), 247.
16 Katerina Kolozova, *Toward Radical Metaphysics of Socialism: Marx and Laruelle* (Brooklyn: Punctum Books, 2015).
17 Laruelle, *Philosophie*, 17–22.
18 Laruelle, *Philosophie*, 54; Althusser, 1969.
19 Donna Haraway, *Primate Visions: Gender, Race, and Nature in the World of Modern Science* (London: Routledge, 1990).
20 A contested term by some of those associated with it, in particular those that build on to a lesser or greater extent on Laruelle's non-philosophy or nonstandard philosophy; consider Ray Brassier's statement in the interview given for *Kronos* in 2011 (Brassier, Ray. "I am a Nihilist Because I Still Believe in Truth," interviewed by Marcin Rychter. *Kronos* 16, no. 1 [2011]. https://kronos.org.pl/numery/kronos-1-162011/ [accessed February 20, 2021]).
21 Anthony Paul Smith, *A Non-Philosophical Theory of Nature: Ecologies of Thought* (New York: Palgrave Macmillan, 2013).
22 Marx, *Grundrisse*, 41.
23 François Laruelle, *Philosophy and Non-Philosophy*, trans. Taylor Adkins (Minneapolis: University of Minnesota Press-Univocal Publishing, 2013), 25, 26, 30.
24 Laruelle, *Philosophie*, 56.
25 Laruelle, *Philosophie*, 13–14; François Laruelle, *Introduction to Non-Marxism*, trans. Anthony Paul Smith (Minneapolis: University of Minnesota Press-Univocal Publishing, 2014), 144, 161.
26 Karl Marx and Frederick Engels, "Manifesto of the Communist Party," in *Selected Works Vol. 1: 1845–1859*, ed. Karl Marx and Frederick Engels (Moscow: Progress Publishers, 1969), 30.

27 Karl Marx, *Capital Vol.1*, trans. B. Fowkes (London: The Penguin Group, 1976), 927.
28 Marx, *Manuscripts*: "Critique of Hegel's Philosophy in General."
29 When I say "generically conceived dialectics" I am referring to the use of the notion we find in Marx's doctoral thesis, where he seems to be relying mainly on the original meaning of the term in Greek philosophy, and sees Hegel's appropriation of the notion as one of the possible correct uses—true to the original, Greek or etymological meaning—Marx himself would, however, amend with the perspective of "historical necessity." (Karl Marx and Frederick Engels, *Collected Works Vol. 1* [Moscow: Progress Publishers, 1975], 491–2).
30 Marx, *Manuscripts*: "Critique of Hegel's Philosophy in General."
31 François Laruelle, *Theory of Identities*, trans. Alyosha Edlebi (New York: Columbia University Press, 2016), 39, 61–2.
32 Judith Butler, *Bodies That Matter* (London: Routledge, 1993).

13

Are We Human? Or, Posthumanism and the Subject of Modernity

Matthew Flisfeder

Žižek's Inhuman Humanism: Repetition Without a Return

Although he is likely to disagree with me, I want to make (perhaps) a bold claim and argue that Žižek's antihumanist modernism, in fact, and within the context of contemporary debates over anthropocentrism and popular discourses about the Anthropocene, accomplishes a humanist gesture and helps us to rethink and revise the concept of humanism for the era of posthuman capitalism or what others now refer to as the Capitalocene.[1] The discourse on posthumanism is far from univocal and must be understood, at least, in two different modalities. It is a theory of post-HUMAN-ism, on the one hand, examining a kind of transhumanist technological augmentation to the human body, the kind of which Žižek writes about in various texts, but nowhere more focused than in his book, *Hegel in a Wired Brain*. In terms of the rise in digital automation and the prospects of a technological "singularity," tethering humans to machines as a material assemblage of technological objects of different kinds (both organic and inorganic), posthumanism strikes us as an inevitable direction for capitalism to take as part of its ceaseless logic of accumulation. In some ways, then, we can argue, as Žižek does, that to survive capitalism must become posthuman; or, as he puts it, "what we are witnessing today is nothing less than an attempt to integrate the passage to posthumanity with capitalism" (*LTBD*, 46).

But posthumanism is also, on the other hand, a theory of post-HUMANISM, in the sense of being a critical theory seeking to escape the contradictions and deficiencies of various humanist philosophies, from premodern religious and Renaissance humanisms of the early and pre-Enlightenment period, to the modern liberal secular humanisms that followed, and up to and including the various socialist, Marxist, and Stalinist humanisms of the twentieth century. Posthumanism in its various guises (such as object-oriented ontology, speculative realism, vitalist materialism, and actor-network theory) seeks to displace the role and agency of the human subject and philosophies that privilege Promethean humanist exceptionalism. For some of the posthumanists of this variety, their objective is to expand human agency onto all things through the extension of subjectivity, anthropomorphizing all that exists.[2] For others, the goal is to see all that exists as commonly objective: all objects of various kinds.[3] In both cases, the ethic is one of building a "democracy of objects," or a kind of "flat ontology," that nevertheless leads into a performative contradiction that points the finger at human subjects for the ecological crises of the Anthropocene, while at the same time claiming, paradoxically, that humans are nothing special in the first place.

The anti-anthropocentrism of the posthumanists should be distinguished from antihumanisms of the 1960s (the period that saw the development of the theories of Althusser and Lacan, which have influenced Žižek's own brand of antihumanist philosophy) by the fact that it sought to deconstruct the subject in discourse. As Lévi-Strauss argued in *The Savage Mind*, against Sartre, the goal of the human sciences is not to constitute but to dissolve human subjectivity.[4] However, as Kate Soper notes, antihumanism remains limited to Kantian critique insofar as it takes as its object, not reality as such, but merely human representations of reality. As Foucault argues in *The Order of Things*, the object of the human sciences is "neither biology, nor economics nor even philology that comprise the human sciences, but our representations to ourselves of the activities they study."[5]

Contemporary posthumanisms, however, seek to withdraw the human as such. For them, even the antihumanists remain caught in the Kantian, "correlationist" problematic of the distinction between the phenomenal and the noumenal realms of intelligibility. As the speculative realist philosopher Quentin Meillassoux proposes, we have to assume, instead, unreason (as opposed to human reasoning and aesthetics/representation) as, itself, an ontological priority.[6] Like other new materialist and posthumanist thinkers, Meillassoux's postcritical philosophy strikes at the heart of modernist theory in its goal to resolve the Kantian problematic of the thing-in-itself through a return, in some ways, to precritical and premodern investments in realism. For Meillassoux, the only necessity is contingency, rendering human ethical and free agency obsolete, the kind of which that is most responsible for modernist and Enlightenment thought that takes human reasoning as a methodological priority. For many who view as primary the conundrum of the Anthropocene, withdrawing human ethical agency can only but make sense, even if this draws them into an intractable contradiction: why even bother with polemics against anthropocentrism in the first place if there is nothing exceptional about the human subject? Who is even the target of such polemics? The irony, not to be missed, is that even the new materialist posthumanists still seem to show their belief in the agency of the Lacanian big Other confirming meaning on existence; or else, they find themselves caught in premodern, precritical mysticisms.

Both antihumanism and posthumanism are therefore anti-anthropocentric; however, whereas antihumanism sees the subject as the product of ideology and discourse, posthumanism sees the human/nonhuman distinction as altogether harmful to nature, assigning priority to it over the human subject. As the most famous of the object-oriented ontologists, Graham Harman, puts it (quite jubilantly), finally, we are in a position to "oppose the long dictatorship of human beings in philosophy."[7] Žižek's response to contemporary posthumanisms of these kinds has been twofold: it has been inspired by his Hegelian reinterpretation of dialectical materialism, but it has also, I claim, pushed him to more persuasively defend human subjectivity methodologically, as well as a universalist ethics, in a way that encourages us to repeat the kind of humanism that has its foundations in modernist conceptions of freedom, Truth, and universality. However, this repetition, to be sure, is a far cry from both bourgeois-liberal and older Marxist-humanist and existentialist defenses of human freedom and universality. Žižek's humanism is grounded, less in the pursuit of the Absolute than in the acknowledgment that Truth remains actual only through the *failed* Absolute—that is, in the failure of its actualization, in its betrayal. And this failure of actualization of the Absolute is the place where the position of the subject is inscribed in the picture (*SFA*, 375).

Žižek's "humanism" goes missing in much of the discourse around his work and his ties to the Enlightenment tradition, his atheist (Hegelian) reading of Christianity, and in his ongoing questioning of modern humanisms in both their liberal and socialist varieties. Implied in this, I claim, we find the seeds for the potential to reinvent a radical, universal, and dialectical humanism appropriate for coming to grasp the contradictions of a looming posthuman capitalism in the twenty-first century. While Žižek often speaks of the inhuman core of human subjectivity, I propose instead that his own groundwork in an Enlightenment and modernist tradition, read through German Idealism and the antihumanism of Althusser and Lacan, in fact, helps us to develop what I will call a *humanism of the not-all*.

My claim, of course, appears counterintuitive since not only does Žižek consistently attack and challenge socialist humanisms (Stalinism with a "human face"), as well as liberal humanisms and postures of "human rights" (capitalism "with a human face"), but he also writes out of the Lacanian and

Althusserian antihumanist traditions. Against those who, like Althusser, claim Hegel as a humanist influence on Lukács, Lefebvre, and Sartre, for instance, in the Marxist humanism of the twentieth century, Žižek has been quick to assert that Hegel is not a humanist (*LN*, 98) and has used his Lacanian rereading of Hegel to develop an antihumanist theory of the inhuman core of human subjectivity. Nevertheless, much of his writing continues to be premised on answering the question: What is the human subject? This is a question that in some ways flies in the face of the antihumanism of Althusser and Foucault, in their own ways both declaring the end of the subject and seeing the subject as a mere by-product or epiphenomenon of ideology and discourse. But much more recently, especially in his writing about the various new materialisms and posthumanisms of the twenty-first century, Žižek encourages a rereading of Enlightenment thought and German Idealism through the lens of antihumanism, as well as through a post-Cold War communist critique of global capitalism. For him, the only way to resuscitate the Marxist goal of communism is via a turn back to Hegel. It's through his return to Hegel that I find in Žižek's writing the potential to rethink the terms of a humanist critical theory for the twenty-first century.

It is against the posthumanists, and especially with his much sharper and clearer turn toward Hegel in his books *Less Than Nothing* and *Absolute Recoil*, the reinvention of dialectical materialism beginning with *The Parallax View*, and his return to the Cartesian *cogito* in *The Ticklish Subject*, that we see not a *return* to humanism, as he often likes to claim about his writing on Lenin; rather, what we find here is a line of questioning that forces us to *repeat* core humanist thinking, not merely to answer the question: What is the *meaning* of humanity? Such a boring question is far less important than those that pertain to the survival of humanity and human ethics, in the face of looming ecological catastrophe, and the rise of digital automation, AI, or technological singularity. Here, Žižek's inhuman humanism pushes us to ask much more relevant ethical questions about our survival and how we need to think our agency in non-moralistic terms and against the kinds of moralizing we might find in other varieties of liberal consequentialist thought or in the virtue ethics of identity politics liberalism.

As he puts in *HWB*, "One often hears that, in order to confront appropriately the threat of an ecological catastrophe, we have to renounce 'anthropocentrism' and to conceive of ourselves (humanity) as a subordinated element in the great chain of Being." He goes on, noting the posthumanist claim that we (humanity) are posing a threat to mother Earth. Yet, it is not Earth that we need to be worried about:

> *we* are in trouble, Earth is indifferent, it has survived much worse disasters than the possible self-destruction of one of its species. What is under threat is *our* environment, *our* habitat, the only one in which we can live. From the imagined standpoint of Earth it would be much better for its

global ecosystem if we (humanity) disappeared, so what is under threat in 'ecological crisis' is *our* survival, the survival of our society. (*HWB*, 165)

Here, he points out, we find the hidden anthropocentrism of posthumanist anti-anthropocentrism. And, I would add, it's here in his criticism of the performative contradiction of the posthumanists that we can also locate Žižek's own repetition of the foundational (modernist) humanist gesture: of showing how it is we humans who "make history."

By tackling the ambiguities of biogenetics and cognitive sciences, as well as the anti-anthropocentric theories and concerns of the new materialists and posthumanists amid rising uncertainties of humanity in the face of environmental and ecological catastrophe, and the rise of new digital media, automation, AI, and the forecasted technological singularity, we find in Žižek encouragement for repeating the modernist intrigue with the figure of the human and the human subject at precisely the moment when everywhere we hear about its untimely death. In large part, the repetition of the question of the human subject is forced by a demand to consider ethical questions about our political conjuncture, as in the Leninist question: What is to be done? But here it is worth noting a semantic distinction between terms like human, subject, and humanism, which tie back into some of the deficiencies with the Marxist and socialist humanisms of the twentieth century, particularly those that base themselves on the early Marx of the 1844 manuscripts.

To put it bluntly, the difficulty with a Marxist humanism that draws on some conception of "Total Man," as Lefebvre put it,[8] is that it assumes a completed and self-reconciled conception of humanity with itself or with its own nature—that is, it is a dream of achieving a reconciled *balance* with nature. Ironically, we find the same hope here of a balanced nature in much of the discourse on posthumanist new materialisms and realisms, which see the birth of human subjectivity and reason as something akin to an ontological deviation from the nature of reality, as noted earlier via Meillassoux. This is similar to the rise of the "biopolitical" scientisms of the early Soviet period, in the projects of biocosmism and tech-gnosis (as Žižek calls it),[9] from which, according to him, we see the rise of the kind of Stalinist romantic humanism that formed as a reactionary position against the failures of the Soviet new materialists.[10] But it was also this turn that caused, according to Althusser, the Stalinist deviation away from the Marxist science of historical materialism, and toward the tripartite flaws of economism, historicism, and humanism.

Since the publication of *The Parallax View*, and even slightly before in his Leninist turn, and after in *In Defense of Lost Causes*, Žižek has shown that so much of the contemporary posthumanisms and new materialisms reproduce dimensions of the Soviet projects to transcend human existence. In a way, what he shows is that with the rise of Stalinist humanism, and the turns toward socialist realism, as well as traditional Russian culture, which are more or less a response to the failures of the posthumanist Soviet projects, biocosmism, and so on, we can see an equation between humanism and forms of terror expressed by the regime of late Stalinism. Nevertheless, Žižek maintains that this guise of humanism in late Stalinism is still what exercises its inner greatness. Not necessarily in the sense espoused by Merleau-Ponty in his book, *Humanism and Terror*, which claims that the violence of the communist terror is justified by the struggle to realize the actuality of communism. For Žižek, rather, it is the guise of humanism that in fact prevented full-scale nuclear holocaust during the Cuban Missile Crisis, for instance, as in the displays of politeness that allowed the two powers to prevent outright catastrophe (*IDLC*, 214–15). This shows, in other words, that at least at the level of appearances, modernist humanism has the potential to save us from near catastrophe.

Part of Žižek's fear, though, about the growth of new posthumanist movements is that they potentially raise the specter of a much more brutal reactionary humanism. However, and in contrast with many of the left posthumanist movements, Žižek shows, too, that the posthuman turn also signals a change or a transformation in the capitalist mode of production. He shows that in order to save itself capitalism must become posthuman. Posthumanism, then, in its different guises, works either as an underlying defense of this new stage in capitalist production at the same time that it advocates inaction and unreason on the part of the human subjects it opposes.

Unlike Althusser, who saw in Stalin's humanism a deviation from Marxist science, Sartre was one who turned toward a humanist reading of historical materialism, precisely against the antihumanism of Stalinism; and, in fact, much of the debate that has followed in subsequent decades rests on the question of whether or not Stalinism is a humanism. The trouble with Sartre, though, as Žižek notes, and I agree, is that his humanism expresses too much of a voluntarism that dismisses the structural aspects of ideology that Althusser so significantly drew out in his theories of ideology and subjectivity. But as an entry point, then, for how I conceive Žižek's inhuman humanism, a humanism of the not-all—or, perhaps more appropriately, a repetition of the humanist gesture based on Žižek's return to the *cogito*, the dialectic, and the subject of modernity—Althusser's theory of subjectivity offers a first point for articulating Žižek's strategy for thinking the human subject and the way this is tied into his return to the Enlightenment and modernist theories of German Idealism, especially Kant and Hegel, against, for instance, the Spinoza of Althusser and the contemporary posthumanists.

The Vagaries of Choice

Perhaps the best way to see the difference between an older Marxist humanism and the kind of inhuman humanism that I am claiming here in Žižek's writing can be summed up in the difference he identifies between

Sartre and Lacan. For Sartre, according to Žižek, "the basic free act by means of which the subject 'chooses itself,' formulates the existential project that defines its identity, is an act of self-consciousness" (*HWB*, 93–4). Sartre's subject of choice is one that is fully present to itself, or experienced by the subject, a point that is consistent with his well-known dismissal of the Freudian unconscious.[11] It is easier, in response to the centered Sartrean subject, to grasp Althusser's point about the overlap between Marx and Freud in troubling the bourgeois subject of modernity. For Althusser, what is common in both Marx and Freud is the challenge they present to the subject of the bourgeois individual: Marx, with his conception of the class struggle, proves the masses, rather than the individual subject, are the motor of history; Freud, with the discovery of the unconscious, shows that the subject's agency is never fully present to itself. In contrast, bourgeois and humanist ideology (and here, too, we might see what is problematic with Sartre's existential humanism and his dismissal of the Freudian unconscious) sees the individual free and fully conscious subject as the condition of ethical and self-accountable agency. As he explains, "the ideology of man as a subject whose *unity* is ensured or crowned by consciousness is not just any fragmentary ideology; it is quite simply *the philosophical form of bourgeois ideology*"; and, in his critique of political economy, "Marx was criticizing its 'economic' version in rejecting any idea of 'homo economicus,' in which man is defined as the conscious subject of his needs."[12] For Lacan, then, in opposition to bourgeois and existentialist humanisms, "the primordial choice is unconscious since the Unconscious is not a substantial determination of the subject but the most basic level of reflexivity" (*HWB*, 94). For Sartre, the act of choice that founds subjectivity is self-conscious, whereas for Lacan it is not merely an act of the unconscious; rather, it is the primordial forced free choice that forms the unconscious in the first place, thereby creating the foundational subjectivization of the subject. We can read this difference further via Žižek's return to Descartes and the *cogito*.

Descartes and the *cogito* are perhaps most commonly associated with the origins of modern humanism, as opposed to the Renaissance humanism, where humanity aspires to the divine. Modern humanism, in contrast, notably privileges humanity as the creator of its own material conditions. This view is due in no small part to Descartes's rationalist methodology. Nevertheless, Žižek identifies Descartes as an antihumanist thinker and claims that "his *cogito* should be strictly distinguished from what we call 'human personality,' all the wealth of inner life." Against the Renaissance humanism that sought to elevate human beings above all creatures, according to Žižek, the Cartesian subject "is quite another thing: an inhuman void, an empty point of self-relating negativity" (*HWB*, 181). His point is surely provocative, but I want to argue that it makes sense in the context of reading the *cogito* according to the Lacanian logics of sexuation and their associated ethical dimensions; and, through this, we can see how

Žižek's antihumanism of the inhuman core of human subjectivity develops a humanism of the not-all, of the feminine logic of sexuation in Lacan. It's through this logic, too, that Žižek's Hegelian dialectical materialism contrasts with the posthumanist new materialism of twenty-first century postmodern capitalism and its contradictory anti-anthropocentrism. Rescuing the *cogito* and the subject proves pivotal in this regard.

In several places in his early writing, but most notably in *For They Know Not What They Do* and in *Tarrying with the Negative*, Žižek writes that for Lacan the Cartesian *cogito* is the subject of the unconscious, a point that is again developed in other ways in *The Ticklish Subject*. He notes that in Lacan's *Seminar XI: The Four Fundamental Concepts of Psycho-Analysis*, Lacan proposes dividing Descartes's *cogito ergo sum*, "I think, therefore I am," into two parts: thinking ("I think") and being ("I am"). The subject is thus forced to choose between the two. Here, Lacan claims that the subject—in the process of subjectivization—is condemned to the forced choice of thinking, thereby losing being. However, later, in *Seminar XIV*, on the logic of fantasy, Lacan reverses his earlier statement, now claiming that the subject is forced to choose being, with thought then relegated to the position of the unconscious. Here, in this sense, we see how, as noted earlier, Žižek claims that for Lacan the primordial forced choice is an act of the unconscious, since, according to him, it is a mistake to see the later formulation, in the logic of fantasy, as a correction of the earlier one. Instead, we should read the two formulas as a reflection of the antagonistic logic of the sexual difference, and as tied to the foundational forced choice that forges the subject in its relationship to its enjoyment. The masculine subject, he claims, chooses being over thought, which is relegated to the position of the unconscious; the feminine subject, then, chooses thought over being, losing the latter in the process, which is why, according to Lacan, *la femme n'existe pas*.

To understand this, we have to think of the subjectivization in terms of the binary opposition between a foundational affirmation, as well as a complementary act of negation; or, to be more precise: the foundation here is one of an initial free choice of negation that, in Lacanian terms, alienates the subject into the affirmed position of the Symbolic order, or into the community of other human subjects. In subjectivization, the choice in question (of negation and affirmation) is that of the forced choice between thought and being. Typically, the subject will choose or affirm being; but in every act of affirmation there is likewise and simultaneously an act of negation—that is, the negation of the choices not chosen, that is, thought. What Lacan calls symbolic castration is the process of being interpellated as a lacking subject. The subject lacks the choice not chosen, the "lost object" or the Lacanian object a. In the choice of affirming being, the subject can then externalize the cause of the negated choice onto the Other, in whose name it appears to have renounced or negated the lost choice, and in this way becomes alienated within the Symbolic order. In so far as the lost, negated choice, *stays* lost, the subject remains capable of enjoying loss in the form of the desire that it forever pursues. What proves crucial is the fact that, by enjoying loss itself, the subject continues enjoying its own foundational forced choice, even if it experiences this enjoyment as painful since it can never recover the lost object.

The point here is that, contrary to the liberal conception of the fully self-conscious subject, the Lacanian subject is one formed by an unconscious relation to itself and to its own enjoyment. Enjoyment, not the conscious pursuit of needs, in other words, becomes the driving motivation of subjective freedom. While the subject appears to pursue its desire—the lost object of the choice not chosen—what it nevertheless repeats is the enjoyment in failing to find the lost object. In doing so, the subject repeats the enjoyment in the foundational moment of free negation, marking itself as lacking and alienated, forever incomplete. Beginning with the Lacanian subject in this sense, it would appear as though Žižek's alienated subject remains distant from the humanist subject of modernity, and even the Marxist-humanist subject seeking to disalienate. However, it's when we grasp the difference between the masculine and feminine subjects in Lacan's logics of sexuation that we start to see how Žižek's ethics of the feminine not-all helps us to revive or rethink a humanism appropriate to our era: one, that is, that sees alienation as constitutive rather than merely contingent.

In the Lacanian logics of sexuation, the masculine position represents a universal function founded upon a particular limit (all X are submitted to the universal function F; there is at least one X that is not submitted to the universal function F). The masculine logic is, thus, limited and finite, bearing upon the logic of the phallic master-signifier. It is oriented toward the phallus as the signifier of its symbolic castration. By affirming the phallus as its limit, the masculine subject produces itself as lacking, that is, the choice of being over thought. Or, again, rather, by negating thought, the masculine subject affirms being in the form of the phallic (paternal) signifier. On the feminine side of the logics of sexuation, a particular negation implies that there is no exception, there is no limit (not all X are submitted to the function F; there is no X that is not submitted to the function F), and in this sense, the feminine subject is the one capable of *thinking* the contradiction at the heart of being, that is, the choice of thought over being. To put this difference in Hegelian terms, we could say that the masculine subject is the one of the understanding (*verstand*)—its limit is one of mere knowledge, as in the Lacanian university discourse. The best it can do is understand what is. The feminine subject, however, is the one of thinking or reasoning (*Vernunft*); it becomes unlimited, precisely in the very form of questioning and bombarding the Other with a demand to think. The hysterical neurotic is, after all, the subject who produces for the analytical discourse the very knowledge that becomes its basis and foundation. It's through unceasing questioning and reasoning that the subject here forces a continuous negation that is ultimately driven toward a transformative act.

If the masculine subject is, then, the subject of the All (the universality founded upon its exception), the feminine subject is the one of the not-All. But for this reason, the feminine subject of the not-All becomes the ethical subject of reasoning. In the place of the understanding subject of the *verstand*, the subject can go on enjoying the pursuit of desire; but the subject of reason, of the *Vernunft*, is the one capable of traversing the fantasy tied to being in order to think the limits of desire, thereby being interpellated according to the logic drive. The subject of the All, then, the subject of desire, remains according to Žižek the Kantian subject, limited by its inability to get beyond the antinomies of pure reason, to perceive the thing-in-itself. The subject of the not-All, however, is the one who, by grasping the contradiction at the heart of being, is *un*-limited, and can grasp the infinite in being that allows her to perform an ethical act. This subject, according to Žižek, the subject of the not-All, the subject of the drive, is Hegelian (*AR*, 372; *SFA*, 375).

Both the masculine and feminine subjects are oriented toward the phallic signifier; however, whereas the masculine subject is oriented in the mode of affirming the signifier, the feminine subject is oriented toward the negation of the signifier. As the subject of the mere understanding, the masculine subject we might say represents the subject caught in ideology— the bourgeois-liberal ideology of the fully self-conscious, self-aware subject of limited rational agency. Its limit is one of mere external reflection. As the subject of reason, however, the feminine subject is oriented toward thinking and reasoning, and is in this way positioned as ethical, where ethics is the process of taking reasoning all the way to the end, to the point of ethical action or duty; thinking to the point where it cannot but act, producing the new (concept/signifier).[13] Put differently, in negating the phallic signifier, the feminine subject identifies, not the futility in masculine understanding, but the very self-relating contradiction of the structure of understanding itself. It therefore grasps the paradoxical freedom of the contingent but necessary foundational choice. Noting this paradox, the presupposing of the positing gives the subject the ultimate freedom to act; and, as Joan Copjec notes, for Lacan, an ethical act is feminine.[14] As the reasoning subject, the feminine subject of the not-all, I claim, is the one that best suits or models what I am calling Žižek's humanism of the not-all. I claim this because the human subject of the not-all, for Lacan, as well as for Žižek's Hegel, becomes the methodological and ethical center for thinking the terms of alienation, universality, freedom, and Truth. It is this subject, the feminine subject of the not-all, that in Žižek's Lacanian-Hegelian interpretation, is the quintessential subject of modernity. Humanism of the not-all registers the foundational alienated disparity of modernity, itself.

The Disparity of Alienated Being

For Žižek, one of the primary differences between premodern and modern ontology lies in the way that the latter, in its scientific bent, turns away from subjective enchantments toward the raw, meaningless, and cold "objective reality." Sexual difference is seen as a mere historicist, subjective humanizing of the real reality. For modern transcendental philosophy, as he puts it, "sexual difference is deontologized, reduced to the ontic sphere of the human race." Ontologizing sexual difference, one runs the risk of being accused of illegitimate anthropomorphism, "of projecting onto the universe what is merely an empirical (biological and psychic) feature of human beings" (*LN*, 739). However, for Lacan, it's not that sexuality remains merely an ontic dimension of human reality; rather, sexuality registers an ontological cleavage already present in reality, itself; and this, Žižek notes, is a cleavage already acknowledged in modern philosophy by German Idealism, from Kant to Hegel.

As Copjec has shown, the Lacanian logics of sexuation express, similarly, the logics of the Kantian antinomies of pure reason, with the masculine logic falling on the side of the dynamic antinomies, and the feminine logic falling on the side of the mathematical antinomies.[15] Žižek explains that the antinomies are "indications of the inability of finite reason to grasp the noumenal reality: the moment we apply our categories to what can never become an object of our experience, we become caught up in insoluble contradictions" (*LN*, 740): for instance, the question of whether the universe has a beginning or an ending in time and space, or if it is in fact infinite and expansive. For Kant, the resolution of such a problem is to produce the distinction between phenomena of human experience, and noumena, or things-in-themselves, which can never truly be objects of human knowledge and understanding. To put it bluntly, for Kant, we can know only our knowledge of things, but we cannot know things-in-themselves. Human knowledge, for Kant, remains limited in this sense, and it is not too hard to see here how Kant represents the masculine subject of mere understanding (*verstand*) par excellence. The Hegelian subject, however, of the determinate reflection, and of the infinite judgment, is the one capable of grasping, through reasoning, an intractable contradiction at the heart of being. This is where, for me, a humanist premise returns in our grasping of reasoning and ethics; but humanism here operates somewhat closely to the Kantian idea of the heuristic concept. We begin with the modern humanist subject of limited agency only to arrive at the not-All, alienated, inhuman core of the subject: from positing the presuppositions (in Kant) to presupposing the positing (in Hegel). This alienated humanity is what Žižek calls the disparity.

Disparity refers to the way that Žižek redefines the being of being-human as alienated, or as incomplete. The failure to be what one is, he writes, is constitutive of being-human (*D*, 28). This is a failure that triggers human creativity and reasoning. Or, as he puts it elsewhere, deficiency is a core feature of being-human (*HWB*, 183). In this sense, there can be no in-humanism without the betrayal of humanism—that is, without the prior positing of the humanist subject so that through the processes of reasoning, the inhuman subject becomes capable of presupposing the positing of its foundational humanist gesture. It's only from the perspective of our inhumanity that the universality of humanism is even comprehensible. Or, yet another way to make this point is the claim that the subject is, precisely, the failure of its own actualization (*LN*, 750). Therefore, there is no inhuman subject without humanism; or, in other words, the ethical subject only emerges through the (creative) failure of the humanist subject to realize itself. Its universality is perceived only in its betrayal, and this betrayal, I claim, *is* the humanist subject.

Žižek, therefore, accomplishes a rethinking of humanism on the grounds of alienation and negativity as opposed to a humanist Marxist conception of unalienated or disalienated species-being, fully reconciled toward itself; and, it is via his psychoanalytic reading of Hegel and German Idealism that we find the distinction between the latter, which sees alienation as contingent, and a view of alienation as constitutive, both of subjectivity as well as of reality itself. For Žižek, the development of human sexuality, which as we saw earlier bears upon a fundamental antagonism with regards to the foundational moment of subjectivization, is in fact not a product of the humanization of nature. Quite the opposite. Sexuality, according to Žižek, is the product of our subjectivization of an incompleteness within ontological reality. Human sexuality is the very way in which we come to grasp the very incompleteness at the heart of reality. Or, as Žižek explains, "'sexuality' is the way the ontological deadlock, the incompleteness of reality in itself, is inscribed into subjectivity. It is not a subjective distortion of objective reality, but a subjective distortion which is directly identical with the non-All, the inconsistency, out-of-jointness, of reality itself. This is why sexuality is, at its most radical, not human, but the point of inhumanity, the '*operator of the inhuman*'" (*LN*, 745). Nevertheless, the humanism of human sexuality is still, as it reflects an ontological deadlock, the royal road toward subjectivizing the overlapping not-All of substance and subject.

Put differently, if reality is ontologically complete, that leaves human subjects impotent, having no true ability to impact upon the Real. But we are told we have produced an Anthropocene in which too much of the world has been impacted, changed, and transformed, by the human footprint. If, however, we acknowledge the incompleteness of ontological reality, we may grasp the human subject as the very place of this ontological gap in the parallax of reality. This positions (alienated) human subjects as ethical agents, with the ability to either destroy or take care of the world. It is our ontological incompleteness, as well as the ontological incompleteness of reality, that gives us the sense in which human ethical action is made capable of materially transforming the world, for better or worse. And it is the modernist universalist ethic that drives us forward, in contrast with the postmodernist anti-universalist ethic, that sees only the end of history and dystopia as the folding back in on the present, the perpetual present, that cautions us to only "stay with the trouble," as Donna Haraway puts it. Against such a posthumanist perspective that sees the human subject as the culprit of planetary demise, we see how Žižek's humanism of the not-all, his inhuman humanism, provides the model for seeing through toward the salvation of humanity, as the reaching of its own Notion of the modernist project of universal emancipation.

Here, I am not proposing to add meaning or meaningfulness to being-human; rather, we are called to grapple with the fact of a human subject that always sticks out and, in the face of this and other impulses tied to enjoyment, to ask how we might act according to the ethics of the modernist emancipatory project. This doesn't mean that the subject of modernity has passed its time. Rather, we see that the humanist subject of modernity set in motion a process that still troubles us for thinking the dimensions of Truth, reasoning, universality, and freedom. And this is still a project to which Žižek remains devoted. This idea, of a human subject of the not-all, capable of making reality just as much as it makes us, is not only an arm in the dialectics of nature, but it is also a project with a view to which humanist modernism continues to set its sights. The point is not, as Habermas put it, that modernity is an incomplete project. Rather, it's that incompleteness, as grasped by the humanist subject of modernity, is the Truth of every identity.

Notes

1. See, for instance, Andreas Malm, *Fossil Capital: The Rise of Steam Power and the Roots of Global Warming* (New York: Verso, 2016); and, Jason W. Moore, *Capitalism in the Web of Life: Ecology and the Accumulation of Capital* (New York: Verso, 2016).

2. For instance, see Steven Shaviro, "Consequences of Pansychism," in *The Nonhuman Turn*, ed. Richard Grusin (Minneapolis: University of Minnesota Press, 2015), 19–44. Shaviro also elaborates on his pansychism in his book on Whitehead, *The Universe of Things: On Speculative Realism* (Minneapolis: University of Minnesota Press, 2014).

3. Levi Bryant, for instance, argues that all things are machinic objects of different kinds in *Onto-Cartography: An Ontology of Machines and Media* (Edinburgh: University of Edinburgh Press, 2014). Bryant's object-oriented ontology draws similarly from the object-oriented philosophy of Graham Harman who, likewise, also argues that all things are objects of various kinds. See *Object-Oriented Ontology: A New Theory of Everything* (New York: Pelican, 2018).

4 Claude Lévi-Strauss, *The Savage Mind* (Chicago: University of Chicago Press, 1966), 247.
5 Cited in Kate Soper, *Humanism and Anti-Humanism* (La Salle: Open Court Press, 1986), 97.
6 Quentin Meillassoux, *After Finitude: An Essay on the Necessity of Contingency*, trans. Ray Brassier (New York: Continuum, 2008), 53.
7 Graham Harman, *Tool-Being: Heidegger and the Metaphysics of Objects* (Chicago: Open Court, 2002), 2.
8 Henri Lefebvre, *Dialectical Materialism*, trans. John Sturrock (Minneapolis: University of Minnesota Press, 2009).
9 See also, Boris Groys (ed.), *Russian Cosmism* (Cambridge, MA: MIT Press, 2018).
10 On this point, see Slavoj Žižek, "Sexuality in the Posthuman Age," *Stasis* 4, no. 1 (2016): 54–69.
11 Jean-Paul Sartre, *Being and Nothingness*, trans. Hazel E. Barnes (New York: Washington Square Press, 1984), 728–9.
12 Louis Althusser, "Marx and Freud," in *Writings on Psychoanalysis: Freud and Lacan*, trans. Jeffrey Mehlman (New York: Columbia University Press, 1996), 114–15.
13 On this point, see Anna Kornbluh, *The Order of Forms: Realism, Formalism, and Social Space* (Chicago: University of Chicago Press, 2019), 139–55.
14 Joan Copjec, *Imagine There's No Woman: Ethics and Sublimation* (Cambridge, MA: MIT Press, 2002), 7.
15 Joan Copjec, "Sex and the Euthanasia of Reason," in *Read My Desire: Lacan Against the Historicists* (Cambridge, MA: MIT Press, 1994).

PART III

Glossary

14

Fantasy

Todd McGowan

One of Slavoj Žižek's favorite lines of attack targets those who invoke the importance of stories. He opposes categorically the attempt to understand others through paying attention to their stories. This is because their stories—and narrative as such—have a hidden fantasmatic function. When we tell a story about ourselves, we do not relate our history but our fantasy about this history. We erect this fantasy in order to avoid the basic antagonism that haunts our desire—the impossibility of discovering an object that could provide the satisfaction that it promises. For Žižek, it is only by confronting the fundamental antagonism of subjectivity that we can make any political or theoretical advance. Taking a critical approach to fantasy is requisite for the confrontation with antagonism.

All narrative is rooted in fantasy. Narrative places events in chronological order so that they no longer appear contradictory. As Žižek puts it in *The Plague of Fantasies* (his work most devoted to the logic of fantasy), "fantasy is the primordial form of *narrative*, which serves to occult some original deadlock" (*PF*, 10). Every subject confronts a deadlock relative to its own desire. The object is desirable only insofar as it is impossible. But fantasy intervenes with a story that narrates a barrier to accessing the object.

Fantasy's fundamental operation consists in transforming an impossible object into a prohibited object. It makes the impossible object possible. Fantasy provides a matrix through which the subject can discover an otherwise impossible enjoyment attached to the impossible object. By narrating the subject's relation to the object, fantasy tells the subject what it is supposed to desire. The fundamental question that the subject confronts in its existence is the desire of the Other.

The desire of the Other is always a blank space for the subject. The Other cannot simply tell the subject what it wants because the Other doesn't know its own desire. This blank space is the source of trauma for the subject. But fantasy intervenes to rescue the subject from this trauma. In *The Sublime Object of Ideology*, Žižek explains, "fantasy functions as a construction, as an imaginary scenario filling out the void, the opening of the *desire of the Other*: by giving us a definite answer to the question 'What does the Other want?'" (*SOI*, 114–15). Thanks to fantasy, the problem of the Other's desire becomes manageable.

Even though fantasy obscures the fundamental antagonism of subjectivity, we cannot simply do without it. Fantasy isn't just the imagined realization of desire. It sets down the path for desire in the first place. Fantasy shows us how we are to desire. It tells me that I want, for instance, a strawberry cake or a brand new car. Its narrative structure provides a matrix that teaches me how to desire.

Through its narrative structure, fantasy always domesticates trauma. By placing the trauma of subjectivity in a chronological form, fantasy obfuscates the nature of the trauma. This is why psychoanalysis is not about constructing a narrative about our trauma and integrating it into a coherent narrative. Narrative describes a history of loss, but what it occludes is that the loss is constitutive of subjectivity and not the result of any specific event. Fantasmatic narrative hides the constitutive status of trauma for the subject.

But Žižek's view of fantasy is not simply negative. While fantasy obfuscates the subject's inherent antagonism and translates this antagonism into narrative, it also enables the subject to encounter the Real of its desire in a way that it cannot within social reality. In this sense, fantasy has a radicality for Žižek that reality lacks. As he puts it in *The Fragile Absolute*, "in the opposition between fantasy and reality, the Real is on the side of fantasy" (*FA*, 67). In this sense, traversing the fantasy, as Žižek understands it, does not involve abandoning fantasy or moving beyond it.

When talking about traversing the fantasy, Žižek often cites a passage from Richard Boothby's *Freud as Philosopher* that points toward a different understanding of this idea. Boothby writes, "To traverse the phantasy in the Lacanian sense is to be more profoundly claimed by the phantasy than ever, in the sense of being brought into in ever more intimate relation with that real core of the phantasy that transcends imaging."[1] Traversing the fantasy doesn't take us away from fantasy but enables us to adopt a different relation to it. It enables us to confront the point of loss in the fantasy. By being "more profoundly claimed" by it, we cease to allow it to operate as the supplement of ideology and instead foreground the enjoyment that fantasy provides. We go all in for fantasy at the expense of considerations for our social reality.

After traversing the fantasy, Žižek believes, we move from the domain of desire to that of drive. Drive is desire without fantasy functioning as its hidden supplement. Traversing the fantasy shifts fantasy from being an obscene supplement to one's subjectivity to being openly the form of one's enjoyment. Fantasy becomes central and no longer plays the role of ideology's underside.

Because every symbolic structure needs this underside, it is always vulnerable. When we are able to traverse the fantasy, we are able to act. This act is what breaks up the ideological consensus. After the traversing of the fantasy and the entrance into the domain of the drive, we are able to act.

The point of psychoanalysis, as Žižek sees it, is radically opposed to that of other forms of therapy. Whereas therapy helps the subject to construct a coherent narrative of identity that smooths out the disturbances of psychic life, psychoanalysis is "radically *anti-narrativist*: the ultimate aim of psychoanalytic treatment is *not* for the analysand to organize his confused life experience into (another) coherent narrative, with all the traumas properly integrated, and so on" (*PF*, 10). By wrenching us out of the narratives that we tell about ourselves, psychoanalysis blocks the everyday functioning of fantasy. Rather than allowing us to remain comfortably immersed in our fantasies, we must, according to Žižek, take up the logic of fantasy so much so that it radically undermines our sense of reality. It is only by going through the fantasy that we can change our reality.

Note

1 Richard Boothby, *Freud as Philosopher: Metapsychology After Lacan* (New York: Routledge, 2001), 275–6.

15

Ideology

Glyn Daly

Ideology is a complex notion that Žižek has continued to develop and refine throughout his work. Drawing on Lacanian categories, Žižek states that the basic "function of ideology is not to offer us a point of escape from our reality but to offer us the social reality itself as an escape from some traumatic, real kernel" (*SOI*, 45). In the first instance, ideology serves as a form of defense against the Real-as-impossible. As the inherent limit of the symbolic order, the Real is always in excess of that order (it cannot be symbolized) and threatens to overrun it. Ideology is a reaction to this and seeks to augment the symbolic order of what we call "reality" and to bestow upon it a fantasmatic consistency that is capable of mediating and displacing the negative excesses of the Real. In this way, ideology attempts to generate a sense of reality as a coherent intelligible order. Put in other terms reality *itself* is the fantasmatic distortion, a distortion that ideology deploys in order to counteract the disintegrative effects of the Real.

Ideology should thus be understood as thoroughly *realist* in orientation. Far from being limited to an idealist or normative vision of the world, the central function of ideology is to naturalize an existing power framework of reality—which in the modern age is capitalism—and to impose a kind of spontaneous lifeworld for its ongoing reproduction in an everyday sense. This relies simultaneously on a process of externalization. The paradigmatic example here is twentieth-century fascism where the fantasmatic figure of "the Jew" came to symbolize fundamental social blockage (the central impossibility that prevents society from becoming a full identity) and as the point at which "social negativity as such assumes positive existence" (*SOI*, 143). In this way the inherent negativity that thwarts all society from within—the failures, inconsistencies, antagonistic disruptions, and so on—is projected into the image of the "Jew" who appears as a foreign intruder threatening social decay and corruption from the outside. By providing a "cause" (a convenient explanation) for all the symptoms of social blockage in 1930s Germany (deflation, mass unemployment, economic stagnation, etc.), Nazi ideology was able to preserve both the basic framework of capitalist relations and the image of potential holistic unity ("Free Germany from the Jews" was a common Nazi slogan along with "One People, One Empire, One Leader").

This externalization of social negativity is the hallmark of all ideology and can be seen at work in today's forms of nationalism and populism where various groups (Muslims, Mexicans, immigrants, etc.) are made responsible for the ills of society. Such negativity can also be projected more widely into images of institutional corruption. With Brexit, for example, we see how the repeated emphasis on the idea of a Eurocratic elite (the "Brussels Grandees") was used to convey the sense of external blockage and to reinforce Johnson's idea of an EU-free "Golden age for Britain." Trump, on the other hand, combined barely concealed racist and xenophobic discourse with the idea of a covert "deep state" sustaining decadent liberal privilege and conspiring against the people, preventing America from becoming "great again."

Žižek's critique of ideology contains within it a radical theoretical innovation in respect of the dimension of antagonism. In contrast to the post-Marxist view of antagonism, where "the presence of the 'Other' prevents me from being totally myself,"[1] Žižek affirms that antagonism is rather a manifestation of *auto-negativity*. Through the persistence of the subject (the void of $), identity is always-already blocked and this is projected onto a specific Other, construed as responsible for that blockage. As mediated through ideology, concrete antagonisms are essentially a *symptom*, a way of trying to cover up the more radical dimension of auto-negativity and avoid the traumatic knowledge of the pure inherent antagonism that resides at the heart of all identity. This is also what allows Žižek to retain a certain notion of *false consciousness*, not in the sense of a failure to recognize an external positive truth but precisely the opposite: a failure to recognize that there is no access to such positivity and that the negativity of the Real is not an external obstacle that can be overcome but is something radically inherent, a constitutive limit of the socio-symbolic order as such.

According to Žižek, ideological subjects are particularly disturbed by the idea of the Other's *jouissance* or enjoyment: the Other as a figure who is stealing our enjoyment by ruining our "way of life" and/or has access to perverse forms of enjoyment that can be fantasized about (the attributed dark desires and excesses of the Other that are perceived as both threatening and fascinating). At the same time, ideology also seeks to "bribe" the subject directly with enjoyment. In fascism, for example, the public discourse of sacrifice/duty served simultaneously as private license for its followers to indulge in all manner of violence and cruelty against Jews and other "inferiors." In the contemporary era, however, this public/private distinction is breaking down. With the rise of the alt-right movement and the global expansion of right-wing populism, for example, the public baiting of "snowflakes" along with sexist machismo, obscene language, and the dismissal of traditional forms of polite public discourse as "cuckservative" has become commonplace—all of which are openly enjoyed.

Ideology is further distinguished in providing forms of agency but in such a way that they are deprived of their malignant quality: that is, the capacity to act, to break free of the existing order of possibility. Put in other terms, all current forms of impossibility can be overcome (via advances in neurotechnology, genetic manipulation, augmented reality, etc.) *except* for the impossibility of overcoming the capitalist system as such—this persists as today's silently operating magisterium. This is especially the case with today's discourse on ecology and sustainability where the subject is encouraged to do their duty (conserve energy, recycle, etc.) but precisely as a way avoiding more searching questions about the realities of the capitalist system (e.g., the fact that just 100 companies are responsible for almost three-quarters of global emissions). Rather than a straightforward consistency of message, the ideological operation consists in developing forms of reflexive critique (opposition to waste, pollution, overconsumption, etc.) that remain crucially *within* the terms of the capitalist horizon. This brings us full circle to the realist character of ideology in its naturalization of capitalism as an unquestioned reality.

Does this consequently mean that we can never escape ideology? The answer to this cannot be unambiguous. Insofar as there exists no positive critique (we cannot transcend all distortion to see the world as it really is), we remain within the terms of ideology. Yet this does not preclude the possibility of a certain kind of negative critique. Here Žižek draws upon the Hegelian notion of reconciliation, which consists not in the positive overcoming of the distortion of negative excess but in the opposite recognition that negative excess is both inherent and constitutive of existence as such. In a countermove to the ideological externalization of negativity into a concrete blockage, reconciliation shows that the true blockage is precisely this externalization as such. While there is nothing tangible beyond ideology, it nonetheless remains as always non-all.

Note

1 Ernesto Laclau and Chantal Mouffe, *Hegemony and Socialist Strategy* (London: Verso, 1985), 125.

16

Universality

Ilan Kapoor

If the postmodern Left tends toward jettisoning the Enlightenment idea of universality, Žižek vigorously defends it: for him, now more than ever, the universalist project that is capitalism needs to be matched politically, not by a skepticism toward but an embrace of a Left universality. The challenge though is doing so without falling into "abstract universalism," which more often than not, yields to a politics of exclusion, if not neocolonialism.

Indeed, the problem with abstract universalism is that it asserts an *a priori* category (rooted in, say, nature, humanism, or reason), which is then applied to all circumstances. It gives way to an indifference to particularity, "disinterestedly" deploying an assumed or self-evident truth to all specifics ("All men are born equal," "Europeans are civilized," "reason trumps passion," etc.). It thereby masks as neutral and objective while being enunciated from a particular position. Take today's liberal human rights discourse, for example: based on a rational-moral account of the requirements for human flourishing, it famously promulgates universal rights and protections (e.g., equality before the law, private property rights, civil and political freedoms). But the problem is that such a conception is a Western liberal one parading as universal: it secretly privileges, for instance, individual rights over group ones, civil and political rights and protections over socioeconomic ones, and by favoring private property rights in the context of patriarchy, white male property owners over workers, racialized groups, and women. Moreover, in recent decades it has been used to justify neocolonial and military-foreign policy objectives: as is well known, the 2003 US invasion of Iraq, and takeover of its oil fields, was justified on the basis of "bringing freedom and democracy" to the country, pointing up anew the extent to which abstract universalism can serve as a façade.

Žižek offers instead an alternate conceptualization of universalism—a negative universality—that averts these problems while enabling a universal political project. Given abstract universalism's limitation of identifying the universal with a *positive* content (an *a priori* or particular essence), Žižek's proposal, drawing on Hegel and Lacan, is to identify universality *negatively*, that is, through that which is absent rather than present: "every universality can only present itself 'as such' in a negative way" (*ET*, 335), he writes. Since, according to Hegel,[1] every identity/thought depends on that to which it stands in opposition (e.g., positive universalism is meaningful only in relation to an Other, i.e., particularism), contradiction is not to be seen as its limitation or weakness but its very driving force. Antagonism (the Real), for Žižek, is therefore the "internal condition of every identity" (*SOI*, 6). In this sense, what is universal is neither identity nor thought but the antagonism that structures both.

Since the universal is the name of the gap (the Real) that prevents the particular from achieving its self-identity (*CHU*, 217), it is always particularized. But this is only to rehearse the aforementioned point that every identity is always unstable, that is, at odds with itself, unable to be identical with itself, as when the "universal" rights of white male property owners inevitably bump up against the rights of women, racialized groups, workers, and so on. As Žižek states, "the Universal emerges within the Particular when some particular content starts to function as the stand-in for the absent Universal—that is to say, the universal is operative only through the split in the particular" (*TS*, 176).

Several important political implications follow. First, because negative universality is (and can only be) taken up from a particular vantage point, it is always partial, partisan, contingent (*LN*, 285). The paradox here is that universality can only be articulated from a specific standpoint, making it possible to avert the postmodern trap of insisting on particularity while denying truth. Žižek avers in fact that "*universal Truth is accessible* [but] *only from a partial engaged subject position*" (*PV*, 35). In part, this is definitional, since any claim to the particular cannot be made without recourse to the universal. As Hegel famously notes, the master *needs* the slave-as-Other in order to be recognized as master (i.e., the very claim to masterhood is unintelligible without a shared universal language). In the same vein, Balibar[2] points out that a racist anti-universalism (e.g., "whites are superior to Blacks") must invoke a universal benchmark (the notion of what it is to be human) to enable the comparison between white and Black in the first place. Particularity needs an Other (and a shared language) to distinguish itself as unique, thus always proclaiming its particularity from a universal standpoint.

But partly, the universal truth-dimension of every particular stems from the antagonism at its very heart. Truth emerges from both the specific configuration that makes particularity particular and the universality of the antagonism to which such particularity responds. This is to say that truth is both contingent *and* universal. Every situation may well articulate a particular truth, but the emergence of that truth arises due to the universal-as-Real that besets all situations (*CHU*, 315). The Real is thereby a contextualized antagonism: it is not some unchanging substance but is immanent to every sociohistorical order, reflecting any such order's inability to fully constitute itself. As Žižek declares, "What all epochs share is not some trans-epochal constant feature; it is, rather, that they are all answers to the same deadlock" (*CZ*, 76).

Second, it is the antagonism at the hub of every particular that enables the possibility of shared struggle. When each particular (e.g., an identity-based movement, worker's struggle, or anti-globalization protest) discovers that the deadlock which stymies it is also the deadlock that stymies others, then their common predicament becomes the basis for political solidarity. What each particular shares is not a positive content (e.g., an identity, which can end up dividing people across class, gender, North-South, or racial lines) but an inability to complete itself (as a result of common patterns of socioeconomic marginalization, exploitation, etc.): "a particular demand . . . starts to function as a metaphoric condensation of the global [universal] opposition against Them, those in power, so that the protest is no longer just about that demand, but about the universal dimension that resonates in that particular demand" (*TS*, 204). It is this shared universality-as-antagonism that, for Žižek, lays the groundwork for a global Left politics today.

Finally, and most importantly for Žižek, negative universality foregrounds the "part of no-part" (the slum dwellers, rural subalterns, refugees, Indigenous communities, the homeless, the precariat, the permanently unemployed, the gendered, disabled, and racialized poor, etc.). This is because any positive universalism such as global capitalism has a symptom, an element that must remain an exception for the very constitution of that universalism—the part of no-part. They are symptomatic of capitalism's founding gesture—socioeconomic and spatial inequality—and although excluded from the System, they are its ultimate support. Žižek designates them as the "concrete universal," since it is from their *particular* vantage point that the truth of the System is revealed (*TS*, 92). And because they are outcasts, when they present themselves as exemplars of the universal, they do so legitimately since, unlike all other groups, they have no stake in the System. Their exceptional particularity enables them, paradoxically, to embrace universality, standing not for exclusive but universal interests.

Notes

1 G. W. F. Hegel, *The Science of Logic*, trans. George Di Giovanni (Cambridge: Cambridge University Press, 2010), 360. G. W. F. Hegel, *Phenomenology of Spirit*, trans. John Niemeyer Findlay (Oxford: Clarendon Press, 1977), 138.
2 Étienne Balibar, *Politics and the Other Scene* (London: Verso, 2002), 146.

17

The Subject

Russell Sbriglia

At the outset of his book *The Ticklish Subject*, Žižek, troping on the opening lines of *The Communist Manifesto*, proclaims that "A spectre is haunting Western academia [. . .] the spectre of the Cartesian subject" (*TS*, 1). As he elaborates, regardless of their differences from—even, in some instances, their outright hostilities toward—one another, virtually "all academic powers," from the "New Age obscurantist," "Deep Ecologist," "cognitive scientist," and "Heideggerian proponent of the thought of Being" to the "postmodern deconstructionist," "critical (post-)Marxist," "feminist," and "Habermasian theorist of communication," are united in their desire to reject the Cartesian subject and "exorcize this spectre" once and for all (*TS*, 1). Standing firmly against this tide, Žižek insists not merely on the continued relevance, but on the very necessity of the Cartesian subject for proper philosophical thinking, especially in a materialist vein. What he means by "Cartesian subject," however, is considerably different from its classic understanding.

According to the classic understanding, the Cartesian subject, as epitomized by the dictum *cogito ergo sum*, "I think, therefore I am," is a rational, self-present, self-transparent entity, an autonomous, atomized agent that stands both apart from and above other types of being. Žižek's understanding of the Cartesian subject, however, is shaped by its retheorization—and radicalization—throughout the two traditions that most inform his thought: German Idealism and Lacanian psychoanalysis, both of which advance theories of a fundamentally "irrational," opaque, abyssal subject, a subject inherently "out of joint" not only with itself but with the rest of the "great chain of being" as well.

This retheorization/radicalization begins with Kant, who draws attention to the "parallax gap," as Žižek would put it, between the Cartesian *cogito*, the "I think," and the *res cogitans*, the "thing which thinks." Whereas

Descartes presumed that the act of the *cogito* renders self-present and self-transparent the *res cogitans*, Kant reveals the impossibility of these two entities ever coinciding or overlapping. In Kant's idealist nomenclature, the "I" of "transcendental apperception" and the "I or he or it (the thing) which thinks" are forever incommensurable; the former can only ever be a "simple, and in itself completely empty, representation" of the latter, an emptiness which Kant designates via an "X."[1] The upshot of this discovery, Žižek explains, is that "the 'I' exists only as ex-sisting, at a distance from the 'thing' that it is" (*SFA*, 66). This is the paradox of self-consciousness with which Kant confronts us, that "I am conscious of myself only insofar as I am out of reach to myself qua the real kernel of my being ['I or he or it (the thing) which thinks']," that "I cannot acquire consciousness of myself in my capacity of the 'Thing which thinks'" (*TN*, 15).

Enter Lacan, who, thinking Kant's "Copernican revolution" alongside that of Freud's, posits this gap between *cogito* and *res cogitans* as the unconscious. Drawing upon Freud's crucial insight that the unconscious thinks—an insight best encapsulated by his famous claim that "*the ego is not master in its own house*"—Lacan asserts that the dictum of the subject is not "I think, therefore I am," but rather, "I am thinking where I am not, therefore I am where I am not thinking," or, as he rephrases this, "I am not, where I am the plaything of my thoughts; I think about what I am where I do not think I am thinking."[2] That the "I" is the plaything of thoughts of which it is not conscious of thinking is why Lacan insists that the subject is the subject of the unconscious. Hence his transposition of the "X" that is the Kantian transcendental subject into "$," his symbol for the "barred subject," the subject "split" or "divided" by the unconscious. Like Kant's transcendental subject, the Lacanian subject, as the matheme $ is intended to convey, is ineluctably estranged from itself. And yet, as Žižek stresses, in both cases, this self-estrangement, this self-division, is not a sign of the subject's undoing or "deconstruction," but rather its constitution as such, for *the subject is nothing but this very estrangement*.

And this finally brings us to Hegel, the (not so vanishing) mediator between Kant and Lacan, whose system Žižek uses Lacanian psychoanalysis as a means of "reactualiz[ing]" (*SOI*, 7). As Žižek explains, though Kant correctly identified the "problematic" of the "transcendental constitution" of self-consciousness (*TN*, 39)—its "*possib[ility] only against the background of its own impossibility*" (*TN*, 15)—he failed to take the next step of identifying this parallax gap or antinomy, this empty, unfathomable X, with the subject as such. More precisely, he failed to accomplish the "Hegelian reflexive reversal of *recognizing in this 'nothing' the very negativity that defines the notion of the subject*" (*ME*, 143). This, Žižek explains, is why "Hegel rails at Kant more than at any other philosopher"—not because he is anti-Kantian but, on the contrary, because he is "*more Kantian than Kant himself*" (*ME*, 187). Hegel excoriates Kant because he saw that "Kant was already there" but "radically misrecognized" (*ME*, 187) his discovery of "the subject *qua* the void of negativity" (*ME*, 47), a void which Hegel famously dubs the "night of the world," the "empty nothing" we discover when we descend into "the interior of [human] nature" and arrive at the "*pure Self*."[3] For Žižek, the pure Self that one encounters in the Hegelian night of the world prefigures the Lacanian subject of the unconscious (*ME*, 43; *TN*, 63); in other words, Hegel accomplishes the passage from X to $ *avant la lettre*. Properly grasping this prefiguration, however, requires reading Hegel "*avec* Lacan" (*MSH*, 1–5), a reading that enables us to see that Hegel's system revolves not around the reconciliation or sublation of any and all differences, however recalcitrant, but rather the emergence of the subject as an irreconcilable, unsublatable kernel of (self-) difference.

Any discussion of Žižek's understanding of the subject would be incomplete, however, if it simply stopped at identifying it as a substanceless void and didn't also attend to the crucial dialectical reversal whereby the emergence of this abyssal subject effectuates a rift or rend in substance itself, thereby preventing it from being entirely "substantial," self-identical. Žižek here follows Hegel's famous adage that "everything turns on grasping and expressing the True, not only as *Substance*, but equally as *Subject*."[4] As Žižek glosses this often misunderstood line, Hegel's point is not that the subject is a mega-actant that "swallow[s] up or internaliz[es] the whole of reality" (*LTN*, 258), but rather that the subject is "a kind of ontological 'crack'" in reality (*TN*, 26), a "crack in the edifice of Being" (*SFA*, 70) that renders reality "ontologically incomplete" (*SFA*, 376), in a state of perpetual becoming. This, above all else, is why Žižek maintains that the subject is indispensable to any sort of materialist (and/or realist) philosophy whatsoever. The specter of the subject can never be exorcized, for as the negativity that "grounds the very positive ontological order" (*TS*, 158), the subject is a being that constitutively haunts being from within, that functions "hauntologically."[5] Were we able to subtract the subject, Žižek insists, we would simultaneously lose the very reality it posits.

Notes

1 Immanuel Kant, *Critique of Pure Reason*, trans. N. Kemp Smith (London: Macmillan, 1929), 331.

2 Sigmund Freud, "A Difficulty in the Path of Psycho-Analysis," in *The Standard Edition of the Complete Psychological Words of Sigmund Freud*, ed. and trans. James Strachey, vol. 17 (London: Hogarth, 1955), 143; Jacques Lacan, "The Instance of the Letter in the Unconscious, or Reason since Freud," in *Écrits: The First Complete Edition in English*, trans. Bruce Fink (New York: Norton, 2006), 430.

3 G. W. F. Hegel, *Hegel and the Human Spirit: A Translation of the Jena Lectures on the Philosophy of Spirit (1805–6)*, trans. Leo Rauch (Detroit: Wayne State University Press, 1983), 87.

4 G. W. F. Hegel, *Phenomenology of Spirit*, trans. A. V. Miller (New York: Oxford University Press, 1977), 10.

5 For Žižek's use of the Derridean neologism "hauntology," see his essay "Against the Populist Temptation," *Critical Inquiry* 32, no. 3 (2006): 565.

18

Symptom

David J. Gunkel

Slavoj Žižek has been concerned with the concept of the symptom from the very beginning. In fact, "The Symptom" comprises the subject matter of the first part of his first book published in English, *The Sublime Object of Ideology* (first published in 1989, second edition issued in 2008). This text begins in a way that is rather characteristic of all Žižek's writings—with a statement from Jacques Lacan that seems, at first, to be counterintuitive: "According to Lacan, it was none other than Karl Marx who invented the notion of symptom" (*SOI*, 3). And the two chapters that follow this statement, "How Marx Invented the Symptom" and "From Symptom to Sinthome," are designed to explicate and develop this insight. In doing so, Žižek provides a characterization of the symptom that can itself be considered symptomatic of Western metaphysics.

The word "symptom" is typically used to indicate a mode of indication. As Todd McGowan explains in the entry "symptom" in the *Žižek Dictionary*, "the usual idea of the symptom in both psychoanalysis and traditional medicine sees it as an indication of an underlying disorder that some form of therapy (either analytic or medicinal) will attempt to cure and thereby eliminate."[1] Formulated in this way, "symptom" is understood as a sign that refers to and is the external manifestation or indication of something that is more fundamental and often hidden from direct perception. We therefore commonly distinguish the symptom from its underlying cause, and this common understanding not only adheres to the standard formula of semiotics but is also informed by an original ontological decision that differentiates between mere external appearances and the more profound substance that is its ultimate cause and referent. Characterized in this fashion, the usual understanding of "symptom" can be accommodated to and explained by a metaphysical arrangement that is at least as old as Plato.

According to the standard account of Platonism, or what is often called (not without controversy) "Plato's theory of the forms," appearances are nothing less than symptoms of more substantial transcendental ideas, and the task of thinking is to learn to penetrate or see beyond these mere external apparitions and gain access to the true form and original cause.

For Žižek, however, the symptom is formulated in a way that is entirely otherwise. "Symptom" is not the sign of some hidden kernel of truth that is more substantial or profound; it is the necessarily excluded other of the system that makes the system possible in the first place. As Žižek explains, "the 'symptom' is, strictly speaking, a particular element which subverts its own universal foundation, a species subverting its own genus . . . a point of breakdown heterogeneous to a given ideological field and at the same time necessary for that field to achieve its closure, its accomplished form" (*SOI*, 16). For this reason, "symptom" possesses a "radical ontological status" (*SOI*, 81); it is the constitutive part of a system that is necessarily excluded from the system as such. Or as Žižek explains by way of a passage he appropriates from Jacques Rancière, it is "the part of no part" (*TS*, 188). The symptom, therefore, comprises the constitutive exception that "threatens the functioning of the system, even though it is the necessary product of this same system."² It is a kind of unacknowledged (and always-already unacknowledgeable) excremental remainder that is necessary for something to produce itself and function as the system that it is. And it is this characterization of the symptom—this "constitutive exception"—that Žižek, following Lacan, identifies with the name "Sinthome."

This alternative conceptualization of the symptom—a conceptualization that is simultaneously dependent on Lacan's work and beyond the circuit of its determinations—turns out to be symptomatic of Platonism. And the fact that Žižek himself never actually acknowledges this as such is just one more symptom of the symptom. It is, in fact, only by excluding this particular concept of the symptom (the very idea of the "constitutive exception"), that Platonism can become what it is. One might recall that Socrates, as was described in Plato's *Apology*, explains and tries to defend his own philosophical efforts as a response to the Oracle at Delphi³. The Delphic temple, as is reported in *Protagoras*,⁴ famously had two laconic statements inscribed above its gate: "Know thyself" and "Nothing in Excess." Although the latter has typically been interpreted as a call to moderation in all things, it can also be read as the trace of the symptom, inscribed at the very gateway to philosophy. In this way, the statement "Nothing in excess" may be interpreted as an exclusive operation, indicating that whatever might come to exceed the grasp of self-knowing is to remain unacknowledged, unknowable, or nothing. Consequently, every attempt to demarcate the proper boundaries of a system and cordon off its internal workings from what it is not, always and without exception, produces an exceptional externality that it must deny—an absolutely other that is cast off, externalized, and remains nothing.

Notes

1 Todd McGowan, "Symptom," in *The Žižek dictionary*, ed. Rex Butler (Durham: Acumen, 2014), 242.
2 McGowan, "Symptom," 242.
3 Plato, *Apology*, trans. H. N. Fowler (Cambridge, MA: Harvard University Press, 1982), 21a.
4 Plato, *Protagoras*, trans. W. R. M. Lamb (Cambridge, MA: Harvard University Press, 1977), 324b.

19

Class Struggle

Matthew W. Bost

Marx and Engels famously argued that under capitalism, "all that is solid melts into air." Through strategies from settler colonialism and the enclosure of common lands to the abstractions of contemporary finance capital and mediated globalization, capital violently uproots subjects from their symbolic coordinates, splitting subjectivity between constantly proliferating identities and communal orientations. For Žižek, class struggle names the material kernel of antagonism organizing this "multitude of perspectives" (176), a kernel that emancipatory struggles must engage if they are to contest contemporary forms of domination.[1]

Žižek argues that theories of identity as fluid, multiple, and overdetermined get at crucial aspects of contemporary subjectivity. Such perspectives nonetheless tend to treat some features of life (especially the economy and parliamentary democracy) as depoliticized defaults, exempting them from critique. While the empirical fact of socioeconomic class can be reduced to one dimension of identity among others, "the class and commodity structure of capitalism is not just a phenomenon limited to the particular 'domain' of economy, but the structuring principle that determines the social totality" (332, n. 167). Class is thus inscribed in contemporary politics as an empirical category *and* as the logic whereby elements of subjectivity and consumer objects alike are abstracted and circulated through commodity exchange, shaping identity according to the relational forms of the market. Class struggle occupies the position of the Lacanian Real of capitalism: a point of immanent failure that structures the constitutive tensions at the heart of this logic and an antagonism that saturates the entire social body (182). "[C]lass struggle is ultimately the struggle for the meaning of society 'as such'" (210), determining not just who will occupy the empty signifiers of contemporary political authority (e.g., "the People") but also the boundaries between society and what is excluded from social community *tout court* and designated as "the destruction of, the threat to, society" (210).

Žižek's rethinking of class struggle leads to a further rethinking of the Marxian figures of the working class and proletariat. Class struggle is actualized through multiple layers of social composition, from feminist, antiracist, and anti-imperialist social movements to the host of uprisings that have confronted capitalism with its violent exclusions over the past several decades (300). Class struggle provides a "formal generative matrix" (190) for understanding the solidarities uniting these movements, as well as how they might avoid the trap of a politics that argues in the name of a specific identity position without engaging the structures that produce identity under capitalism. Similarly, the Marxian proletariat as agent of world history does not simply describe the empirical working class but is the structural position delineating the point of failure or contradiction that limns capital's Symbolic order. Many different groups can occupy the proletarian position of "the embodiment of social negativity" (336, n. 208). The crucial question is, therefore, "who is able to subjectivize" (336) the proletarian position in a given moment, challenging capital at the level of its governing logic.

Žižek's reconsideration of the proletariat leads him to endorse a Hegelian "concrete universality" (300) that centers partisanship and antagonism as the true universal positions, and locates universality in the tension between particulars that shape what different versions of "the universal" look like. In contrast, capital proffers an abstract universality that represses, disavows, or forecloses particularity completely. Abstract universalism underwrites neoliberal discourses of multiculturalism, appeals to universal human rights, and so-called religious fundamentalisms alike, all of which locate social antagonism in the concrete figure of an Other who is treated as outside the national or global community. Neoliberal multiculturalism tolerates its Others (as long as they remain exploitable, one-dimensional, and safely at a distance), but the same logic manifests in the obscene supplement of new fascisms and so-called religious fundamentalisms that treat the Other as an enemy to be exterminated, as well as in military interventionism in the name of universal "humanity." The forms of subjectivity fostered by these discourses displace the histories of violent dispossession and exploitation that are internal to capitalism's global order. By contrast, class struggle provides a way to produce a universal position that grapples with the violence of capital head-on *and* that enables a working-through of the structural inequalities that generate contemporary racialized, gendered, sexual, national, and socioeconomic differences.

The political task of class struggle is to find organizational forms that can sustain this antagonism. One such form is the Leninist vanguard Party, often written off as elitist and authoritarian. On Žižek's reading, the Party does not lead the masses toward "determinate positive knowledge" (188) but functions similarly to the psychoanalytic "subject-supposed-to-know," orienting political knowledge production around a "collective ... subject" (188) that sustains dissent and conflict *within* the orientation toward antagonism provided by the Party. The "externality" (189) of the Party relative to individuals recognizes the fact that class consciousness is never spontaneous but requires mediation through collectives that allow "the working class to perceive its own place within the social totality" (187) and that create transferential relationships between individual subjects and collective struggles.

As the reference to Lenin suggests, Žižek also advocates a reckoning with historical revolutionary projects from the Jacobins to twentieth-century communism. We can acknowledge that such projects "failed, even failed monstrously," while affirming the "field of possibilities" they opened up (310), especially in moments from the Paris Commune to the early 1920s Soviet Union to the Shanghai Commune where masses of people, taking the egalitarian promise of revolutionary slogans at their word, "act[ed] *as if* the utopian future" was directly at hand (259). Repeating these moments in the present entails a direct reckoning with the anxiety and terror that accompany revolutionary change and a rejection of the "attitude of 'innocence'" toward political struggle that, in practice, means "saying 'yes' to existing relations of domination" (194). It also entails fidelity to missed revolutionary opportunities, moments where things might have gone completely differently. In their untimeliness with respect to the present, such moments (similarly to the Party) offer the potential for reorganizing subjectivity around a set of histories and political forms that throw the inevitability of capitalism into question.

Note

1 Slavoj Žižek, "Afterward: Lenin's Choice," V. I. Lenin, in *Revolution at the Gates: A Selection of Writings from February to October 1917*, ed. Slavoj Žižek (London: Verso, 2011), 167–336.

20

Violence

Oxana Timofeeva

In the language of today's media and everyday social life, the word "violence" has exclusively negative connotations. All sorts of violence—domestic, police, gender, terrorist, racial, psychological, and so on—are associated with actual forms of intimidation and abuse. In the domain of public morality, violence is categorically denounced as evil or treated as rather an embarrassing obstacle to the progressive development of human values. However, this strategy of rejection does not really help to eliminate violence altogether. Moreover, the liberal ideology of nonviolent tolerance has as its side effects, unprecedented outbursts of violence here and there, as if we were dealing with the processes of the return of the repressed, already described in Freudian psychoanalysis. As the old Russian proverb has it, "we drive it out the door, and it climbs in through the window."

Against this background, there is an alternative intellectual tradition of interpreting violence rather in political terms, outside of the field of public morals. This underlying tradition is opposed to widespread commonsensical experiences. Left-wing thinkers especially, from the very beginning of the twentieth century, discuss violence within the domain of actual and historical political struggles. Basically, according to this line of thought, which unites such different and outstanding authors as Vladimir Lenin, Georges Sorel, Walter Benjamin, Frantz Fanon, and some others, there are two kinds of violence. Violence of the first kind comes from the strongest, from those in power. It can be the violence of police against protesters, the violence of the state, colonial violence, and so on. This oppressive violence is often recognized not as violence but as the norm, and that can also be referred to, in Hannah Arendt's terms, as the "banality of evil"[1]: one commits it, for instance, because it is his or her job, or because they simply obey the law. Against this normalized, banalized violence, and as a response to it, another kind of violence emerges, which is the violence of the oppressed. This second kind of violence is generally associated with the people's struggles for liberation or other spontaneous and organized reaction to the injustices of the world. Thus, Sorel opposes the general proletarian strike to the violence of the state, whereas Fanon calls for the armed resistance of the native people in the colonies.

Slavoj Žižek definitely belongs to this radical tradition, which, in terms of Walter Benjamin, can be called the tradition of the oppressed and which keeps fidelity to the spirit of great revolutions. The main reference in Žižek's own theory of violence is Walter Benjamin, who differentiated between the two kinds of violence as the mythic and the divine.[2] The mythic violence, according to Benjamin, is the violence of the law. It can be either law-making or law-preserving: these two functions perfectly coincide in such an "ignominious" institution as the police, which does violence in the name of the law.[3] Benjamin's divine violence, on the other hand, is antagonistic to the mythic in all respects: "If mythic violence is lawmaking, divine violence is law-destroying; if the former sets boundaries, the latter boundlessly destroys them; if mythic violence brings at once guilt and retribution, divine power only expiates; if the former threatens, the latter strikes; if the former is bloody, the latter is lethal without spilling blood."[4] Importantly, Benjamin does not idealize or romanticize divine violence: in fact, it can be as glorious, as monstrous. Revolutionary terror is one of the examples of this violence, which is called "divine" not because it is committed in the name of God or sanctioned by God, but precisely because there is no God, Law, or any authority behind it. Therefore, Benjamin also defines it as "sovereign." In Žižek's words: "there is no big Other guaranteeing its divine nature" (V, 200). Katerina Kolozova comments on this: "Enacted in radical solitude, without the support of the 'big Other,' pure violence, conceived as blind attack 'demanding immediate justice,' seems indeed to be carried out as divine."[5]

Apart from Benjamin's theory, three sources and three component parts constitute Žižek's concept of violence (as well as other concepts of his philosophy). The first is Hegel. The essential methodological and conceptual element that comes from Hegel is negativity, the idea of the cut that breaks the regular flow of things. The second source is Marx and his critique of capital. The third is Lacanian psychoanalysis with its differentiation between reality and the Real as the structure that we do not perceive. This constellation creates Žižek's own version of dialectical materialism, wherein the concept of violence is interpreted through philosophical negativity laid on the analysis of the Real as "the inexorable, 'abstract,' spectral logic of capital that determines what goes on in social reality" (V, 13).

Žižek's two kinds of violence are objective and subjective.[6] Subjective include the most visible things, such as crimes, whereas the first type, objective, is invisible, normalized, and itself divides into two kinds—

symbolic (the violence of language or symbolic order) and systemic. Regarding the first kind of violence, Sorel speaks of the violence of the state, Benjamin of the violence of the law, Fanon of the violence of the colonizers, whereas Žižek unmasks the systemic and objective violence of capitalism, which is in the Real, and he develops strong philosophical arguments for the violence that is opposed to it. Rejecting tolerance as an ideological category, he claims that "The formula of revolutionary solidarity is not 'let us tolerate our differences,' it is not a pact of civilizations, but a pact of struggles which cut across civilization, a pact between what, in each civilization, undermines its identity from within, fights against its oppressive kernel. What unites us is the same struggle" (V, 157). Most important is that, according to Žižek, what gives to this solidarity its main transformative and emancipatory drive is the negativity of love. As he states in the concluding chapter of his book on violence: "The notion of love should be given here all its Paulinian weight: *the domain of pure violence*, the domain outside law (legal power), the domain of the violence which is neither law-founding nor law-sustaining, is the domain of love" (V, 205).

Notes

1 See Hannah Arendt, *Eichmann in Jerusalem: A Report on the Banality of Evil* (London: Penguin Classic, 2006).
2 Walter Benjamin, *Critique of Violence: Selected Writings Vol. 1 1913–1926* (Cambridge, MA: Harvard University Press, 1996), 236–52.
3 Benjamin, *Critique*, 242–3.
4 Benjamin, *Critique*, 249–50.
5 Katerina Kolozova, "Violence: The Indispensable Condition of the Law (and of the Political)," *Angelaki: Journal of the Theoretical Humanities* 19, no. 2 (June 2014): 107.
6 For the more detailed analysis of the concept of violence in Žižek, see K. Wood, *Žižek: A Reader's Guide* (Hoboken: Wiley-Blackwell, 2012), 257–66.

21

The Death Drive

Zahi Zalloua

Sigmund Freud's death drive—and psychoanalysis as a whole—represents a direct assault on philosophy's pursuit of knowledge and its phantasms of autonomy, sovereignty, and self-sufficiency. The idea of the death drive casts doubt on all curative philosophies. As Žižek avers, there is really no place for the death drive in the history of philosophy. "What is unthinkable for [Spinoza]," Žižek writes, "is what Freud terms 'death drive': the idea that *conatus* is based on a fundamental act of self-sabotaging" (*OWB*, 34). The Freudian death drive scandalizes philosophical discourse, since it discloses human existence itself as an irremediable problem.

Later psychoanalysts, especially those following Lacan's interpretive lead, have downplayed Freud's so-called biologism and reinterpreted the death drive in relation to the symbolic order and the emergence of subjectivity as such. Lacan leaves no doubt about the importance of Freud's notion of the death drive to a psychoanalytic approach: "To evade the death instinct in [Freud's] doctrine is not to know his doctrine at all."[1] For Lacanians, the death drive comes to name an ontological lack, a desire for plenitude, a yearning to return to a state of complete *jouissance* or enjoyment, to what has been lost as a result of one's entry into language, one's symbolic castration. Phantasmatically speaking, the goal is to attain the mysterious, transcendent object (*das Ding*)—"to reproduce the initial state, to find *das Ding*, the object"[2]—that would fully satisfy desire and thus put an end to one's alienation and the suffering one feels when faced with one's mortality. In exposing its illusory character (in showing that the object is not a timeless or immortal being), psychoanalysis hopes to "traverse" this human fantasy of wholeness.

While generally sympathetic to this larger Lacanian framing of the death drive, Žižek gives the Freudian notion still a different twist, highlighting, or better yet harnessing the drive's unruly excess and its self-sabotaging or short-circuiting ways. Two passages illustrate Žižek's position particularly well:

> I think that Freud, to put it in fashionable terms, isolates a certain excess. He calls it death drive, a certain excess of destructability that is, as it were, undermining, destabilizing the social order, an excess that is ambiguous in the sense that it can be a source of constructive energy or it can be purely destructive. The idea is that Freud isolates this space of excess, which then, of course, opens up the space for possible change. I think Freud's basic answer would have been: psychoanalysis just does this elementary job of showing how there is a gap, a failure, a nonfunctioning excess in society.[3]
>
> "Death drive" is not a biological fact but a notion indicating that the human psychic apparatus is subordinated to a blind automatism of repetition beyond pleasure-seeking, self-preservation, accordance between man and his milieu. Man is . . . "an animal sick unto death," an animal excoriated by an insatiable parasite (reason, *logos*, language). In this perspective, the "death drive," this dimension of radical negativity cannot be reduced to an expression of alienated social conditions, it defines *la condition humaine* as such: there is no solution, no escape from it; the thing to do is not to "overcome," to "abolish" it, but to come to terms with it, to learn to recognize it in its terrifying dimension and then, on the basis of this fundamental recognition, to try to articulate a *modus vivendi* with it. All "culture" is in a way a reaction-formation, an attempt to limit, canalize—to *cultivate* this imbalance, this traumatic kernel, this radical antagonism through which man cuts his umbilical cord with nature, with animal homeostasis. (*SOI*, 4–5)

For Žižek, the death drive is constitutive of the human condition (a mixture of language and automatism). There is no transcending this unruly remainder or excess, only acceptance or affirmation. Living with the death drive requires us, then, to abandon its identification with the "Nirvana Principle." Like Lacan, Žižek is emphatic about decoupling the death drive from "the craving for self-annihilation" (*PV*, 62). It is in fact quite at odds with the biological desire for self-destruction:

> The paradox of the Freudian "death drive" is . . . that it is Freud's name for its very opposite, for the way immortality appears within psychoanalysis, for an uncanny *excess* of life, for an "undead" urge which persists beyond the (biological) cycle of life and death, of generation and corruption. The ultimate lesson of psychoanalysis is that human life is never "just life": humans are not simply alive, they are possessed by the strange drive to enjoy life in excess, passionately

attached to a surplus which sticks out and derails the ordinary run of things. (PV, 62)

The death drive is aligned with pure evil, since it always risks undermining the predictability of self-interest, sabotaging the subject's conformity with the pleasure principle:

> The true opposite of egotist self-love is not altruism, a concern for common good, but envy, *ressentiment*, which makes me act against my own interests. Freud knew it well: the death drive is opposed to the pleasure principle as well as to the reality principle. The true evil, which is the death drive, involves self-sabotage. It makes us act against our own interests. (V, 87)

Rereading the death drive as "a 'natural' glitch in human nature"[4] and a hunger for immortality counterintuitively foregrounds the unruly "inhuman" at the core of the human, *what is in us more than us*.

Notes

1 Jacques Lacan, "The Subversion of the Subject and the Dialectic of Desire in the Freudian Unconscious," in *Écrits: The First Complete Edition in English*, trans. Bruce Fink (New York: Norton, 2006), 681.

2 Jacques Lacan, *The Ethics of Psychoanalysis, 1959–1960, The Seminar of Jacques Lacan, Book VII*, ed. Jacques-Alain Miller, trans. Dennis Porter (New York: Norton, 1992), 53.

3 Slavoj Žižek, "Unbehagen and the Subject: An Interview with Slavoj Žižek," *Psychoanalysis, Culture & Society* 15 (2010): 422.

4 Adrian Johnston, *Žižek's Ontology: A Transcendental Materialist Theory of Subjectivity* (Evanston: Northwestern University Press, 2008), 183.

CONTRIBUTORS

Matthew W. Bost is Associate Professor of Rhetoric, Writing, and Public Discourse at Whitman College. His work focuses on the relationship between rhetoric, philosophy, and social change, with an emphasis on histories of communism, feminism, and rhetorics of the posthuman. His work has been published in *Rhetoric Society Quarterly*, *Philosophy and Rhetoric*, and other spaces. His recent publications have explored the role of trope in Karl Marx's *Eighteenth Brumaire of Louis Bonaparte*, the nonhuman element in Marx and Engels' rhetoric, and the relationship between debt and political community in Marx's *The Civil War in France*.

Geoff Boucher is Associate Professor in Literary Studies at Deakin University in the Faculty of Arts and Education. He has written extensively on psychoanalysis and politics, including numerous book chapters and journal articles in the psychoanalytic field. He is the author of several books on Marxism, including *Understanding Marxism* (2012), *Adorno Reframed* (2012), and (with Matt Sharpe) *Zizek and Politics* (2010). His critique of so-called post-Marxism is presented in *The Charmed Circle of Ideology* (2008).

Clint Burnham is Professor of English at Simon Fraser University, in Vancouver, Canada. He is the author of *Does the Internet Have an Unconscious? Slavoj Žižek and Digital Culture* (2018) *Fredric Jameson and The Wolf of Wall Street* (2016), and co-editor, with Paul Kingsbury, of the collection *Lacan and the Environment* (2021), as well as recent essays on psychoanalysis, decolonization, the pandemic, and the digital, in collections from transcript and Routledge and in the journals *Canadian Literature*, *CLCweb: Comparative Literature and Culture*, *Rethinking Marxism*, *Continental Thought and Theory*, *The International Journal of Žižek Studies*, *Historical Materialism*, and *Psychoanalysis, Culture, and Society*.

Glyn Daly is Senior Lecturer in Politics Faculty of Health, Education, and Society at the University of Northampton. He is the author of *Speculation: Politics, Ideology, Event* and co-author of *Conversations with Žižek* and has written many essays on politics, ideology, and political economy.

Jeffrey R. Di Leo is Professor of English and Philosophy at the University of Houston-Victoria, USA. He is Editor-in-Chief of the *American Book Review*, Founding Editor of the journal *symplokē*, and Executive Director of the Society for Critical Exchange and its Winter Theory Institute. He is the author or editor of more than thirty books on philosophy, literature, higher education, book culture, and literary theory. His recent books include *American Literature as World Literature* (2017), *The Bloomsbury Handbook of Literary and Cultural Theory* (2019), *The End of American Literature: Essays from the Late Age of Print* (2019), *Biotheory: Life and Death under Capitalism* (2020, with Peter Hitchcock), *Philosophy as World Literature* (2020), *What's Wrong with Antitheory?* (2020), *Vinyl Theory* (2020), *Philosophy as World Literature* (2020), *Catastrophe and Education: Neoliberalism, Theory, and the Future of the Humanities* (2020), *Contemporary Literary and Cultural Theory* (forthcoming), and *Selling the Humanities* (forthcoming).

Matthew Flisfeder is an associate professor of rhetoric and communications at the University of Winnipeg, Canada. He is the author of *Algorithmic Desire: Toward a New Structuralist Theory of Social media* (2021), *Postmodern Theory and Blade Runner* (2017), and *The Symbolic, The Sublime, and Slavoj Žižek's Theory of Film* (2012) and is co-editor of *Žižek and Media Studies: A Reader* (2014).

Agon Hamza, assistant professor of philosophy, is the author of *Reading Hegel* (2020; with Frank Ruda and Slavoj Žižek), *Reading Marx* (Polity, 2018; with Frank Ruda and Slavoj Žižek), *Althusser and Pasolini: Philosophy, Marxism, and Film* (2016), and *From Myth to Symptom: The Case of Kosovo* (2013; with Slavoj Žižek). In addition, he is the editor of *Althusser and Theology: Religion, Politics and Philosophy* (2016) and *Repeating Žižek* (2015), as well as co-editor, with Frank Ruda, of *Slavoj Žižek and Dialectical Materialism* (2016). He is founder and co-editor (with Frank Ruda) of the international philosophy journal *Crisis and Critique*. He served as a political advisor to the prime minister of the Republic of Kosova.

David J. Gunkel is Professor in the Department of Communication at Northern Illinois University. He was the founding co-editor of the *International Journal of Žižek Studies* and is the author of fourteen books including: *The Machine Question: Critical Perspectives on AI, Robots and Ethics* (2012), *Heidegger and the Media* (2014), *Of Remixology: Ethics and Aesthetics After Remix* (2016), *Robot Rights* (2018), and *Deconstruction* (2021).

Ilan Kapoor is Professor of Critical Development Studies at the Faculty of Environmental and Urban Change, York University, Toronto. His research focuses on psychoanalytic and postcolonial theory and politics, and ideology critique. He is the author of *The Postcolonial Politics of Development* (2008), *Celebrity Humanitarianism: The Ideology of Global Charity* (2013), and *Confronting Desire: Psychoanalysis and International Development* (2020); editor of the collected volume, *Psychoanalysis and the GlObal* (2018); and co-author, with Zahi Zalloua, of *Universal Politics* (2022), and with Gavin Fridell, Maureen Sioh, and Pieter de Vries, of *Global Libidinal Economy* (2023 forthcoming).

Katerina (Katarina) Kolozova is Senior Researcher and Full Professor at the Institute of Social Sciences and Humanities, Skopje, and visiting faculty at Arizona State University-Center for Philosophical Technologies. Prof. Kolozova was a visiting scholar at the Department of Rhetoric at the University of California-Berkley in 2009 (under the peer supervision of Prof. Judith Butler), and a Columbia University NY-SIPA Visiting Scholar at its Paris Global Centre in 2019. She is a member of the Board of Directors of the New Centre for Research and Practice—Seattle WA and co-director of the School of Materialist Research (Tempe AZ, Vienna, Eindhoven, Skopje). Kolozova is the author of *Capitalism's Holocaust of Animals: A Non-Marxist Critique of Capital, Philosophy and Patriarchy* published in 2019 and *Cut of the Real: Subjectivity in Poststructuralist Philosophy*, published in 2014. She has published numerous articles, most recently in *Philosophy Today* Volume 65, Issue 2 (Spring 2021) Philosophy after Automation Pages 359–74 https://doi.org/10.5840/philtoday2021420402. Kolozova has contributed to a number of edited books, most recently a chapter titled "Poststructuralism" part of the Oxford *Handbook of Feminist Philosophy* (April 2021).

Todd McGowan teaches theory and film at the University of Vermont. He is the author of *The Racist Fantasy* (2022), *Universality and Identity Politics* (2020), *Emancipation After Hegel: Achieving a Contradictory Revolution* (2019), *Only a Joke Can Save Us: A Theory of Comedy* (2017), and *Capitalism and Desire* (2016), among other books.

James Penney is Professor of Cultural Studies and French and Francophone Studies at Trent University (Canada). He is the author of *Genet, Lacan and the Ontology of Incompletion* (2023) and three other books: *After Queer Theory: The Limits of Sexual Politics* (2014), *The Structures of Love: Art and Politics Beyond the Transference* (2012), and *The World of Perversion: Psychoanalysis and the Impossible Absolute of Desire* (2006).

Ed Pluth is Professor of Philosophy at California State University, Chico. He is the author of *Signifiers and Acts: Freedom in Lacan's Theory of the Subject* (2007), *Alain Badiou* (2010), and *On Silence: Holding the Voice*

Hostage with Cindy Zeiher (2019). His translation of Jean-Claude Milner's *L'Œuvre claire* (*A Search for Clarity: Science and Philosophy in Lacan's Oeuvre*) was published in 2021.

Frank Ruda is Senior Lecturer in Philosophy at the University of Dundee, Scotland and Professor of Philosophy at the European Graduate School. He is inter alia the author of *Reading Marx* (2018), *Reading Hegel* (2022) (both authored with Slavoj Žižek), and Agon Hamza), of *The Dash – the Other Side of Absolute Knowing* (2018) (with Rebecca Comay), and of *Abolishing Freedom: A Plea for a Contemporary Use of Fatalism* (2018), among other books.

Russell Sbriglia is Associate Professor and Director of Undergraduate Literature Studies in the Department of English at Seton Hall University. He is the editor of the books *Everything You Always Wanted to Know about Literature but Were Afraid to Ask Žižek* (2017) and (with Slavoj Žižek) *Subject Lessons: Hegel, Lacan, and the Future of Materialism* (2020).

Laurence Simmons is Professor of Film Studies in Media and Screen at the University of Auckland, New Zealand and has written extensively on critical theory. In addition to books on Derrida and Baudrillard, he has co-edited a volume of essays on the relevance of the work of Slavoj Žižek to Australasia *From Z to A: Žižek at the Antipodes* (2005). His most recent book-length publication explores Hitchcock's films in order to identify the core commitments that inform Žižek's own work, *Žižek through Hitchcock* (2021).

Oxana Timofeeva is a professor at "Stasis" Center for Philosophy at the European University at St. Petersburg, member of the artistic collective "Chto Delat," deputy editor of the journal "Stasis," and the author of books *Solar Politics* (2022), *How to Love a Homeland* (2020), *History of Animals* (2018), *This Is not That* (2022), *Introduction to the Erotic Philosophy of Georges Bataille* (2009), and other writings.

Erik Vogt is Gwendolyn Miles Smith Professor of Philosophy at Trinity College (CT, USA), as well as Privat-Dozent of Philosophy at the University of Vienna (Vienna, Austria). He is the author and (co-)editor of twenty-four books. Recent book publications include *Slavoj Žižek und die Kuenste* (2022, forthcoming), *Rancière und die Literatur*, ed. with M. Manfé (2020), *Zwischen Sensologie und aesthetischem Dissens. Essays zu Mario Perniola und Jacques Rancière* (2019); *Adorno and the Concept of Genocide*, ed. with R. Crawford (2016); *Bruchlinien Europas*, ed. with G. Unterthurner (2016); *Aesthetisch-Politische Lektueren zum "Fall Wagner"* (2015).

Zahi Zalloua is the Cushing Eells Professor of Philosophy and Literature at Whitman College and Editor of *The Comparatist*. He is the co-author, with Ilan Kapoor, of *Universal Politics* (2021), and the author of *Solidarity and the Palestinian Cause: Indigeneity, Blackness, and the Promise of Universality* (forthcoming), *Being Posthuman: Ontologies of the Future* (2021), *Žižek on Race: Toward an Anti-Racist Future* (2020), *Theory's Autoimmunity: Skepticism, Literature, and Philosophy* (2018), *Continental Philosophy and the Palestinian Question: Beyond the Jew and the Greek* (2017), *Reading Unruly: Interpretation and Its Ethical Demands* (2014), and *Montaigne and the Ethics of Skepticism* (2005). He has edited volumes and special journal issues on globalization, literary theory, ethical criticism, and trauma studies.

Cindy Zeiher is Senior Lecturer in the School of Language, Political and Social Sciences at the University of Canterbury, Christchurch, New Zealand. Her writings focus on questions of subjectivity relating to Freudian-Lacanian psychoanalysis, feminist theories, and politics. She is currently completing her first sole authored book which reads from a Lacanian perspective, French philosopher and musicologist, Vladimir Jankélévitch's refusal of German culture and idealism.

INDEX

absolute knowledge 20, 35–7, 65
absolute recoil 32–6
absolute reflection 33
  determining 33
  external 33
  positioning 33–4
actor-network theory 197
Adorno, Theodor W. 154–60,
  167–71, 176, 180
aesthetics 27–9, 136–7, 165, 197
Age of Innocence, The (Wharton) 77
alienated being, disparity of 206–8
Altemeyer, Bob 167–8, 170–1
alterity 6, 8, 20–1, 114, 139
Althusser, Louis 14, 197–202
Ambassadors, The (Holbein the
  Younger) 145
analysts 93–5
anamorphosis 145
Anglo-American gender 65
annihilation 155
anthropocentrism 186, 191–2, 196,
  198–200
anti-Blackness 4
anti-ethics 96, 98
anti-philosophy 27
anti-Semitic proto-fascism 156–7
anti-Semitism 154–6, 159, 161
anxiety 13, 99, 143, 168, 171, 175,
  178–80, 231
aphanisis (disappearance) 110
aphanisis, subject of 108–12
aporias 94
Aristotle 90, 94
astonishment 114–15
Australian sexual rights law 71
authoritarian aggression 169
authoritarianism 56, 167–80

authoritarian personalities 167–80
  authoritarian aggression 169
  authoritarian submission 169
  as durable syndrome 168–9
  fetishism, logic of 174–6
  Frankfurt School's discovery
    of 169–71
  Lacanian theorization of 167–80
  Lacan's modernist rethinking of
    Freud 178–80
  left-wing 176
  as perverse subjectivity 171–3
  psychoanalytic pattern 170
  right-wing 167
  rigid conventionalism 169
  totalitarian perversions 176–8
  Žižekian interpretation of 167–80
authoritarian submission 169
authority 13, 56, 111–12, 114, 147,
  159–61, 168–80, 229, 233

Badiou, Alain 29, 48, 54–6,
  60 n.10, 98
Badmington, Neil 145
Balibar, Étienne 4
Bartleby paradox 122–33
Baudrillard, Jean 125–7
Belsey, Catherine 110
Benjamin, Walter 29, 49
Benna, Ziad 14 n.2
Bentham, Jeremy 99
Beyond the Pleasure Principle
  (Freud) 91
Bielski, Andrew 78–9
big Other, the 83–4, 126, 158–9,
  164–5, 173–7, 198, 233
biologism 235
biopolitics 200–1, 206

INDEX

Black Lives Matter (BLM)   4–5, 79, 100
Black people   4
Black subjectivity   4
BLM; *see* Black Lives Matter (BLM)
Bonilla-Silva, Eduardo   82
Boothby, Richard   214
Borromean knots   28
Bostonians, The (James)   86
bourgeoisie   55, 69
Bratton, Benjamin   83–4
Breuer, Josef   91
Burrage, Henry   86
Butler, Judith   190
Butler, Rex   148

Cahiers du cinéma   139
Calvo, Luz   79–80, 83
Cambridge Analytica   98
capitalism   52–3, 55, 148
Capitalocene   196
Cartesian subject   2, 11, 21–2, 107, 202, 222
castration   3, 66, 68, 97, 117, 143, 160, 179–80, 203–4, 235
cats   7–8
Chancellor, Olive   86
Charron, Pierre   111
"Child Is Being Beaten: Earth or Negro, A"? (Freud)   78–80, 83
Chinese Cultural Revolution   45–59
    Badiou on   54–8
    failure of   49
    Mao writing on   48–56
    Paris Commune and   56–7
    Žižek reflections on   45–59
choice, vagaries of   201–5
Christianity   33, 38–43
    God within   38–41
    Good Friday   38–9
    Hegel on   39–43
    materialist reading of   38
    as religion of atheism   41
    Žižek and   39–43
Civilization and Its Discontents (Freud)   92
civil society   186
class struggle   36, 51, 169, 202, 229–31

climate crisis   83–4
cogito   19–29, 108–12, 202
communism   43, 53, 96, 148, 176–8, 199, 201, 231
Communist Manifesto, The (Žižek)   21, 187, 222
community   4–5, 42, 59, 108, 114, 159–64, 177, 203, 230
contradiction   31–2, 36–7, 48, 50–1, 58, 64, 70, 84, 110, 124, 137, 161–2, 169, 174, 180, 187, 190, 197–200, 204–6, 220
Copjec, Joan   61, 65
cosmopolitan Jew   5
Covid-19   83
Critique of Hegel's Philosophy in General (Marx)   184, 189–90
Critique of Pure Reason (Kant)   85
Critique of Violence (Benjamin)   29
cynicism   1, 175–6

Darvay, Daniel   137
Das Capital (Marx)   2
das Ding   141–2
death   155
death drive   11, 91, 103 n.46, 158, 235–7
death of God   41
Declaration of Independence   99
deconstruction   130, 185
Defense of Lost Causes (Žižek)   5–6, 96, 98–100, 116, 200
Deleuzian theory   185
DeMorgan's law   23
Derrida, Jacques   6–8, 139
Descartes, René   19, 22, 24–5, 107–11, 115, 117, 202, 223
desires   13, 20, 23, 54, 63, 67, 69, 75, 79–86, 93, 96, 100
determining reflection   33
dialectics   55, 78, 146, 184, 190, 192, 195 n.29, 208
disavowal   2, 7, 13, 84, 163, 168, 174, 178, 180
"Don't You See I'm Burning?" (Lacan)   81
drive   11, 91, 103 n.46, 158, 235–7
Dworkin, Andrea   72

égaliberté 4
Eichmann, Adolph 172
empathy 169
enjoyment (*jouissance*) 2–3, 13, 72, 78, 82, 95, 100, 116–17, 143, 159–61, 168, 170–80, 203–4, 208, 213
Enlightenment 5, 14, 184
 humanism 190
 idea of universality 219–20
 and modernist tradition 198
 project 184
 republican 186
 self-discipline of 111
 thought 197–9
 tradition 97–8
envy 72, 237
epistemology
 to Hegel's dialectical materialism 64
 versus ontology 64
 Sohn-Rethel's 188–90
equality-freedom 4
Eros 91–2, 163
Essays (Montaigne) 111, 116–17, 120 n.36
ethics 98
Everything You Always Wanted to Know About Lacan (But Were Afraid To Ask Hitchcock) (Žižek) 135–6, 144–6, 149–50
exceptionalism 197
exemplarity 8
external reflection 33

face 5–7, 84, 99, 123–4, 128, 137, 199–200
Faith and Knowledge (Hegel) 38–9
false consciousness 1–2, 217
Fanon, Frantz 5, 80
fantasy 80–4, 213–15
fascism 160–2, 169, 177–8
Fechner, Gustav Theodor 99
feminine logic 3–4, 11, 14, 66, 117, 203, 206
feminine masochism 136
femininity/feminism 66–9, 116–17
Fernandez-Alvarez, Hilda 81

fetishism, logic of 174–6
films 138–41
Fink, Bruce 23, 109
flat ontology 197
Floyd, George 80, 83
Flying Dutchman, The 157
Fontaine, Jean de La 141
foreclosure 13, 168, 183, 190, 192
formulas of sexuation 2, 65
For They Know Not What They Do: Enjoyment as a Political Factor (Žižek) 95, 203
Foucault, Michel 1, 116
Fragile Absolute, The (Žižek) 214
Frankfurt school 167, 169–71
freedom 35
French Revolution 46–7, 58–9
Freud, Sigmund 77–86, 87 n.11
 Beyond the Pleasure Principle 91
 "Child Is Being Beaten: Earth or Negro, A"? 78–80, 83
 Civilization and Its Discontents 92
 death drive 103 n.46
 on happiness 91–5
 Lacan's modernist rethinking of 178–80
 phraseologies 84
 primal repression 61–4
 on principles of mental functioning 82
 "Repression" (Freud) 62
 secondary repression 62
 theory of femininity 66–7
 "Unconscious, The" 62–4
Freud as Philosopher (Boothby) 214
Fromm, Erich 170
fundamentalism 174–5
Furet, Francois 46

Galileo 19–29
 Lacan, Jacques on 19–29
 Žižek, Slavoj on 19–29
gaze 143–6
German Ideology 184
GNH; *see* Gross National Happiness (GNH)
GNP; *see* Gross National Product (GNP)

God 33, 38–9
    death of 41
    existence 174
    of fundamentalism 174–5
    Other 174
Good Friday 38–9
Gothic
    modernism 136–8
    in *Rebecca* 139–40
Götterdämmerung 162–5
Grail community 159–60
Grenzgänger 129–30
Gross National Happiness
    (GNH) 99, 103 n.47
Gross National Product (GNP) 99

happiness 11
    Freud's views on 91–5
    and its discontents 91–5
    Lacan on 92–5
    as pagan concept 97
    science of 90
    as unethical category 95–9
    Žižek's critique of 90–100, 101 n.4
Harari, Roberto 79
Haraway, Donna 189, 208
hauntology 138–41
Hegel, G. W. F. 19–29
    absolute knowledge 20, 35–7
    absolute recoil 32–6
    Absolute Recoil (Žižek) 199
    on Cartesian cogito 24–5
    dialectic 34
    epistemology *versus* ontology 64
    Faith and Knowledge 38–9
    on French Revolution 47, 58–9
    Lacan, Jacques on 19–29
    legacy of subjectivity-centered
        thought 185
    Less Than Nothing (Žižek) 199
    Phenomenology of Spirit 31–
        2, 39–41
    Philosophy of History 42
    Reason in 20
    religion, views on 39–43
    Science of Logic 32–3
    Spirit 37–8
    and Žižek, Slavoj 19–29, 31–43

Hegel in a Wired Brain (Žižek) 196,
    199–200, 202, 207
Hegemony, Contingency, Universality
    (Žižek) 190
hermeneutics 4, 8, 111, 114
heterology 8
historicism 200
Hitchcock, Alfred 135–50, 151 n.5
    films 136–50
    Gothic imagery and
        architecture 136–50
    and Manderley 133–44, 148–9
    modernism 135–50
    as postmodernist 149–50
    Psycho 145
    Rebecca 136–50
    vanishing mediator 147–8
Hitlerism 177–8
Hogle, Jerrold 137
Holbein, Hans 145
Hook, Derek 79
Horkheimer, Max 170
Horney, Karen 67
How to Read Lacan (Žižek) 7, 77,
    81, 84, 111–12, 115, 173
humanism 98
    alienated being, disparity of 206–8
    inhuman 196–201
    Marxist 199–200
    Stalin's 201
    vagaries of choice 201–5
    Žižek's 198
Humanism and Terror (Merleau-
    Ponty) 201
humanity 4–5, 186–7
human rights 4, 70–1, 180, 198,
    219, 230
Hussein, Saddam 85
hysteria 112, 131, 157–8, 179

idealism 189
ideology 1–2, 216–18
Imaginary 27, 29, 81, 115, 127,
    164, 186
immortality 236–7
imperfection 112, 117
incompleteness 4, 11, 63, 67–8, 107,
    117, 207–8

Indivisible Remainder, The
(Žižek) 146
inhuman
  core of Montaigne 112–17
  ethics 98–100
  face 98–100
  gaze 7
  humanism 14
  neighbor 6
  subject 98
"Instance of the Letter, The"
  (Lacan) 23
interpellation 3, 113, 117, 145
Interrogating the Real (Žižek) 141
Introduction to Non-Marxism
  (Laruelle) 190
Iraq: The Borrowed Kettle (Žižek) 85
Irigaray, Luce 66
Izcovich, Luis 125

James, Henry 77, 85–6
Jameson, Fredric 20, 135–6, 148
Jevons, William Stanley 99
Jewish Question, The (Marx) 186
Jones, Ernest 110
jouissance (enjoyment) 2–3, 13, 72, 78, 82, 95, 100, 116–17, 143, 159–61, 168, 170–80, 203–4, 208, 213
Judaism 33

Kant, Immanuel 5, 25, 35, 100, 197
  Critique of Pure Reason 85
  Ding-as-sich 66
  on marriage 72
  metaphysics of morals 184
  phenomenal *versus* noumenal worlds 35
  practical philosophy of morals 184
Kay, Sarah 141

labor 187
Lacan, Jacques 2–3, 6, 9–11, 14–15
  on cogito 19–29
  and Montaigne 110–12
  "Don't You See I'm Burning?" 81
  on happiness 92–5
  Hegelianism 19–29

"Instance of the Letter, The" 23
  on logic of Real 124–5
  on modern Galileo 19–29
  modernist rethinking of Freud 178–80
  "Presentation on Psychical Causality" 110
  reading of Descartes 22
  sexuation, formulas of 2–3, 65–6
  theory of femininity 66–8
  unconscious 63–4
lack 6, 12, 21, 32, 37, 62, 64, 66–8, 72, 84, 97, 107, 127–8, 131, 136, 143
Laclau, Ernesto 108, 190
Lama, Dalai 97
Lang, Fritz 137
La Peste (Camus) 84
Laruelle, François 114, 183–5, 190, 192
Leader, Darian 79
Lenin, V. I. 42, 46, 49–50, 56–7, 60, 187, 189, 199–200, 230–2
Less than Nothing (Žižek) 4, 7–8, 26–9, 33–6, 40, 46, 118, 149, 186, 199, 206–7, 220
Levi, Primo 6
Levinas, Emmanuel 5–6
LGBT+ discourse 74
Liebestod 157–8, 160
linguistic turn 185
logocentrism 100
logos 236
love 6, 72, 77, 91, 98, 158–60, 163–4, 170, 234, 237
Lyotard, Jean-François 118 n.4

McGowan, Todd 84
MacKinnon, Catherine 72
Manderley 133–44, 148–9
Mannoni, Octave 174
Mao Tse-Tung 45–59, 60 n.10
marriage 72
Marx, Karl 14, 36, 39, 41, 48–53, 183–93
  Capital 189
  Critique of Hegel's Philosophy in General 184, 189–90

Das Capital 2
Grundrisse 189
Jewish Question, The 186
modernism/modernity 183–8
objectivity of subject 188–90
posthumanism/non-
 humanism 191–3
revolution 49
Sohn-Rethel's epistemology
 and 188–90
Marxism 14, 36, 39, 41, 48–53, 183–93
masculinity 2–4, 66, 68–9, 116–17
mastery 6, 107, 112, 114–17, 120, 143
materialism 185
 Christianity 42
 dialectical 9, 32, 36–9, 64, 197–200, 233
 Feuerbach's 184
 historical 200–1
 Marxist 200
 philosophical 189
 as politico-epistemic project 14
 Posthumanist 203
 radical 14
 and religion 39, 41–2
Mbembe, Achille 4
Meillassoux, Quentin 197
Melville, Herman 122–3, 128
MeToo movement 61, 70–4
Milbank, John 20
Miller, Jacques-Alain 146
Milner, Jean-Claude 24, 27–8, 30 n.14, 73
modernism/modernity 1–9
 authors/thinkers 77–86
 and *Das Ding* 141–2
 frame 146–7
 Galileo 19–29
 genealogy of 137
 Gothic 136–8
 on happiness 91–100
 hauntology 138–41
 Hitchcock's modernist
  hauntology 135–50
 Lacan *versus* Žižek
  thinking 19–29
 legacy of 183–8

Marxism and 183–8
 ontology 61–75
 perplexed gaze 143–6
 posthumanism and 196–208
 self-reflexion 136 (*see also*
  Rebecca (Hitchcock))
 symptomal reading 142–3
 through lens of non-
  philosophy 183–8
 vectors of 183–8
 of Wagnerian art 154–65
 Wagner's 154–65
 Žižek's universalism and 183–8
Modleski, Tania 136, 147–8
Möebius strip 39
monsters 116
Monstrosity of Christ, The (Žižek and
 Milbank) 20, 40–1, 146
Montaigne, Michel de 107–17
 aphanisis, subject of 108–12
 Essays 111, 116–17, 120 n.36
 inhuman core of 112–17
 and Lacan, Jacques 110–12
 "Of Cripples" 113, 115
 "Of Idleness" 116
 scepticism 110–12
 self-mastery 116
Mulvey, Laura 143
Murnau, F. W. 137
Muselmann (Levi) 6, 8

narcissism 143
National Socialism 155
Nazism 175–7
negativity 23
Negro 78–80
neighbor 7–8, 180
neoliberalism 10–11, 100, 230
Nirvana principle 236
non-all 9, 11, 14, 117, 207
non-Marxism 183
non-philosophy 13–14, 183–5, 189, 192
noumena 9, 35, 197, 206
Nyong, Tavia 79–80

object 28, 32, 35, 112–13, 131–2, 136
 displacement 34

knowledge of 64
Montaigne as 117
of primal repression 62
revolution 45–6
of thinking's desire 23, 96
woman and 68
writing history and 47–8
object-oriented ontology 10, 61, 197
"Of Cripples" (Montaigne) 113, 115
"Of Idleness" (Montaigne) 116
On Belief (Žižek) 95
ontology
   versus epistemology 64
   flat 197
   modern 61–75
   modernism/modernity 61–75
   object-oriented 10, 61, 197
Order of Things, The
   (Foucault) 25, 197
Other/Otherness 6–8, 174–9
Oudart, Jean-Pierre 143

parallax 35–6
Parallax View, The (Žižek) 5, 34–5,
   77, 86, 117, 122, 124, 129–31,
   220, 236–7
Paris Commune 56–7
Parsifal (Wagner) 156–60, 162–5
particularism 220
"part of no-part" 4–5, 221; see also
   Other/Otherness
passage à l'acte 2, 14 n.2
Passions of the Soul, The
   (Descartes) 108–9, 115
patriarchy 66–7, 72, 219
Pauline redemption 162–5
performative contradiction 31, 174,
   180, 197, 200
perverse subjectivity 171–3
perversion 75, 159, 173–4, 176–80
Peterson, Jordan 95
phalluses 3, 20, 66–8, 97, 179–80, 204
phantasmagoria 155
phenomenal *versus* noumenal
   worlds 35
Phenomenology of Spirit (Hegel)
   31–2, 39–41
philosophical materialism 189

Philosophy of History (Hegel) 42
Piglia, Ricardo 146
pleasure principle 13, 82, 91–3, 97,
   100, 168, 237
Pluth, Ed 109
Poizat, Michel 159
political state 186
Ponelle, Jean-Pierre 158
positioning reflection 33
posthumanism 191–3, 196–208
postmodernism 142, 149–50,
   153 n.39, 192–3
poststructuralism 184–5
PPS; *see* principle of philosophical
   sufficiency (PPS)
"Presentation on Psychical Causality"
   (Lacan) 110
primal repression 61–4
principle of philosophical sufficiency
   (PPS) 183–4, 188, 191–2
proletarian position 4, 50, 230
proletariat 50, 57, 69, 190, 230
Protestantism 148
Psycho (Hitchcock) 145
psychoanalysis 8–9, 11–12, 68–9,
   75 n.7
   cogito for 23
   Freudian 65
   gender ideology and 65
   Hegel 26–7
   Lacanian 1, 12, 27, 92–6
   modernist route for 27
   and modernity 12
   for ontology 10, 61
   and philosophy 12
   sexual difference 65
   sexuality as 70
   transcendental aesthetic for 27
   Žižek 29, 70–2, 107
Puppet and the Dwarf: The Perverse
   Core of Christianity, The
   (Žižek) 20, 38, 141

QAnon 180
queer theory 61, 65, 70

racism 4, 81–3
Ragland, Ellie 81

Rancière, Jacques 4
Ransom, Basil 86
Real, logic of 2, 8, 11, 14, 21, 23, 28, 124, 142–3, 145–6, 175, 190–3
    Bartleby on 127
    das Ding 141
    dreams 81
    human-in-human 193
    indifference 190
    Lacan, Jacques on 124–5, 141
    of neighbor 6
    of sexual difference 69
    skepticism 111
    and thought 183–5
    Žižek, Slavoj on 3–4, 160
reality principle 82, 237
Reason 20
Rebecca (Hitchcock) 136–50
religion 33; *see also* Christianity; Judaism
    of atheism 41–2
    versus materialism 38–43
    as self-sublating process 42
    Žižek views on 38–43
renegades 55
repetition 22, 26, 28, 36, 54, 57, 126–9, 149, 196–201
repression
    Freud on 61–4
    primal 61–4
    secondary 62
"Repression" (Freud) 62
revolution 45–59
    French Revolution 46–7, 58–9
    history 46–7
    Mao writing, Žižek reflections on 48–56
    Marxist revolution 49
    Russian Revolution 46
    writing history from 46–8
right-wing authoritarians 167
rigid conventionalism 169
Ring of the Nibelung, The (Žižek) 155–6, 160–5
Riquelme, John Paul 137
Russian Revolution 46

Savage Mind, The (Lévi-Strauss) 197

Science of Logic (Hegel) 32–3
scopophilia 143
secondary repression 62
secularism 186
self-consciousness 202
self-critique 49
self-instrumentalization 175
self-reflexion 136
self-reflexivity 2
self-sacrifice 177–8
Selznick, David O. 143
sexual binary 69
sexual difference 65–6, 68–9, 206
sexual identity 69
sexual relations, contracts in 71
sexuation/sexuality 2–3, 61–75
    femininity 66–9
    Hegel's on 66–7
    inequalities 71–2
    Lacan formulas of 2–3, 65–6
    masculinity 66, 68–9
    sexual difference 65–6, 68–9, 206
    Žižek on 61–75
Shaoqi, Liu 60 n.10
Shaw, Tamsin 98
skepticism 11, 107–8, 110–14, 219
Smith, Anthony Paul 189
social relations 188–9
Sohn-Rethel, Alfred 187–90
Sohn-Rethel's epistemology 188–90
solidarity 221, 234
Soper, Kate 197
spectrality 137–41
speculative realism 10, 61, 197
Speculum of the Other Woman (Irigaray) 66
Spirit 36–8
Stalinism 177–8
state violence 78–80, 83–4
stricto sensu 184
Studies on Hysteria (Breuer) 91
subject 222–4
subjectivity
    Black 4
    Hegel, G. W. F. legacy of thought 185
    perverse 171–3

Sublime Object of Ideology, The (Žižek) 214
subtraction 4–5, 63, 130, 146
superego 67, 100, 170, 172
Symbolic Law 174, 179
Symbolic Order 179
symptom 226–7
symptomal reading 142–3

Tarrant, Verena 86
Tarrying with the Negative (Žižek) 25, 203
Taylor, Breonna 83
temporality 83
Thanatos 91
Theale, Milly 86
Theses on Feuerbach (Marx) 184
They Know Not What They Do (Žižek) 3, 95, 172, 176, 203
thinking *versus* being 23
Ticklish Subject, The (Žižek) 21–2, 199, 203, 220–4, 227
totalitarianism 95, 171–6
"Total Man" 200
Totem and Taboo (Freud) 3
transhumanism 14
Traoré, Bouna 14 n.2
Tristan and Isolde (Wagner) 157–9
Truffaut, François 147
Trump, Donald 167

Uncle Tom's Cabin (Nyong and Calvo) 80
"Unconscious, The" (Freud) 62–3
universalism/universality 2–5, 198, 205, 219–21
　climate crisis 78
　of humanity 2–5, 207–8
　Mao's 55–7
　of masculine castration 66

Valdes, Carlotta 147
value 187–9
vanishing mediator 148
Vernunft 205
Vertigo (Hitchcock) 147

violence 10, 29, 47, 71–2, 77–8, 80, 83, 86, 112, 155–6, 161, 170–1, 201, 217, 230, 232–4
"Visual Pleasure and Narrative Cinema" (Mulvey) 143

Wagner, Richard 154–65
　ambivalent attitude 155
　anti-Semitism in 154–6, 161–2
　artistic theory and practice 154–65
　authentic Christianity 163–4
　fantasy of redemption 155
　fascism, theory of 160–2
　modernity 154–65
　music dramas 154–60
　myth/mythology, use of 155–6
　Parsifal 156–60, 162–5
　and Pauline redemption 162–5
　sexualized politics 156–9
　Tristan and Isolde 157–9
Webster, Jamieson 79
Welcome to the Desert of the Real: Five Essays on 9/11 and Related Dates (Žižek) 96–8, 114
Wharton, Edith 77, 85
"What Is Enlightenment?" (Kant) 5
white supremacy 83
Wings of the Dove, The (James) 77, 85–6
Wolfreys, Julian 142
Women Who Knew Too Much: Hitchcock and Feminist Theory, The (Modleski) 136
wonder 5, 40, 97–8, 108–9, 115, 123

xenophobia 180
Xiaoping, Deng 46, 60 n.10

YouTube 90, 96

Žižek, Slavoj 1–9, 14 n.2
　absolute recoil 32–6
　on Adorno's ideological-critical reading 154–65
　authoritarian personality, critique of 167–80

and Bartleby paradox 122–33
Chinese Cultural Revolution, thought to 45–59
and Christianity 38–43
on cogito 19–29, 108–12
Communist Manifesto, The 21, 187, 222
In Defense of Lost Causes 5–6, 96, 98–100, 116, 200
with Montaigne 107–17
with Derrida 7–8
Descartes and 19, 22, 24–5, 107–11, 115, 117, 202, 223
dialectical materialism 32–6 (*see also* absolute recoil)
Everything You Always Wanted to Know About Lacan (But Were Afraid To Ask Hitchcock) 135–6, 144–6, 149–50
For They Know Not What They Do: Enjoyment as a Political Factor 3, 95, 172, 176, 203
Fragile Absolute, The 214
happiness, critique of 11, 90–100
and Hegel 19–29, 31–43
Hegel in a Wired Brain 196, 199–200, 202, 207
Hegemony, Contingency, Universality 190
How to Read Lacan 7, 77, 81, 84, 111–12, 115, 173
on ideology 1–2
Indivisible Remainder, The 146
inhuman humanism 196–201
Interrogating the Real 141
Iraq: The Borrowed Kettle 85
on Lacanian logic of feminine/masculine 2–4
Less than Nothing 4, 7–8, 26–9, 33–6, 40, 46, 118, 149, 186, 199, 206–7, 220

on Levinas's ethical petrification 6
on logic of Real 3–4
Mao writing, reflections on 48–56
Marxism 41
on modern Galileo 19–29
modernism/modernity, commitment to 1–9
modernist authors/thinkers, approach to 77–86
modern ontology 61–75
Monstrosity of Christ, The 20, 40–1, 146
neighbor, examples of 7–8
"non-all," logic of 2–6
On Belief 95
Parallax View, The 5, 34–5, 77, 86, 117, 122, 124, 129–31, 220, 236–7
performative contradiction 31–2
Plague of Fantasies, The 213
on Plato 118 n.5
Puppet and the Dwarf: The Perverse Core of Christianity, The 20, 38, 141
Ring of the Nibelung, The 155–6, 160–5
sex in recent work of 61–75
Sublime Object of Ideology, The 214
symptomal reading 142–3
Tarrying with the Negative 25, 203
Ticklish Subject, The 21–2, 199, 203, 220–4, 227
on Wagner's ambivalent modernity 154–65
Welcome to the Desert of the Real: Five Essays on 9/11 and Related Dates 96–8, 114
Zupančič, Alenka 61

www.ingramcontent.com/pod-product-compliance
Lightning Source LLC
Chambersburg PA
CBHW062130300426
44115CB00012BA/1872